Queen Anne Goes to the Kitchen

The artwork for this cookbook is taken from the artwork on the arch framing the altar area or apse in St. Paul's, and depicts the grapes and vine, which symbolize Christ and his disciples. "I am the vine, ye are the branches; He that abideth in me and I in Him, the same bringeth forth much fruit." [John 15: 1]

Symbols of the Eucharist are woven into the vine branches: The fish (early Christian symbol of followers of Christ [Mark 1:17]) with the cup of salvation [Psalm 116:13]); and the cross (symbol of Christ's resurrection) with the bread of life [John 6:35]).

Other symbols of Christ's life are woven into the branches: At the top of the arch is a crown (depicting the glory, righteousness, and the life that the Lord has promised to those who love Him) [James 1:12]; the shields represent faith [Eph. 6:16] and salvation [Psalm 18:35]; the cross of Christ [Gal. 6:14]; the descending dove is the symbol of the Holy Spirit; [Matt. 3:16]; the trefoil has historically represented the Holy Trinity [I John 5:7]; and the boat is the symbol of courage and faith (that Christ will bring our boats safely to harbor) [Matt. 14:22-33].

QUEEN ANNE GOES TO THE KITCHEN

THIRD EDITION

by
The Episcopal Church Women
of St. Paul's Parish

TIDEWATER PUBLISHERS
Centreville, Maryland

The following publishers have generously given permission to use recipes from copy-
righted works: From *Eat, Drink and Be Merry in Maryland: An Anthology from a Great
Tradition,* compiled by Frederick Philip Stieff. Copyright © 1932 by F. P. Stieff and renewed
1960 by Frederick Philip Stieff. Reprinted by permission of The Putnam Publishing Group:
Veal Pâté, Clabber or Buttermilk Griddle Cakes, Custard Pone, Imperial Deviled Crab,
Oyster Stew, Hominy Chafing Dish, German Fried Potatoes, Eastern Shore Salad, Sweet
Potato Pudding or Pie, and Queen of Puddings. From *The Gun Club Cook Book* by Charles
Browne. Copyright © 1930 by Charles Scribners Sons. Reprinted by permission of the
publisher: Panned Oysters à la Gun Club.

Library of Congress Cataloging-in-Publication Data

Queen Anne goes to the kitchen / by the Episcopal Church Women of St.
Paul's Parish. — 3rd ed.
      p.   cm.
   Includes index.
   ISBN 0-87033-438-7 (pbk.)
      1. Cookery, American.   I. St. Paul's Parish (Centreville, Md.).
Episcopal Church Women.
TX715.Q55   1993
641.5973—dc20   93-18270
                                                        CIP

This book was comb bound by clients of the Chesterwye Center, Inc.,
Grasonville, Maryland.

Manufactured in the United States of America
First edition, 1962. Third edition, 1993

CONTENTS

REFACE

The first edition of *Queen Anne Goes to the Kitchen* was published in 1962, ten years after the first bridge to span the Chesapeake Bay changed life on the Eastern Shore. Where once the only means of reaching this remote peninsula was a ferry boat, now multitudes of travelers and commuters came to visit and to live, eager to enjoy "the land of pleasant living."

Over three hundred years before, in 1631, the first settlers had come to the area that is now Queen Anne's County. The wealth of food sources from land and water provided the pioneers with abundant opportunities to develop a culinary tradition second to none. A taste for savoring the best of this Chesapeake country bounty has brought to Eastern Shoremen and -women a reputation for superb food presented with renowned hospitality.

The Episcopal Church Women of St. Paul's Parish, spurred on by fund-raising obligations, selected recipes that were collected from parish families and friends for the first edition of the cookbook. It was simply constructed, with cardboard covers and pages bound by metal rings. A second edition followed in 1969. With each version, the cookbook has been revised and updated, but both older editions are now out of print. The copies that survive are tattered and stained from years of happy use in the kitchen.

In 1992 the Episcopal Church Women undertook the production of a third edition to commemorate the tricentennial of the founding of St. Paul's Parish. All that is lasting and treasured from the past has been gathered together with contemporary selections of merit. Collectors familiar with the earlier cookbooks will remember the charming illustrations by Lynette Nielsen. In this edition the artwork has been designed to reflect the symbols of Christian life and is particularly inspired by the arch art near the altar in St. Paul's Church.

The three women most responsible for the successful completion of the first two editions of the cookbook—Lynette Nielsen, Isabel

Lieber, and Margaret Ashley—brought varied backgrounds to the project; its rich flavor is derived both from their experiences as worldwide travelers and from their love of Queen Anne's County tradition. We like to think that this new offering continues to reflect both cosmopolitan and rural touches through the diversity of our contributors.

In the same spirit, funds generated from sales of the cookbook are used to support local and diocesan outreach programs, and range from county daycare, mental health centers, and scholarships to Camp Wright to services for those in need around the world.

The following people made the third edition of *Queen Anne Goes to the Kitchen* possible.

COMMITTEE
Janet Doehler, *Chairperson*
Mary Davy Pippin, *Cochairperson*
Jane Corey
Shirley Freestate
Diane Freestate
Nancy Gribbon
Dicky Long
Stephanie Thompson
Joann Valliant

ARTWORK
Stephanie Thompson, *Chairperson*
Sally Clark
Hallie Rugg

HISTORIC RESEARCH
Sandy Ross

TYPING
Diane Freestate
Arline Mayer

TESTERS AND PROOFREADERS
Bettie Altfather
Janie Ashley
Judith Conley
Jane Corey
Nina Curran

TESTERS AND PROOFREADERS
(continued)
Janet Doehler
Sydney Doehler
Kathy Draper
Lou Eby
Barbara Efland
Diane Freestate
Shirley Freestate
Bob Gribbon
Nancy Gribbon
Louisa Heilman
Marty LaGiglia
Dicky Long
Cecily Lyle
Helen Mann
Barbara Mason
Arline Mayer
Susan Miller
Mary Davy Pippin
Reed Rogers
Sandy Ross
Hallie Rugg
Sarah Senecal
Stephanie Thompson
Debbie Travers
Joann Valliant
Joan Withington

St. Paul's History

Enter this door as if the floor were gold,
And every wall of jewels, all of wealth untold
As if the choir in robes of fire were singing here;
Nor shout, nor rush, but hush For God is here.

The calligraphy in the foyer of St. Paul's was created by Melissa Clark, who copied the
verse from a plaque hanging at St. Mary's Church, Ashbury, in Oxfordshire,
England. It has been attributed to the Reverend J. Mackey.

John Moll

*S*t. Paul's Episcopal Church observed its 300th anniversary in 1992, celebrating its official establishment as a parish by the Vestry Act of 1692. The original parish church was known as "Chester Church" and is believed to have been built sometime between 1640 and 1660 outside the present town of Centreville. The second church building on the same site began construction in 1697 and the vestry rebuilt the church a third time after the Revolutionary War. In 1794, the town of Centreville was established, leaving the church across the river from its parishioners.

In 1834, some of the ancient bricks of the old Chester Church were removed and placed in the new building erected on the present site in Centreville. The church was extended in 1855 to reflect the shape of the cross and stands today as the fourth building to serve the congregation of St. Paul's Parish. In honor of St. Paul's 300th anniversary, the Episcopal Church Women (ECW) celebrate the continuing life of St. Paul's history through this special cookbook project, the third edition of *Queen Anne Goes to the Kitchen.*

RECTORS OF ST. PAUL'S PARISH

The Reverend John Lillingston 1694–1709	The Reverend John Reynolds 1806–1809
The Reverend John Hindman 1710–1713	The Reverend Daniel Stevens 1811–1816
The Reverend Christopher Wilkinson 1714–1728	The Reverend William I. Bulkley 1817–1820
The Reverend James Cox 1729–1753	The Reverend Grandison Alsquith 1821–1823
The Reverend Alexander Malcolm 1754–1763	The Reverend Bennett S. Glover 1824–1825
The Reverend Samuel Keene 1763–1766	The Reverend Thomas K. Peck 1825–1828
The Reverend Hugh Neill 1767–1781	The Reverend Robert W. Goldsborough 1829–1836
The Reverend Robert Smith 1783–1784	The Reverend John Owen 1836
The Reverend Elisha Rigg 1796–1803	The Reverend John P. Robinson 1836–1841
The Reverend Mr. Barclay 1804–1805	The Reverend Henry Brown 1841–1851

The Reverend William G. Hawkins
1851–1852

The Reverend William Cross Crane
1852–1855

The Reverend Erastus F. Dashiell
1856–1862

The Reverend E. J. Sterns
1862–1863

The Reverend Gustavus C. Bird
1863–1866

The Reverend Aristides S. Smith
1867–1872

The Reverend S. H. S. Gallaudet
1872–1873

The Reverend James A. Mitchell
1873–1902

The Reverend Walter B. Stehl
1902–1913

The Reverend Arthur B. Conger
1913–1916

The Reverend J. Derickson Cummings
1916–1919

The Reverend William C. Marshall
1919–1923

The Reverend Alward Chamberlaine
1924–1938

The Reverend Thomas Donaldson
1939–1957

The Reverend David F. Gearhart
1958–1965

The Reverend James E. Cantler
1965–1972

The Reverend William M. Hargett
1973–1986

The Reverend Joseph Tatnall (Interim)
1986–1987

The Reverend Robert T. Gribbon
1987–

BISHOPS OF THE DIOCESE OF EASTON

The Right Reverend
Henry Champain Lay
1869–1885

The Right Reverend
William Forbes Adams
1887–1920

The Right Reverend
George William Davenport
1920–1938

The Right Reverend
William McClelland
1939–1949

The Right Reverend
Allen Jerome Miller
1949–1966

The Right Reverend
George Alfred Taylor
1967–1975

The Right Reverend
William Moultrie Moore, Jr.
1975–1983

The Right Reverend
Elliott L. Sorge
1983–

$\mathscr{B}$IBLICAL HERB GARDEN

IN MEMORIAM

Ethel Andrew
Katherine L. Bordley
Josephine G. Bullock
Ruth Branner Gadd
Collin Rex Harrison

Adrienne Howard
Douglass Mann
Oscar Payne
William Thomas
Charles Carroll Tilghman

Elizabeth B. Tuttle
Genevieve Valliant
David Wharton
Sally Will
Clayton Wright, Jr.

LEGEND

CROSS: Edging Box *Buxus sempervirens suffruticosa* (Isaiah 41:19)
CENTER: Miniature roses *Rosa chinensis* "minima" and lily of
the valley *Convallaria majalis* (Song of Solomon 2:1)

SCENTED

Thyme edging *Thymus* spp. (Song of Solomon 4:16)
Silver thyme *Thymus vulgaris argenteus*
Lemon thyme *Thymus vulgaris citriodorus*
Wooly thyme *Thymus praecox*
Lavender *lavandula vera* "munstead" (Luke 23:56)
Tansy *Tanacetum vulgare* (Song of Solomon 4:14)
Pineapple sage *Salvia elegans* (Exodus 37:17-18)
Golden sage *Salvia officinalis* "Aurea" (Exodus 37:17-18)
Rosemary *Rosemarinus officinalis* "Arp" (John 19:39-40)
Tithing herb: Rue *Ruta graveolens* (Luke 11:42)

MEDICINAL

Chamomile edging *Anthemis nobilis* (James 1:9-10)
Horehound *Marrubium vulgare* (Exodus 12:8)
Hyssop *Origanum syriacum* (Leviticus 14:4,6)
Feverfew *Chrysanthemum parthenium matricaria* (Isaiah 40:6)
Tithing herb: Mint *Mentha* spp. (Matthew 23:23)
Apple mint *Mentha suaveolens*
Peppermint *Mentha piperita*
Pineapple mint *Mentha suaveolens* "Variegata"
Spearmint *Mentha spicata*

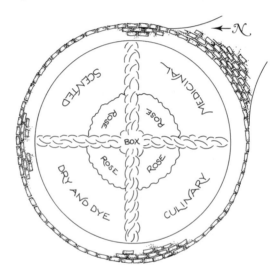

DRY AND DYE

Marigold edging *Calendula arvensis* (Isaiah 40:6)
Garlic chives *Allium sativum* (Numbers 11:5-6)
Egyptian onion *Allium cepa* (Numbers 11:5-6)
Golden flax *Linum flavum* (Genesis 41:42)
Blackberry lily *Belamcanda chinensis* (Hosea 14:5)
Golden marguerite *Anthemis tinctoria* "Kelway" (Peter 1:24-25)
Tithing herb: Dill *Anethum graveolens* (Matthew 23:23)

CULINARY

Watercress edging *Nasturtium officinale* (Deuteronomy 32:2)
Sweet woodruff *Gallium odoratum* (Song of Solomon 4:16)
Dill *Anethum graveolens* (Matthew 23:23)
Marjoram *Origanum majorana* (Exodus 12:22)
Chives *Allium schoenoprasum* (Numbers 11:5-6)
Rosemary *Rosmarinus officinalis* "Arp" (John 19:39- 40)
Coriander *Coriandrum sativum* (Numbers 11:7)
Sage *Salvia officinalis* (Exodus 37:17-18)

The Biblical Herb Garden came about by the energies of the Queen Anne's County Garden Club, the Junior Garden Club, and St. Paul's Sunday School, who prepared the garden for spring planting in the fall of 1991. In the commemorative year of 1992 the fruits of their labor were already providing a hands-on source of learning about herb culture and craft for St. Paul's and the community. Here are some gatherings from the Herb Garden.

MINT BUTTER

6   tablespoons butter, at room temperature
3   tablespoons fresh mint, minced (or 1½ tablespoons dried)
    salt and pepper to taste
1   tablespoon lemon juice

Mix butter with mint. Add salt and pepper, then lemon juice. Refrigerate. Spread on grilled lamb or add a dab to peas.

HOREHOUND CANDY

½   cup dried horehound leaves (or 1½ cup fresh)
2   cups boiling water
3   cups granulated sugar
½   teaspoon cream of tartar
1   teaspoon lemon juice

Make a strong infusion of the horehound leaves by steeping them in 2 cups boiling water. Strain after 10 minutes into 6-quart saucepan. Add sugar and cream of tartar. Boil to crack stage (300 degrees on candy thermometer). Add lemon juice. Pour quickly into buttered jelly roll pan. Mark off into small squares when candy begins to harden. When it shrinks from side of pan sprinkle with sugar and turn out into plastic bag. Break gently.

🐛 *DILL VINEGAR*

> 1 quart white vinegar
> 2 or 3 dill seed heads

Sterilize a quart bottle and keep warm. Bring vinegar just to boiling point in a stainless steel saucepan. Put dill seed heads or branches into bottle. Pour hot vinegar over herbs to within 2 inches of the top. Cork securely. Place in a cool, dark place for a week to 10 days. Decant and remove herbs. A fresh herb sprig may be added. Recork and store.

🐛 *CHAMOMILE TEA*

> dried chamomile flowers
> boiling water
> honey

Steep 5 or 6 chamomile flowers in 1 cup of boiling water for 5 minutes. Strain and add a little honey and drink while hot.

🐛 *MAI WINE*

> 1 gallon Rhine wine
> 10 sprigs sweet woodruff

Stuff bottle of Rhine wine with sweet woodruff sprigs. Steep for a week or longer in the refrigerator. Serve in punch cups with a fresh sweet woodruff sprig and a fresh strawberry.

🐛 *ROSEMARY SHORTBREAD COOKIES*

> 8 tablespoons butter
> ¼ cup confectioners' sugar
> 1½ cups all-purpose flour
> 2 tablespoons fresh rosemary, finely minced
> 2 tablespoons granulated sugar for sprinkling

Process ingredients in processor. Roll out on floured board to ¼ inch thick and cut out using a 2-inch cookie cutter. Bake at 325 degrees on a greased cookie sheet for 15 minutes or until shortbread begins to change color. Cool on wire rack and sprinkle with the extra sugar. Makes 3 dozen cookies.

BEVERAGES AND HORS D'OEUVRES

For every cup and plateful,
God make us truly grateful.

🥬 *MINT JULEP*

This recipe is extracted from a letter of Colonel S. B. Buckner, Jr., U.S. Infantry, Ft. George G. Meade, Md., to Major General William D. Connor, West Point, N.Y., dated March 30, 1937. Colonel Buckner ends: "When all is ready, assemble your guests in the porch or in the garden, where the drama of the juleps will rise heavenward and make the birds sing . . . Being overcome by thirst, I can write no further."

cool, clear spring water (bottled)
lots of fresh mint
a good Kentucky bourbon
sugar bowl
row of silver goblets and spoons
ice

In a canvas bag pound twice as much ice as you think you will need. Make it fine as snow and keep it dry.

In each goblet put a heaping teaspoon of sugar, barely cover with spring water and slightly bruise one mint leaf into this mixture, leaving the spoon in the goblet. Pour bourbon to make about ¼ full. Wipe goblet dry and embellish copiously with mint.

Then comes the important and delicate operation of frosting. By proper manipulation of the spoon, the ingredients are circulated and blended until the goblet is encrusted with frost. "Thus harmoniously blended by the deft touches of a skilled hand, you have a beverage eminently appropriate for honorable men and beautiful women."

—S. B. Buckner, Jr., Col., U.S. Infantry

🥬 *SUE EMORY'S EGGNOG*

Sue Emory always made this at Thanksgiving time for Christmas drinking.

12 eggs, separated
½ teaspoon salt
 1 pound sugar
 1 pint whiskey
 1 pint rum
½ gallon milk, scalded and cooled
   nutmeg

Beat yolks of eggs very light; add salt and sugar to them, then the whiskey and rum. Add milk. Beat whites of eggs very light and add last. Grate nutmeg on top of each cup. Makes approximately 1 gallon.

—Sue Emory

🍃 GLOGG

The ingredients in this are flexible. We make glogg on Christmas Eve as it fits well with a Scandinavian theme and everybody at our house likes it. It is a Swedish answer to darkness, cold, and troublesome trolls. I serve this drink with gravlax, pickled herring, Swedish brown beans, and meatballs.

 3 bottles dry red wine
 1 pint sweet vermouth
10 whole cloves
 1 2-inch piece of fresh or candied ginger
   couple dashes of bitters
 2 cups raisins
 1 cinnamon stick
   peeling of an orange
 2 teaspoons whole cardamom seeds, bruised
 2 cups more or less of aquavit (or vodka will do)
 1 cup sugar
 2 cups blanched almonds

Combine everything except aquavit, sugar, and almonds in a stainless steel kettle. Let stand at least twelve hours. Add aquavit and sugar. Bring to a boil and *immediately* remove from heat, but keep warm. Add almonds and serve. Demitasse spoons can be used to extract almonds and raisins from your mug or glass. Makes 25 servings.

—Joann W. Valliant (Mrs. James W.)

🍃 SHERRY SOUR

 1 fifth dry cocktail sherry
 1 6-ounce can frozen lemonade concentrate, undiluted

Mix the two ingredients in a large pitcher. Chill overnight. Pour over shaved ice in iced stemmed wine glasses. Makes 8 to 12 servings.

—Janet Gadd Doehler (Mrs. William F.)

🍃 GRAPE WINE

> 3 gallons juice
> 1 gallon water
> 2½ pounds sugar per gallon

Select sound ripe grapes, pick from stem, crush and put pulp in tight wooden vessel or barrel for 48 hours. Draw off juice, strain and measure. Pour over pulp 1 gallon water for every 3 gallons juice. Stir and let stand 24 hours. Press mixture to extract all juice. Mix with pure juice first drawn off. For each gallon of this mixture, put 2½ pounds sugar.

Place in a clean keg, filling it, and cover bung hole with mosquito netting to keep out insects. (A five gallon keg will hold only 4 gallons mixture and 10 pounds sugar.)

Let stand 1 month, keeping cask always full by adding juice, as fermenting proceeds. Save some juice to refill keg. At expiration 1 month, bung cask tightly. Fit for use in 3 or 4 months from time it was put in keg, but gains strength and quality by being kept bunged for 6 months or longer.

—Judge Philemon Blake Hopper

The Honorable Philemon B. Hopper (1791-1858): Son and grandson of Col. William Hopper and Col. William Hopper, Jr., active Vestry members in the 18th century development of St. Paul's Parish, Judge Hopper is considered one of the founders of the Methodist Protestant Church in America. Born in Queen Anne's County, Hopper was admitted to the Bar and subsequently elected to the Maryland legislature. In 1826 he was appointed judge of the second judicial district. Known for his hospitality and horticultural interests, Hopper encouraged the planting of mulberry trees for silk and peach orchards for the growing canning industry in the state of Maryland.—Cyclopedia of Methodism, *Mathew Simpson, ed., Philadelphia: Louis H. Everts, 1881.*

🍃 CHRISTMAS PUNCH

> 2 6-ounce cans frozen limeade concentrate
> 2 6-ounce cans frozen lemonade concentrate
> 2 6-ounce cans orange juice concentrate
> 2 quarts cold water
> 2 quarts chilled ginger ale

Combine concentrates with water. Pour over a block of orange ice or ice cubes, whichever you desire. Add ginger ale. Makes 25 servings.

—*Mildred Smith Thompson (Mrs. Philemon Hopper)*

MULLED CIDER

Enjoying mulled cider with doughnuts is part of the fall Apple Festival tradition celebrated on the South Lawn of St. Paul's.

1 quart sweet apple cider
8 whole allspice
1 stick cinnamon
8 whole cloves
dash of salt
¼ cup brown sugar, scant

Put cider into saucepan, add the spices, salt, and sugar. Cover and heat very slowly to the boiling point. Heat should be so low that it takes the cider half an hour to come to a boil. Remove from heat, strain, and serve steaming hot. Makes 5 servings. For larger quantities, reduce proportions of spices and tie in cheesecloth bag.

—*Committee*

CHAMPAGNE PUNCH

1½ pounds sugar
3 pints water
1 quart medium tea
1 quart rum
1 pint lemon juice
1 pint brandy
1 quart orange juice
1 quart soda water
1 quart champagne

Boil the sugar and water until reduced to 1 quart of thick syrup. Blend next five ingredients with the syrup in a glass or stainless steel container. Add soda water and champagne just before serving. Makes 80 4-ounce punch cups.

—*Reba Wright Turpin (Mrs. J. R. E.)*

❧ COFFEE CREAM PUNCH

    3 quarts vanilla ice cream
    2 quarts hot coffee
       nutmeg

Pour coffee over ice cream in a bowl. Stir until partially melted. Sprinkle with nutmeg. Makes 12 servings.

—Mildred Smith Thompson (Mrs. Philemon Hopper)

❧ MARJORIE'S PUNCH

A refreshing drink used for years at Confirmation receptions and Bishop's Teas.

    1 46-ounce can pineapple juice
  ⅔ cup sugar, scant
    1 46-ounce can orange juice
       juice of 3 lemons (⅔ cup)
1½ quarts ginger ale

Combine first four ingredients. Add ginger ale just before serving. At the last moment, add a pretty ice mold of fruit or mint leaves. Makes 36 servings.

—Marjorie Belt Turner (Mrs. Edward)

❧ GRANDMOTHER'S PUNCH

    3 quarts dry sherry
    3 jiggers Cointreau
    1 quart brandy
    1 pint white rum
    3 jiggers white crème de menthe

Mix all ingredients and refrigerate overnight. Serve in thoroughly chilled cocktail glasses. Makes 25 to 30 servings.

—Katherine Nicols Grove (Mrs. J. Robert)

❧ ROSEMARY PUNCH

    3 tablespoons crushed fresh rosemary
    3 tablespoons sugar

¼ teaspoon salt
½ cup water
½ cup apricot nectar
1 cup lime juice
1 quart ginger ale

Simmer first four ingredients for two minutes. Cool and strain. Then combine with remaining ingredients. Makes 12 servings.

—*Ieva Turjanis Ersts (Mrs. Martin)*

WHISKEY SOUR

1 12-ounce can frozen lemonade concentrate, undiluted
1½ cups orange juice
1½ cups Canadian whiskey

Blend in a blender with a handful of ice. Serve over ice with a thin slice of orange and a cherry for color, if desired. Makes 8 to 10 servings.

—*James O. Pippin, Jr.*

WHISKEY SOUR PUNCH

1 or 2 pints simple syrup (see below)
3 quarts blended whiskey (e.g., Seagram's 7)
2 quarts fresh lemon juice (from about 4½ dozen lemons)
1 pint soda water
large hunk of ice

Mix liquids in punch bowl. Add ice and soda a half-hour before serving. Makes 60 to 65 punch cup size servings.

Simple Syrup

4 cups sugar
1 cup water

Bring to a boil and remove from heat at once or it will crystallize. Stir only once or twice. Makes 2 pints.

—*John W. Perry, Jr.*

❧ PUNCH

Very good and potent.

1 fifth bourbon
1 6-ounce can frozen lemonade concentrate, undiluted
1 fifth rum
1 6-ounce can frozen limeade concentrate, undiluted
1 fifth vodka
1 quart sparkling water or ginger ale

Mix all the ingredients, adding sparkling water or ginger ale last. Makes 25 to 30 servings.

—John Goldsborough

❧ SUMMER TEA

This is served at the Bishop's reception at St. Paul's and is very refreshing.

8 teabags
½ cup sugar
3 quarts boiling water
3 or 4 sprigs fresh mint (optional)
1 12-ounce can frozen lemonade concentrate, undiluted
1 liter ginger ale

Add teabags and sugar to boiling water. After tea has cooled, add mint. Before serving, add lemonade concentrate and ginger ale. Makes 55 to 60 servings.

—Lois Gompf Radcliffe (Mrs. Edmund)

❧ BEN BAKER

3 lemons
1 cup of water
   rind of 2 lemons
2 cups whiskey
½ cup sugar

Combine all ingredients. Stir. Pour into a quart jar and top with more water. Chill for 24 hours. Strain. Makes 6 servings.

—*Pearle E. Bishop*

HOT TEA TODDY TO FIGHT A COLD

boiling water
1 teaspoon black tea such as orange pekoe or Earl Grey
1 jigger bourbon
1 tablespoon honey or sugar
1 teaspoon fresh lemon juice

Heat a Jefferson cup with hot water. Discard water and refill three-fourths full with additional hot water. Add tea and brew tea in cup. Add remaining ingredients. Stir well. Drink with both hands wrapped around cup. Refill if desired and go to bed immediately upon finishing toddy. Sleep well.

— *Committee*

PHILADELPHIA UNION LEAGUE SPECIAL

1 ounce Cointreau
1 ounce orange juice
1½ ounces Myers's rum
½ ounce lemon juice
1½ ounces bourbon

Place all ingredients in a cocktail shaker. Add ice, shake, and strain. Makes 1 serving.

—*Paul Marshall Long*

CREAM CHEESE APPETIZER

8 ounces cream cheese
½ cup shrimp cocktail sauce
½ cup chopped canned shrimp or ½ cup crabmeat

Place cream cheese on a serving plate. Top with cocktail sauce. Top sauce with shrimp or crabmeat. Serve with crackers. Makes 2 cups.

—*Joyce Mason Jeswilkowski (Mrs. Charles)*

❧ CURRY CHUTNEY DIP

8 ounces cream cheese
½ cup English walnuts, chopped
1 tablespoon minced onion
3 tablespoons Major Grey's chutney, chopped
1 teaspoon lemon juice
½ teaspoon curry powder (or to taste)
  cream

Mix well all ingredients except cream. Thin to spreading consistency with cream. Serve with bland crackers such as Carr's water biscuits or sesame wafers. Makes approximately 1½ cups.

—*Marjorie McSweeney Orr (Mrs. Arnold J.)*

❧ DEVILED HAM IN MUSHROOM CAPS

1 pound large mushrooms
2 tablespoons butter plus melted butter for topping
  juice of 1 lemon
  salt and pepper to taste
1 tablespoon brandy plus additional for topping
½ pound cooked ham
½ tablespoon mayonnaise
½ teaspoon dry mustard
½ cup Parmesan cheese

Clean mushrooms. Remove stems and sauté caps in 2 tablespoons of butter for 1 to 2 minutes. Add lemon juice, salt, and pepper to taste. Add 1 tablespoon brandy (or to taste). Cool and set aside. Chop mushroom stems. Grind ham and sauté with mushroom stems. Add enough mayonnaise to hold mixture together. Season mixture with dry mustard. Stuff each cap with the filling, using a large pastry bag or spoon. Top each with Parmesan cheese, a little melted butter, and a drop of brandy, if desired. Bake at 425 degrees for 10 minutes or until brown. Serve hot. Fills about 2 dozen mushroom caps, depending on size.

—*Marybelle Weatherford Henry (Mrs. Elmer T.)*

The late Reverend Elmer Henry was assisting priest at St. Paul's from 1976 to 1990.

CHAFING DISH DIP

Nice for a winter cocktail party.

1 5-ounce jar Kraft Old English spread
1 11-ounce can undiluted cream of celery or mushroom soup
1 bouillon cube (beef)
1 clove garlic, minced
  salt and pepper
  dash of Tabasco sauce

Mix ingredients together and serve warm in chafing dish. Provide your favorite crackers to dip. Makes 2 cups.

—*Mary Ashley Long (Mrs. Paul M.)*

WAUS'S WILD GOOSE OR DUCK PÂTÉ

1 wild goose or duck (legs, breast, or both)
  salt and pepper
  celery seed
  baking bag
  several small onions
  several stalks celery
  Worcestershire sauce
  mayonnaise

Soak bodies of picked and cleaned birds in cold water 30 to 60 minutes. Remove from water and rub inside and out with salt, pepper, and celery seed. Bake at 350 degrees in baking bag 30 minutes for duck, 60 minutes for goose, or until desired doneness. Cool. Cut up onions, celery, and cold meat. Grind, alternating meat, celery, and onions. Add salt and pepper to taste. Add several dashes of Worcestershire sauce. This mixture will keep in the refrigerator or it may be frozen until needed. When ready to use, add mayonnaise to form desired consistency of pâté. Makes 12 servings.

—*Frank W. Draper III*

🌿 *MARGARETANNE CAMPBELL'S INDIAN CURRIED CHICKEN BALLS*

    4 ounces cream cheese
    2 tablespoons mayonnaise
    1 tablespoon chutney
    1 teaspoon curry powder
    1 cup chopped cooked chicken
    ¼ teaspoon salt
    ¾ cup sliced blanched almonds
    ½ cup flaked coconut or ½ cup chopped peanuts

Beat cream cheese and mayonnaise until fluffy. Add remaining ingredients except coconut or peanuts. Chill for 1 hour. Remove from refrigerator and form into balls about the size of a quarter. Roll balls in flaked coconut or chopped peanuts. Serve immediately or refrigerate overnight. Serve at room temperature. Makes 35.

—Marybelle Weatherford Henry (Mrs. Elmer T.)

🌿 *CURRIED MEATBALLS*

    1 pound ground beef
    2 teaspoons curry powder
    1 cup stuffing mix
    ½ teaspoon salt
       freshly ground pepper
    ½ cup butter

Mix beef, curry powder, stuffing mix, salt, and pepper together. Shape into small balls and sauté in butter over high heat for 5 minutes or until brown. Drain. Place colored toothpick in each. Serve at once. Makes 32.

—Jean Tubman (Mrs. S. Alexander)

🌿 *SMOKED TUNA AND WHITE BEAN SPREAD*

    1 19-ounce can white (cannellini) beans
    3 tablespoons olive oil
    ¼ pound smoked tuna
    3 tablespoons finely chopped red onion

1 tablespoon fresh herbs: rosemary or dill, etc.
   salt and ground pepper
   squirt of Tabasco

Drain and mash beans with oil. Finely dice/chop tuna. Add other ingredients and chill. Bring to room temperature. Serve with small pumpernickel rounds, plain pita chips, or something similar. Makes 2 cups.

—*Joann W. Valliant (Mrs. James W.)*

❦ CRABMEAT DIP

1   cup flaked crabmeat
2   tablespoons lemon juice
⅓ cup cream
1½ teaspoons Worcestershire sauce
8   ounces cream cheese
1   clove garlic, minced or pressed
    salt and pepper

Mix well together and serve with crackers. Makes 2 cups.

—*Mildred Lee Thompson Murray (Mrs. Gerald)*

❦ CRABMEAT SPREAD

This is too rich for a salad but makes a delicious hors d'oeuvre. Everyone who has tasted this wants the recipe.

¼ cup sweet relish
½ cup mayonnaise
¼ cup chopped onion
1   cup sour cream
2   tablespoons dark Jamaica rum
1   pound fresh backfin (lump) crabmeat

Mix all ingredients together except crab. Then gently toss in crab so as not to break up the large lumps. Let stand in refrigerator several hours before serving. (It will be juicy.) Serve with a teaspoon on crackers or melba toast with cocktails. Makes 2 dozen.

—*Virginia Ingles Freeland (Mrs. Samuel L.)*

❧ CHEESE CAKES

The committee tried this recipe with white cheddar cheese and sharp domestic yellow cheese. Both are excellent. The yellow cheese coarsely grated makes quite a different cake from the cheddar.

1 cup butter
1½ to 2 cups flour
2 cups freshly grated cheese
1 teaspoon salt
cayenne pepper to taste
halves of pecan nuts

Mix butter, flour, and cheese. Add seasonings. Knead thoroughly. Roll out ½-inch thick and cut in small cakes. Place pecan half on top. Bake at 350 degrees for 12 minutes. Makes 3 dozen.

—Reba Wright Turpin (Mrs. J. R. E.)

❧ CHEESE PUFFS

¼ pound grated sharp cheddar cheese
¼ pound margarine
1 cup flour

Blend cheese and margarine. Add flour and beat well. Form into marble-sized balls on cookie sheet. Bake at 400 degrees for 10 to 15 minutes. Makes 2 dozen.

—Harriet Willcox Gearhart (Mrs. David F.)

The Reverend David Gearhart was rector at St. Paul's from 1958 to 1965.

❧ JEAN WETZEL'S PÂTÉ MAISON

Keeps well in refrigerator for 2 weeks.

¾ pound finely ground calf's liver
½ pound finely ground lean pork

    1 clove garlic, crushed
    1 teaspoon salt
    ½ teaspoon thyme
    1 bay leaf, crushed
    ½ teaspoon marjoram
       pinch cayenne powder
       pinch nutmeg
    ½ cup dry white wine
    1 pound lean pork cut into ½-inch thick slices
    ½ pound lean bacon

Combine liver, ground pork, salt, herbs, spices, and wine. Mix well. Line a 9 × 5 loaf pan with strips of bacon. Put in a layer of the ground mixture, a layer of pork slices, another layer of the mixture, and another layer of pork slices. Cover with strips of bacon. Cover all with aluminum foil. Place the loaf pan in a pan of water and bake at 350 degrees for 2 hours. Let cool in pan before unmolding. Makes a 2½-pound loaf.

—Joann W. Valliant (Mrs. James W.)

KOHLBRUSSEL

    30 small Brussels sprouts
     1 tablespoon whipped cream
     3 ounces cream cheese
    1½ tablespoons horseradish

Cook Brussels sprouts for about three minutes in boiling water, only long enough to obtain a brilliant green color. Be sure to remove from the heat before they lose this color. Soften the cream cheese and mix with the whipped cream. Add the horseradish. Cut each Brussels sprout three-quarters of the way through the center and stuff with cheese mixture. Sprinkle the sprouts with salt and let stand at room temperature about 30 minutes before serving. Makes 30.

—Janet Gadd Doehler (Mrs. William F.)

❧ CREAM CHEESE DIP

Delicious as a dip with potato chips. You may vary it by adding
2 ounces of deviled ham or finely cut chipped beef.

8 ounces cream cheese at room temperature
4 tablespoons sour cream
4 tablespoons fresh or dried parsley
2 tablespoons mayonnaise
½ teaspoon onion salt
¼ teaspoon garlic salt

Mix all ingredients together. Makes 1½ cups

—*Elizabeth Trundle Barton (Mrs. Marvin)*
—*Anne Gadd Hennighausen (Mrs. Charles E.)*

❧ VEAL PÂTÉ

This may be used as a first course.

1 pound veal
salt
celery salt
pepper
4 sliced hard-boiled eggs
1 tablespoon unflavored gelatin

Boil veal in small quantity of water until tender. Cut very fine and season to taste with salt, celery seed, and pepper. Fill a buttered mold with alternate layers of the veal and the eggs. Add gelatin to the water in which the veal was cooked and let it boil a few minutes. When this is cool (not cold) pour it over the mold of the veal and eggs and place in a cool place. Serve cold.

—*Miss Clara Hollyday, Readbourne. From* Eat,
Drink and Be Merry in Maryland

❧ LIVER PASTE FOR CANAPÉS

1 medium onion, chopped fine
2 tablespoons butter
1 pound chicken livers

> 5 hard-boiled eggs
> 1 teaspoon mayonnaise
> ¼ teaspoon nutmeg
> ¼ teaspoon Lawry's salt
> salt and pepper to taste

Sauté onion in butter until soft. Add chicken livers and sauté until done. Drain on paper. Put livers and onions through ricer together with eggs. Add mayonnaise and seasoning. Serve cold on crackers. Makes 3 cups.

—Jean Wetzel (Mrs. Frank)

❀ ANCHOVIED CUCUMBERS

> 1 large cucumber
> ¼ cup sweet butter
> 3 2-ounce cans rolled anchovy fillets stuffed with capers, drained
> parsley sprigs

Pare cucumber. Score lengthwise with a fork. Cut into ¼-inch slices. Spread each slice with butter. Top with a rolled anchovy fillet (or a flat piece). Garnish with parsley sprigs. Makes 30.

—Mary Davy Pippin (Mrs. James O., Jr.)

❀ SMOKED OYSTER ROLL

> 8 ounces cream cheese
> 2 tablespoons mayonnaise
> 2 teaspoons Worcestershire sauce
> dash hot pepper sauce
> 2 teaspoons grated onion
> 1 teaspoon salt
> aluminum foil
> 1 4-ounce tin of smoked oysters
> chopped parsley
> paprika

Combine first six ingredients, and spread half-inch thick on foil. Chill. Chop smoked oysters and spread over cheese mixture. Roll up as you would a jelly roll. Sprinkle with chopped parsley and paprika. Makes enough for 12 to 15 people as a spread for crackers or melba toast rounds.

—Katherine Maybeck Draper (Mrs. Frank W., III)

✖ SHRIMP DIP

8 ounces cream cheese
¼ cup mayonnaise
¼ cup salad dressing (Miracle Whip)
1 onion, chopped fine
2 teaspoons prepared mustard
couple of drops of Tabasco
1 8-ounce can small, deveined shrimp, drained

Combine first six ingredients. Add shrimp last. Refrigerate overnight. The recipe can easily be halved. Makes 12 to 15 servings.

—Shirley Tuttle Freestate (Mrs. William M.)

✖ HERB CHEESE FILLING

8 ounces cream cheese
1 teaspoon lemon thyme
½ teaspoon rosemary
1 teaspoon parsley
1 teaspoon garlic chives
dash of Beau Monde [a Spice Islands product]

Mix together. Chill overnight to blend flavors. Use as a stuffing for snow peas or cherry tomatoes. Makes 1 cup.

— Committee

✖ FRESH TOMATO SALSA

6 plum tomatoes, seeded, peeled, and coarsely chopped
⅓ cup chopped red onion
½ to 1 teaspoon seeded, minced jalapeno pepper (canned is fine)
2 to 3 cloves garlic, minced
3 tablespoons minced cilantro
2 tablespoons fresh lime juice

Combine all ingredients and chill. Serve with tortilla chips, or with fish or chicken. Makes about 2½ cups.

—Miss Sydney Cooper Ashley

❧ HOT CHEESE DIP

1 cup shredded very sharp cheese (cheddar)
½ cup chopped onion
½ cup real mayonnaise

Mix together and bake in small dish at 400 degrees for 10 minutes or until brown and bubbly. Serve with toasted and buttered Syrian bread pieces or saltines. Makes 2 cups.

—*Dottie McMinn Wilson (Mrs. Clem)*

❧ ARTICHOKE BITES

1 6-ounce jar marinated artichoke hearts
½ cup chopped onion
1 clove garlic, minced
2 8-ounce packages egg substitute (or 8 eggs)
1 cup shredded sharp cheddar (4 ounces)
1 cup shredded Swiss cheese (4 ounces)
1 cup grated Parmesan cheese (4 ounces)
¼ cup minced parsley
¼ teaspoon pepper
¼ teaspoon basil
¼ teaspoon oregano
⅛ teaspoon Tabasco
dash of Worcestershire sauce
½ cup fine dry bread crumbs or cracker crumbs

Drain artichoke hearts, reserving marinade. In a small saucepan, cook onion and garlic in reserved marinade until onion is tender. In processor bowl or blender combine artichoke hearts and remaining ingredients except bread crumbs. Cover and blend until smooth. Stir in onion mixture and bread crumbs. Spoon mixture into greased 1¾-inch muffin pans or individual tartlet shells, filling about three-fourths full. Bake, uncovered, at 325 degrees for 12 to 15 minutes or until knife inserted comes out clean. Dust with paprika. Remove from pans. Serve immediately.

May be frozen. To serve, remove from freezer, but do not thaw. Follow baking instructions above. Makes approximately 40.

—*Committee*

TACO PIE

4 avocados, peeled, seeded, and mashed in a food
    processor
2 tablespoons lemon juice
1 teaspoon salt
1 cup sour cream
1 package taco seasoning mix
¼ cup mayonnaise
1 bunch scallions, chopped
3 tomatoes, seeded and chopped, or equivalent amount
    of cherry tomatoes
8 ounces cheddar cheese, shredded
1 6-ounce can black olives, sliced

Mix avocados, lemon juice, and salt and spread over the bottom of a fairly deep, straight-sided dish. Mix together sour cream, taco seasoning mix, and mayonnaise. Spread over avocado mixture. Make separate layers of each of the remaining ingredients. Makes 12 servings.

—Ashley Long Tanis (Mrs. Thomas)

CRAB CANAPÉ PIE

1 tablespoon horseradish
½ 3-ounce bottle capers, drained
1 teaspoon grated lemon rind
    a good dash of Tabasco sauce
2 cups mayonnaise
¾ cup grated cheddar cheese
1 pound backfin crabmeat

Mix first six ingredients well. Gently fold in crabmeat. Place in 9 × 13 Pyrex dish. Bake at 350 degrees until thoroughly warm and cheese is melted. Serve with crackers as a spread. Hot crab may be served in tartlet shells and passed while hot. Makes 48 tartlets or 36 servings as a dip.

—Jeanne Kimes Clement (Mrs. David A.)

GOLDEN NUGGETS

4 whole chicken breasts, boned and skinned
¼ cup grated Parmesan cheese

1 teaspoon salt
1 teaspoon dried basil
1 teaspoon dried thyme
1 teaspoon poultry seasoning
½ cup dry bread crumbs
½ cup melted butter

Cut boned breasts into 1½-inch squares. Combine next four ingredients in a bowl. Add chicken squares and toss. In a separate bowl, mix poultry seasoning and bread crumbs. Dip each chicken square in melted butter, then in seasoned bread crumbs. Place on Pam-sprayed foil-lined baking sheets. Bake 10 minutes at 400 degrees. Serve warm with dip of your choice. Makes 60.

—*Committee*

VEGETABLE SPREAD

Suitable for tea sandwiches, as a filling for cherry tomatoes or tartlet shells, or as a spread on crackers, Weasie's Charlotte, N.C., specialty has become a parish favorite when tea sandwiches are called for.

2 carrots
1 small onion, peeled
1 small green pepper, seeded
2 cucumbers, peeled and seeded
   cheesecloth
1 tablespoon salt
1 envelope unflavored gelatin
1 teaspoon dried or 1 tablespoon fresh dill

Chop vegetables in processor. Dampen a double layer of cheesecloth and place it in a colander over a bowl. Pour the finely chopped vegetables into cheesecloth and salt well. Let drain thoroughly into bowl; squeeze gently, saving liquid in bowl. Dissolve gelatin in 3 or 4 tablespoons of vegetable juice over hot water. Mix well with vegetables in a bowl. Add 1 tablespoon lemon juice and 1 cup mayonnaise. Chill overnight. Makes 2 cups.

—*Louisa Smith Heilman (Mrs. Benjamin G.)*

🍃 *VEGGIE SQUARES*

  2 8-ounce packages of crescent rolls
  1 egg, lightly beaten
  2 8-ounce packages cream cheese, softened
  ⅓ cup mayonnaise
  ⅓ cup milk
  ¾ cup shredded cheddar cheese
  1½ teaspoon dried dill or 1 tablespoon fresh
  1 package dry Hidden Valley Ranch dressing mix
  ½ cup broccoli, chopped fine
  ½ cup cauliflower, chopped fine
  ½ cup mushrooms, chopped fine
  ½ cup green pepper, chopped fine
  ½ cup tomato, seeded and chopped fine

Press crescent roll dough flat on a cookie sheet, sealing perforated edges. Spread with lightly beaten egg. Bake as directed on package. Cool.

Mix softened cream cheese, mayonnaise, milk, dill, and dressing mix. Spread on cool crust.

Sprinkle finely chopped vegetables on top of cream cheese mixture and press down lightly. Chill 3 hours. May be made a day before serving. Makes 48 squares.

—*Patricia Callahan Bittner (Mrs. Kenneth R.)*
—*Linda Hirst Leigh (Mrs. Robert A.)*

🍃 *CHEESE MINI-TARTS*

Pastry

  ½ cup margarine
  3 ounces cream cheese
  1 cup flour

Combine margarine and cheese with a pastry blender or in a food processor, then blend in flour. Form into a ball and chill at least half an hour. Pinch off a piece of dough about the size of a walnut, and with floured fingers press into small (1½-inch) tins that have been greased or sprayed. Makes 36 tart shells.

Quiche Filling

4	eggs
2	cups half-and-half
¼	teaspoon salt
	pinch of pepper
1 or 2	dashes of Tabasco sauce
1	cup Gruyère cheese, finely grated

With a whisk, blend eggs, half-and-half, and seasonings. Then stir in Gruyère and pour into pastry-lined cups. Bake at 350 degrees for 20 to 30 minutes. Custard should be firm. Remove from pans as soon as possible and cool on racks. These freeze very well. Serve warm. Fills 54 to 60 mini-tart shells.

Corned Beef Filling

This filling is hearty and especially appealing to those with big appetites!

2	tablespoons butter
½	cup chopped onion
2	tablespoons flour
1½	cups corned beef or 1 12-ounce can
1½	cups tomatoes

Sauté onion in butter for a few minutes until transparent. Stir in flour and cook until golden in color. Add corned beef and tomatoes and cook 10 minutes. Pour into greased, pastry-lined 1½-inch tart pans. Bake at 350 degrees for 20 minutes. Remove carefully after cooling 10 minutes. Fills 48 mini-tart shells.

—*Jane Corey (Mrs. R. Reece)*

❧ *SPINACH BRAID*

1 package (8) refrigerated crescent rolls

3 slices or more Mozzarella cheese

1 10-ounce package frozen chopped spinach, thawed
and drained

1 6½-ounce can tuna, drained (or 2 cups chopped
chicken or turkey)

1 cup ricotta cheese or cream-style small-curd cottage
cheese, drained

½ cup grated Parmesan cheese

1 teaspoon minced garlic (or ½ teaspoon garlic salt)

Remove crescent dough from can and spread out on a greased cookie sheet. Roll out dough with a rolling pin into a rectangle about 14 × 10 inches, pressing perforated edges together. Put Mozzarella slices on dough. Mix remaining ingredients together and pour this filling down the middle of the dough. Make cuts at right angles to the edge of the dough at approximately 1-inch intervals on the long sides. Fold these flaps over filling from alternating sides to give a braided appearance. Bake at 375 degrees for 20 minutes or until golden brown. Makes 4 main-dish servings or 8 appetizer servings.

—*Elizabeth Gannon Woodford (Mrs. Walter E., Jr.)*

❧ *BAKED CHEESE DIP IN BREAD*

This is so good you will need the extra dippers!

8 ounces cream cheese

1½ cups sour cream

¼ cup salsa

8 ounces shredded cheddar cheese

2 round loaves of bread, dark or white

Mix first four ingredients well. Cut off the top of one loaf. Scoop out bread to within 1-inch of crust. Reserve in a plastic bag to keep fresh. Spoon cheese mixture into bread. Replace top. Wrap in foil. Bake for 1½ hours at 400 degrees.

Scoop out the second loaf of bread. Use these pieces and the bag of reserved chunks as dippers. Makes 20 to 24 servings.

—*Nancy Palmatary Pippin (Mrs. Thomas C.)*

✿ *BEAN AND PARSLEY DIP*

  1 15½-ounce can garbanzo beans or 1¾ cups cooked
        beans
  1 large garlic clove, minced
  3 tablespoons lemon juice
  ⅓ cup tahini (sesame seed paste)
  2 green onions chopped
  ½ teaspoon ground cumin
        dash soy sauce
  ½ cup or more chopped parsley
        salt, pepper, cayenne to taste
        garnish: chopped fresh mint and/or parsley

Drain the beans and reserve liquid. Combine in food processor the beans, ¼ cup liquid, and the remaining ingredients. Process. If too thick add more bean liquid. Do not overprocess. Good on pita triangles. Makes 2 cups.

—Joann W. Valliant (Mrs. James W.)

$\mathscr{B}$READS

Bread is a lovely thing to eat.
God bless the barley and the wheat!
—Old English blessing

🌾 *ANADAMA BREAD*

    ½ cup cornmeal
    2 cups boiling water
    2 tablespoons shortening
    ½ cup molasses (light)
    1 teaspoon salt (more if there is no salt in shortening)
    1 yeast cake dissolved in ½ cup warm water
    5 cups flour

Stir meal into boiling water very slowly to avoid lumps. (*Committee note:* Beat with wire whisk while pouring in meal.) Cook about 3 minutes. When thoroughly mixed, add shortening, molasses, and salt. Cool. When lukewarm, add dissolved yeast cake and flour (enough to make a firm dough). Knead well and let rise in a warm place to more than double its bulk. Punch down and form into 2 loaves. Put in loaf pans and let rise until doubled in bulk. Bake at 400 degrees for 1 hour. Makes 2 loaves.

—Madeline Harris Bartlett

🌾 *APPLE-ORANGE NUT BREAD*

    1 large orange
    ½ cup seedless raisins
    1 cup applesauce
    2 cups sifted all-purpose flour
    2 teaspoons baking powder
    1 teaspoon soda
    1 cup sugar
    ¾ teaspoon salt
    ¾ cup chopped nutmeats
    1 egg
    3 tablespoons melted butter or margarine

Squeeze juice from orange. Using a medium blade, put rind through a food chopper with raisins. Add orange juice, rind, and raisins to applesauce. In a separate bowl, sift together all dry ingredients; add applesauce mixture and nutmeats. Mix thoroughly. Separately, beat the egg and add it with the melted butter to the dough, stirring well until thoroughly blended. Pour into a greased loaf pan. Bake at 350 degrees for 70 to 80 minutes. Remove from pan and cool on a wire rack.

—Dorothy Keith Perkins (Mrs. Louis H.)

⚜ *BANANA MUFFINS*

¼ cup butter
¾ cup sugar
1 egg
½ teaspoon vanilla
¾ cup mashed bananas
⅛ cup milk
1¼ cups sifted cake flour
1¼ teaspoons baking powder
¼ teaspoon soda
½ teaspoon salt
⅛ teaspoon cloves
¾ teaspoon cinnamon
¼ teaspoon nutmeg

Cream butter, sugar, and egg. Add vanilla. Combine mashed bananas and milk and add alternately with sifted dry ingredients to shortening mixture. Fill well-greased muffin tins two-thirds full. Bake at 375 degrees for 25 minutes. Makes 16 to 18 small muffins.

—Mary Bishop Keith Jukes (Mrs. J. Herbert Fielding)

⚜ *EASY CHEESE ROLLS*

1 box Pillsbury's hot roll mix
1 cup grated cheddar cheese

Follow directions on package of mix. Before adding flour mixture, blend in grated cheese. Continue as directed on package. Knead very well before shaping rolls. Let rise and bake according to directions. Makes twenty Parkerhouse rolls.

—Jennie V. Chance

❧ *BLUEBERRY MUFFINS*

     2 cups flour
     4 teaspoons baking powder
    ¼ teaspoon salt
    ½ cup sugar
    ¼ teaspoon allspice
    ¼ cup shortening
     1 egg, well beaten
     1 cup milk
        blueberries

Mix dry ingredients. Cut in shortening. Combine egg and milk and add to dough. Add blueberries as desired. Bake at 400 degrees for 25 minutes. Makes 12 muffins.

—Margaret Fesmyer Wolcott (Mrs. Milton)

Mrs. Wolcott was organist at St. Paul's for 30 years.

❧ *BANANA BREAD*

    ¾ cup butter
    1½ cups sugar
    1½ cups mashed banana
     2 eggs
     1 tablespoon vanilla
     2 cups all-purpose flour
     1 teaspoon baking powder
    ¾ teaspoon salt
    ½ cup buttermilk
     1 cup pecans
    ¾ cup walnuts

Cream butter and sugar; then add banana, eggs, and vanilla. Sift dry ingredients and add alternately with buttermilk to banana mixture. Stir in nuts. Put in a greased loaf pan (2-quart size). Bake at 325 degrees for 1½ hours.

—Anna Grace Keith (Mrs. Ronald L.)

❧ *OAT BRAN MUFFINS*

    ¾ cup bran
    1 cup buttermilk or sour milk
    1 egg (can use egg substitute)
    ⅓ cup honey
    ⅓ cup oil
    ¾ cup flour
    ½ cup whole wheat flour
    1 teaspoon baking soda

Combine first five ingredients and let stand for 10 minutes. Then stir in dry ingredients. You may add ½ cup raisins and ¾ cup chopped walnuts. Fill 12 paper cup–lined muffin pans. Bake at 425 degrees for 15 to 20 minutes.

Variations per Batch

    1 chopped, cored, unpeeled apple and 1 teaspoon cinnamon.
    1 cup mashed banana and 1 teaspoon cinnamon.
    ½ cup shredded carrots (squeeze out juice), 1 teaspoon cinnamon, and ½ teaspoon nutmeg.
    1 cup applesauce, 1 teaspoon cinnamon, and a dash of nutmeg.

—Jane Corey (Mrs. R. Reece)

❧ *BRAN MUFFINS*

    1 egg
    1 cup milk (if sour, add ½ teaspoon soda)
    ½ cup molasses
    2 tablespoons melted butter
    1 cup flour
    2 cups whole bran
  1½ teaspoons baking powder (if sweet milk)
    ½ teaspoon salt

Mix together egg, milk, molasses, and melted butter. Add dry ingredients and raisins if desired. Pour into greased muffin tins. Bake at 350 degrees for 25 minutes. Makes 12 muffins.

—Isabel Atkinson Lieber (Mrs Albert C.)

🌿 *BRAN BREAD*

 2 cups All-Bran cereal
 2 cups sour milk (or fresh milk with 1 teaspoon
       vinegar added)
 2 cups sifted flour
 2 teaspoons soda
 1 teaspoon salt
 ½ cup sugar
 ½ cup molasses
 ½ cup raisins

Allow bran to soak up milk in a large bowl. (*Committee note:* Skim milk may be substituted. Add 1 teaspoon vinegar.) Sift dry ingredients together and add to milk mixture. Add molasses and raisins. Put in greased loaf pan. Bake at 350 degrees for 1 hour and 15 minutes, or slightly longer if necessary. Good plain or toasted. Makes one large or two small loaves.

—Mary Bishop Keith Jukes (Mrs. J. Herbert Fielding)

🌿 *BRANDIED PUMPKIN BREAD*

3½ cups flour
 1 teaspoon baking soda
 1 teaspoon cinnamon
 1 teaspoon nutmeg
 1 teaspoon allspice
 4 eggs
2¾ cups sugar
 1 cup oil
 1 16-ounce can pumpkin
 ⅔ cup brandy
 1 cup chopped dates
 1 cup chopped nuts

Sift flour with soda and spices. Set aside. Beat eggs well. Add sugar gradually. Mix in oil, then pumpkin. Blend flour mixture and brandy alternately into egg mixture. Fold in dates and nuts. Bake in 3 greased and floured 9 × 5 × 3-inch loaf pans at 350 degrees for 1 hour.

—Ruby Young (Mrs. Herbert)

❧ *HEALTH NUT BREAD*

This bread makes a nice cream cheese sandwich to serve with fruit salad.

1¾ cups unbleached flour
 ¾ cup sugar
  5 tablespoons non-fat dry milk solids
  2 tablespoons wheat germ
  2 tablespoons rolled oats (quick or old-fashioned)
  1 tablespoon baking powder
  1 teaspoon salt (sea salt)
 ¼ teaspoon mace
 ½ cup chopped nuts
  2 eggs
  1 cup cooked, mashed sweet potato or pumpkin
 ½ cup water
  3 tablespoons oil

Grease and flour a 4½ × 8½-inch baking pan. Line with paper. Preheat oven to 325 degrees. Spoon flour lightly into measuring cup. Level off with knife. Put in medium-sized bowl, add dry ingredients, and stir in nuts. In another bowl, mix and blend eggs, potatoes, water, and oil. Add liquid mixture, all at one time, to dry ingredients. Stir only enough to blend. Pour into prepared pan. Bake for 70 to 75 minutes or until done. Cool 10 minutes before removing from pan. Peel off paper. Cool completely before slicing.

—*Miss Sydney Gadd Doehler*

❧ *CORNMEAL CAKES*

Serve with fried chicken.

  2 cups cornmeal
  1 quart water
  1 teaspoon salt

Cook in double boiler until thick enough to pour or spoon onto a 9-inch square pan. Put in refrigerator overnight. Cut into 12 small squares, sprinkle with flour, and fry. Serve hot with fried chicken. Makes 12 servings.

—*Mary Forman Brown (Mrs. W. Purnell)*

🍃 *WALNUT CHEDDAR LOAF*

This is especially good toasted. It rounds out a soup and salad meal.

    5 cups unbleached flour
    4 tablespoons sugar
    4 teaspoons baking powder
 2½ teaspoons salt
    2 teaspoons dry mustard
    1 teaspoon baking soda
   ⅛ teaspoon red pepper (cayenne)
   ½ cup shortening
    2 cups grated cheddar cheese
    1 teaspoon Worcestershire sauce
    2 eggs, lightly beaten
    2 cups buttermilk
    2 cups chopped walnuts

Sift dry ingredients. Cut shortening and cheese into dry ingredients. Stir well. Combine Worcestershire sauce, eggs, and milk and stir into dry ingredients to moisten. Add walnuts. Mixture will be dry. Pack into pans. It will look lumpy, and Janie Ashley calls it wart bread! Bake in 2 greased and floured 9 × 5 × 2¾-inch pans at 350 degrees for 55 minutes.

—Miss Sydney Gadd Doehler

🍃 *CINNAMON BUNS*

    1 pint milk
    1 teaspoon salt
   ½ cup butter
    2 yeast cakes softened in ½ cup lukewarm water
   ½ cup sugar
    1 tablespoon cinnamon
   ½ cup raisins
    1 egg yolk
       flour (enough to make a soft dough)
   ½ pound butter, melted
    1 cup granulated sugar
    1 egg yolk
    1 tablespoon cinnamon

Heat milk, salt, and ½ cup butter. Cool and add yeast cakes and sugar. Then add cinnamon, raisins, and egg yolk. Mix in enough flour to make a soft dough. Let rise until doubled in bulk. Roll to ¼-inch thickness, making the dough longer than wide. Mix together butter, sugar, egg yolk, and cinnamon. Spread dough with cinnamon butter. Add a few more raisins. Roll like jelly roll and cut in 1-inch pieces.

Place in 15½ × 11½-inch pan side by side allowing a little space between for rising. Let rise slightly. Bake at 350 to 375 degrees for 30 minutes. When almost done, spread with more cinnamon butter and let brown. Makes 24 buns.

—Isabel Atkinson Lieber (Mrs. Albert C.)

CINNAMON BREAD I

    1   cup milk
    ¼   cup butter
    ½   cup sugar
    2   teaspoons salt
    2   packages dry yeast dissolved in ½ cup warm water
    6   cups all-purpose or bread flour
    2   slightly beaten eggs
    ½   cup sugar
    1   tablespoon cinnamon

Scald milk; stir in butter, sugar, and salt. Cool. Put dissolved yeast in large bowl with 3 cups flour, eggs, and milk mixture. Beat 2 minutes. Knead 10 minutes. Place in greased bowl, and turn dough over. Cover and let rise until doubled.

Punch down. Let rise until doubled again. Divide in half and let rest 10 minutes. Roll each half into 12 × 7-inch rectangle. Combine sugar and cinnamon. Sprinkle on rectangles and roll each up like a jelly roll. Seal long edge. Tuck under ends. Place, sealed-edge down in two greased 9 × 5 × 3-inch pans. Cover and let rise until almost doubled, 45 to 60 minutes. Brush tops with softened butter and sprinkle with leftover sugar and cinnamon. Bake at 375 degrees for 35 to 40 minutes. Cover with foil the last 15 minutes if necessary. Remove and cool on wire racks.

—Joann W. Valliant (Mrs. James W.)

🐝 *CINNAMON BREAD II*

Excellent with bacon and fried apples.

      1 egg, beaten light
      ½ cup milk
      2 tablespoons melted shortening
      ½ cup sugar
    1¾ cups flour
      3 teaspoons baking powder
    1½ tablespoons sugar and 1 teaspoon cinnamon, mixed

Mix egg, milk, and melted shortening together. Sift sugar, flour, and baking powder together and stir well into liquid ingredients. Put in cake tin or pie plate. Spread cinnamon and sugar mixture on top. Bake at 350 degrees for about 20 minutes.

—*Elizabeth Trundle Barton (Mrs. Marvin)*

🐝 *CINNAMON CRUMB CAKE*

    1½ cups sifted all-purpose flour
      3 teaspoons baking powder
      ¼ teaspoon salt
      3 tablespoons sugar
      2 tablespoons butter
      1 egg beaten well in a cup
          milk to fill cup
      4 tablespoons sugar
      2 tablespoons flour
      2 teaspoons cinnamon

Sift dry ingredients. Add butter by cutting in with a knife, then flaking with fingers. Add egg-milk mixture to dry ingredients and beat. Spread in 7 × 11-inch pan. In another bowl mix together with a fork the sugar, flour, cinnamon, and butter. Cover batter with crumb mixture. Bake at 400 degrees for 25 minutes.

—*Frances Wright Hilleary (Mrs. Robert)*

❧ CORN CAKES I

    1½ cups cornmeal
     1 teaspoon salt
     2 teaspoons baking powder
     1 egg
     2 tablespoons shortening
        milk

Mix above ingredients together. Use enough milk to thin to desired thickness. Cook on hot griddle.

—Mabel Emory (Mrs. Addison)

❧ CLABBER OR BUTTERMILK GRIDDLE CAKES

These are nice used as pancakes or fritters for dessert by adding fruit and serving with hard sauce.

     1 egg
    1½ cups clabber or buttermilk
     1 cup flour
     1 teaspoon salt
     1 teaspoon baking powder
     ¾ teaspoon soda

Break egg in bowl, beat and add about half the clabber, then sift in the flour with salt and baking powder and mix well, adding rest of clabber. Last add the soda dissolved in a little water. Fry.

    Committee Note: Clabber is a milk product in which the whey and curd are separated. The sweet or sour milk is placed in a crock until it becomes clabber (curdled); then it is put in a curd press (we would use a colander lined with cheesecloth) and drained overnight. Today we buy cultured buttermilk at the supermarket.

—Readbourne Receipts, Queen Anne's County (Courtesy Mr. Swepson Earle).
From Eat, Drink and Be Merry in Maryland

🍂 *CORN CAKES II*

These are the real old-fashioned corn cakes grandmother made.

  1 egg
1¼ cups milk
  1 cup stone-ground white cornmeal
  1 teaspoon salt
  1 teaspoon baking powder

Beat egg well and add milk. Add mixture slowly to cornmeal and salt, stirring well. Stir in baking powder just before cooking. Grease griddle with bacon or ham fat. Griddle must be smoking hot. Makes about 15 cakes.

—*John P. W. Vest*

🍂 *JOHNNYCAKE*

   1 level cup flour
  ¾ cup cornmeal
1½ teaspoons baking powder
  ½ teaspoon salt
   1 egg, well beaten
   2 tablespoons sugar
   1 cup milk
1½ tablespoons melted butter

Add baking powder and salt to flour and meal and sift. Mix in order given. Bake in a greased skillet at 400 to 425 degrees for 15 to 20 minutes. Serves 8.

—*Mrs. Thomas Kibler*

🍂 *SWEET PONE*

Indians used this pone and baked it under live coals and cinders. It is still broadly used on the lower Eastern Shore, particularly in Worcester County.

  4 cups water-ground cornmeal
  1 cup sugar

3 pints (6 cups) boiling water
1 cup molasses
2 teaspoons salt
1 tablespoon shortening
1 cup flour
1 cup cold water

Stir meal and sugar together in large bowl. Slowly stir in boiling water, a cup or so at a time, keeping water boiling and stirring constantly. Add molasses, salt, shortening. Then add 1 cup cold water which has been combined with flour to make a smooth paste. Mix well and pour into greased roasting pan (11 × 15 inches). Bake at 350 degrees until firm, about 2½ hours. This may be baked in smaller loaf pans. If so, reduce baking time.

The end result resembles pound cake. It may be kept in the refrigerator or freezer and brought out, sliced, and steamed when needed.

—A Truitt family recipe

HOLLAND CARROT BREAD

2 cups sifted flour
2 teaspoons baking soda
2 teaspoons cinnamon
½ teaspoon salt
1½ cups sugar
1½ cups cooking oil
3 eggs
2 teaspoons vanilla
2 cups grated carrots
1 cup nutmeats or raisins, if desired

Stir flour, soda, cinnamon, and salt together. Make well in center of flour mixture in bowl and put in sugar, oil, eggs, and vanilla. With an electric mixer, beat on medium speed until well blended. Fold in grated carrots and nuts or raisins. Turn into well-greased and floured 9 × 5-inch loaf pans and bake at 300 degrees for 1 hour, or until bread tests done. Makes 2 loaves.

—Jane Hollingsworth Voshell

🍂 CUSTARD PONE

    3 eggs, well beaten
       lard, a piece the size of a hen's egg
    1 teacup full of sifted cornmeal
    1 teaspoon salt
    3 pints milk
    2 teaspoons yeast powder [baking powder]

After putting in the oven for five minutes, open and stir well, repeat again in five minutes, then bake. If your dish is just large enough for 1 quart of milk, do not put the cup of meal quite full.

—Swepson Earle, Betsy's receipt, Melfield, Queen Anne's County.
From Eat, Drink and Be Merry in Maryland

🍂 CORN MUFFINS

    1   egg, well beaten
    1   cup milk
    ½   cup melted shortening
    ½   cup yellow cornmeal
    1½ cups flour
    2   teaspoons baking powder
    ½   teaspoon salt
    2   tablespoons sugar

Mix egg, milk, and shortening. Place dry ingredients in another bowl; add egg mixture. Beat together. Place in greased muffin tins and bake at 350 to 375 degrees for ½ hour. Makes 12 muffins.

—Given by Isabel Atkinson Lieber from George Rector's recipes

🍂 BUTTERMILK CORN BREAD

> *This is a superb recipe, moist and delicious. Buttermilk makes the difference.*

    1 cup yellow cornmeal
    1 cup all-purpose flour
    2 teaspoons baking powder

¾ teaspoon salt
½ teaspoon baking soda
2 beaten egg yolks
1 cup buttermilk
3 tablespoons melted butter
2 stiffly beaten egg whites

Mix cornmeal, flour, baking powder, salt, and baking soda. Combine egg yolks, buttermilk, and melted butter. Add to dry ingredients, beating until blended. Fold in stiffly beaten egg whites. Pour batter into an 8-inch greased pan. Bake at 350 degrees for 25 to 30 minutes. Makes 8 servings.

Note: When Jij Duffey prepares this recipe, she grinds corn from Chester Farm at Wye Mill where she is a volunteer miller for Preservation Maryland.

—*Reggie Aber,* Wye Miller's Grind
Submitted by Virginia Wilson Duffey (Mrs. Harry J., III)

FRUIT KUCHEN

1 cup all-purpose flour
½ cup sugar
1 teaspoon baking powder
½ teaspoon salt
1 egg
½ cup milk
1 tablespoon salad oil
1⅓ cups drained fruit (14-ounce can)
½ cup sugar
2 tablespoons flour
¼ teaspoon cinnamon
¼ teaspoon nutmeg
3 tablespoons melted butter

Sift dry ingredients together into bowl. Beat egg, milk, and oil, and add to dry ingredients. Pour into greased 8-inch square pan. Scatter drained fruit over batter. Mix sugar, flour, and spices and sprinkle mixture over fruit. Drizzle with melted butter. Bake in preheated hot oven, 425 degrees, for 25 to 30 minutes. Serves 6 to 8.

—*Henrietta Holton Dallum (Mrs. John)*

CORNMEAL GRIDDLE CAKES

1 level cup cornmeal
1 heaping tablespoon shortening
  boiling water, enough to thoroughly melt shortening
    into meal (about 1 cup or slightly more)
1 egg
1 heaping tablespoon flour
1 heaping tablespoon sugar
1 teaspoon salt, level
1 teaspoon baking powder, level
1 cup milk

Mix thoroughly in order given. This batter should be very thin. If it thickens as it stands, add more milk to maintain proper consistency.

Fry on hot griddle, with small amount of grease. Makes 10 to 15 cakes.

—*Helen Thomas Sleasman (Mrs. A.R., Sr.)*

HOUSTON HOUSE ROLLS

These are wonderful.

4 cups flour
1 teaspoon soda
1 teaspoon salt
2 teaspoons baking powder
1 cake Fleischmann's yeast
1 quart cold water
½ cup sugar
½ cup lard shortening
½ cup butter, softened

Sift dry ingredients together. Soak yeast in some of the water. Mix sugar and lard thoroughly. Add dry ingredients and water. Add more flour, if necessary, to make a soft dough. Roll out to ¼-inch thickness. Spread with butter, fold over, and cut with biscuit cutter.

Either put in a cold oven to start or let rise slightly before baking at 350 degrees for 20 minutes. Makes 100 rolls.

Rolls can be made and kept in icebox, baking a few at a time.

—*Isabel Atkinson Lieber (Mrs. Albert C.)*

🌿 *HUNGARIAN COFFEE CAKE*

   1 cup lukewarm milk
   ¼ cup sugar
   1 teaspoon salt
   ¼ cup soft shortening
   1 cake or 1 package dried yeast
   1 egg or 2 egg yolks
   1 tablespoon water
   3½ to 3¾ cups sifted all-purpose flour
   ½ cup melted butter
   ¾ cup sugar
   1 teaspoon mace
   1 teaspoon cinnamon
   ½ cup finely chopped nuts
   ½ cup seeded currants or raisins

Mix together milk, sugar, salt, and shortening. Add yeast. Stir in 1 egg or 2 yolks and water. Mix in flour. Turn dough onto slightly floured board. Cover and let stand 10 minutes, then knead. Cover in greased bowl and let rise until not quite double in bulk (about 45 minutes). Punch down dough. Round up on board and let rest 15 minutes. Cut into walnut size pieces and form into balls. Roll in the melted butter, then in the mixture of sugar, spices, and nuts. Place one layer of balls in a well greased 9-inch tube pan so they hardly touch. Sprinkle with ½ cup currants or raisins. Add another layer of balls, sprinkle with raisins in crevices, pressing in slightly. Cover with damp cloth and let rise at 85 degrees or in warm room, until double in bulk, about 45 minutes. Bake for 35 minutes at 350 degrees. Cover with foil if it gets too brown. Immediately loosen from pan with spatula and invert. Makes 12 servings.

—Janet Gadd Doehler (Mrs. William F.)

On the eve of the American Revolution, the Vestry asked for 80,000 pounds of tobacco "for the building and compleating a new Parish Church at the place where the present Parish stands." The Revolutionary War intervened and the building of this church was not completed until 1793.

🍂 SUGAR CRUMB COFFEE CAKE

       1¼ cups sifted cake flour
       1¼ teaspoons baking powder
        ¼ teaspoon salt
        3 tablespoons butter
        ⅔ cup sugar
        1 egg, unbeaten
        5 tablespoons milk
       1½ tablespoons butter
        4 tablespoons flour
        2 tablespoons confectioners' sugar
        ¼ teaspoon cinnamon
           dash of salt
        ½ teaspoon almond extract
        ¼ cup chopped nuts

Sift flour once; measure, adding baking powder and salt, and sift again. In a separate bowl, cream butter, add sugar, cream well. Add egg and beat until fluffy. Add flour mixture alternately with milk. Put into a 9-inch greased and floured layer cake pan. Cream butter, sift in flour, sugar, cinnamon, and salt. Stir. Add almond extract and nuts. Sprinkle over the cake mixture. Bake at 375 degrees for 30 minutes. Serve warm. Makes 9 servings.

—Lou Snyder Eby (Mrs. J. Walter)

🍂 MUFFINS

        ⅓ cup butter
        2 teaspoons sugar
        ¾ cup milk
        1 egg
        2 cups flour
        ½ teaspoon salt
        1 large tablespoon yeast powder (baking)

Work butter and sugar together. Add milk and egg. Sift dry ingredients together and add to mixture. Put in greased muffin tins. Bake at 400 degrees for 20 minutes. Makes one dozen.

—Mabel Walls Valliant (Mrs. T. Rigby)

❧ *IRISH MUFFINS*

    4 eggs
    2 tablespoons sugar
    2 teaspoons salt
    1 cup melted Crisco
       flour, enough for a stiff batter, about 5 cups
    2 cups milk, scalded and cooled
    1 cake yeast dissolved in ½ cup tepid water with a little
          of the sugar

Beat eggs. Add sugar and salt, Crisco, then flour and milk alternately. Blend well. Stir in yeast. Let rise in bowl until doubled in bulk. Stir well before putting in well-greased muffin tins. Fill tins two-thirds full and let rise again to top of tin. Bake at 375 degrees until golden brown. Makes 2 dozen muffins.

    Note: Make at 1 o'clock for 6 o'clock supper.

—Miss Grace Wilkins

❧ *ORANGE KUCHEN ROLLS*

       1 package active dry yeast
       ½ cup warm water
       2 tablespoons sugar
       1 teaspoon salt
       1 egg
       ½ cup soft butter
      2½ cups sifted flour
       1 cup sugar
  3 or 4 tablespoons grated orange rind

In mixing bowl, dissolve yeast in water. Stir in sugar and salt. Add egg, butter, and half of the flour. Beat with spoon until smooth. Add rest of flour and mix with fingers, squeezing the dough through the fingers until the dough leaves and cleans the sides of the bowl. Knead 20 times on a lightly floured board. Cut in 12 pieces; shape into balls. Roll balls in sugar mixed with orange rind. Place balls in well-greased 9-inch ring mold or 8-inch round layer pan. Let rise until double in bulk, about 1 hour. Heat oven to 375 degrees and bake 25 to 30 minutes.

—Margaret Gadd Ashley (Mrs. John M.)

🥨 *MARYLAND BEATEN BISCUITS*

This recipe is from one of Queen Anne's County's oldest families.

6 pounds flour
1 teaspoon salt
¾ pound lard
1 pint water
1 pint milk

Mix flour and salt; then cut in lard. Mix in water and milk. Beat hard for 20 minutes with back end of an axe. Make into biscuits and bake in hot oven for 20 minutes. Makes 8 dozen.

—Emory recipe

🥨 *OATMEAL BREAD*

2 cups boiling water
2 cups rolled oats
3 tablespoons butter
1 yeast cake
½ cup lukewarm water
½ cup black molasses
2 teaspoons salt
5 cups flour

Pour boiling water over rolled oats and butter and let stand one hour. Dissolve yeast in the warm water. Add molasses, salt, and yeast to oat mixture. Add flour and knead bread about 5 minutes. Let rise 1 hour or longer. Make into 2 loaves and put in greased pans. Let rise again. Brush tops with melted butter. Bake at 375 degrees for 45 to 50 minutes.

—Mabel Walls Valliant (Mrs. T. Rigby)

🥨 *NUT BREAD*

1 egg
1 cup sugar
2 teaspoons melted butter

2   teaspoons molasses

1   teaspoon soda mixed with 1 cup buttermilk

3   cups flour

1   teaspoon yeast powder [baking powder]

1   cup black walnuts, chopped

Mix egg, sugar, butter, and molasses. Stir soda into buttermilk and add to egg mixture. Sift together flour and yeast powder. Stir in the nuts. Blend all ingredients together well. Pour into a greased and floured 9 × 5 × 3-inch loaf pan. Bake from 1 to 1½ hours at 325 degrees.

—Marion Merrick Brower (Mrs. Frank W.)

ORANGE BREAD

This bread cuts better the second day. Slice very thin. Delicious spread with cream cheese or butter to serve with tea.

2   cups flour

2   teaspoons baking powder

¾   cup sugar

¼   teaspoon salt

1   cup candied orange peel (see below)

⅓   cup orange syrup (see below)

1   egg

⅔   cup milk

2   tablespoons melted shortening

Sift all the dry ingredients together. Cut orange peel in small pieces, and add with orange syrup to dry mixture. Beat in milk and egg and stir well. Add melted shortening. Put in greased loaf pan. Sprinkle with a little sugar and let stand 20 minutes. Bake at 350 degrees for about 50 minutes.

Candied Orange Peel

Boil the rind from 6 large or 5 small oranges in water to cover until translucent. Remove the pith. Boil ½ cup water with 1 cup sugar until syrup spins a thread. Cook peel in syrup 5 minutes and drain, reserving syrup.

—Mary Bishop Keith Jukes (Mrs. J. Herbert Fielding)

🌾 *ZUCCHINI BREAD*

          3 eggs
          1 cup salad oil (not olive)
          1 cup granulated sugar
          1 cup brown sugar
          1 tablespoon maple flavoring
          2 cups chopped zucchini
          ½ cup toasted wheat germ
      2½ cups sifted flour
          2 teaspoons baking soda
          ½ teaspoon baking powder
          2 teaspoons salt
          1 cup chopped walnuts
          ½ cup sesame seeds

Preheat oven to 350 degrees. Butter two loaf pans. Beat eggs until foamy. Add oil, sugars, maple flavoring. With a spoon add the zucchini (which has been thoroughly drained and very finely minced). Combine all dry ingredients with batter, taking care not to overbeat. Bake 1 hour at 350 degrees.

—*Cecily Wilson Lyle*

🌾 *POPOVERS*

          2 eggs
          1 cup milk
          1 cup flour
          ¼ teaspoon salt
          1 tablespoon melted butter

Beat eggs slightly. Add the rest of the ingredients. Beat unmercifully! Get iron popover pans hot as blazes. Grease well. Pour in batter and bake at 450 to 475 degrees for 30 minutes. Lower temperature to 350 degrees and bake 18 minutes more. Makes 8 to 10 popovers.

—*Isabel Atkinson Lieber (Mrs. Albert C.)*

🌾 *POTATO REFRIGERATOR ROLLS*

          1 cup mashed potatoes
          ⅔ cup shortening

 3 tablespoons sugar
 1 teaspoon salt
 2 eggs
 1 yeast cake
 ½ cup lukewarm water
 1 cup milk, scalded and cooled to lukewarm
 6 to 8 cups flour

Mash potatoes, add shortening, sugar, salt, and eggs. Cream well. Dissolve yeast in lukewarm water. Add to lukewarm milk, then add to potato mixture. Add sifted flour to make a stiff dough. Toss on floured board and knead well. Put into large bowl and let rise until doubled in bulk. Knead lightly.

Place dough in casserole. Rub over top with melted butter. Cover tightly and place in refrigerator until ready to bake. About 1½ hours before baking time, pinch off dough and shape into rolls as desired. Cover and let rise until doubled in bulk. Bake at 400 degrees for 15 to 20 minutes. Makes 6 dozen rolls.

—Genevieve Hall Valliant (Mrs. Edwin S., Sr.)

POPPY SEED TEA BREAD

 3 cups sifted all-purpose flour
 1 teaspoon salt
 3½ teaspoons baking powder
 ½ cup poppy seed
 ¾ cup sugar
 ¼ cup shortening
 2 large eggs
 1 teaspoon grated lemon rind
 1 cup milk

Sift first three ingredients together and mix with poppy seed. Beat sugar, shortening, and eggs together. Blend in rind and milk. Add all at once to the flour mixture. Mix only until blended (about 30 strokes), folding. Stop at 15 strokes and scrape bowl. Turn into well-greased, lightly floured 9 × 5 × 3-inch loaf pan. Bake at 350 degrees for 1 hour. Cool.

—Janet Gadd Doehler (Mrs. William F.)

🍂 *REFRIGERATOR ROLLS*

½ cup boiling water

1 rounded tablespoon lard, or other shortening

¼ cup sugar

½ tablespoon salt

½ cup milk

1 yeast cake dissolved in ¼ cup water and
　　1 teaspoon sugar

1 egg

4 cups flour

Pour boiling water over lard, sugar, and salt. Add milk, yeast, beaten egg, and flour. Put in refrigerator overnight. Next day, take out of refrigerator, form into rolls, and let rise 3 to 4 hours. Bake rolls at 425 degrees for about 10 minutes. Makes about 4 dozen rolls.

—*Frances Wright Hilleary (Mrs. Robert)*

🍂 *SWEET POTATO ROLLS*

1 cup cooked sweet potatoes

1 teaspoon salt

2 tablespoons sugar

2 eggs

3 tablespoons shortening

¾ cup scalded milk

1¼ cups lukewarm water

1 yeast cake

5 cups flour

Put potatoes in large bowl, mash well. Add salt, sugar, and eggs, and beat well. Add water to the scalded milk. Crumble yeast in milk and water mixture. Let dissolve and add sweet potato mixture and flour. Turn out on mixing board and knead well, adding more flour if the dough is sticky. Put back in bowl and grease well on top. Let rise in warm place until doubled in bulk. Do not mash down at this stage, but pinch enough dough off to make rolls. Let rise in warm place. Bake at 375 degrees for 25 minutes. Makes 5 dozen rolls.

—*Kathryn L. Hagen*

🍃 *CORNMEAL CHEDDAR BREAD*

    1 package active dry yeast
    ¼ cup warm water (at 105 to 115 degrees Fahrenheit)
   2½ ounces sharp cheddar cheese (about ¾ cup shredded)
   3½ cups (17½ ounces) unbleached all-purpose flour
    ⅓ cup yellow cornmeal
    3 tablespoons butter at room temperature, cut into 6 pieces
    2 tablespoons sugar
    2 teaspoons salt
    1 large egg
    5 drops hot pepper sauce
    ¾ cup ice water

Dissolve the yeast in the warm water and let it stand until foamy, about 10 minutes. Insert the shredding disc in a food processor and shred the cheese, using light pressure on the pusher. Remove the shredding disc and insert the metal blade. Add the flour, cornmeal, butter, sugar and salt; process for 20 seconds. Add the yeast mixture and egg. Stir the pepper sauce into the ice water. With the machine running, pour the ice water through the feed tube in a steady stream as fast as the flour absorbs it. After the dough begins to form a ball, let the machine run 45 to 60 seconds to knead. With floured hands, remove the dough and shape it into a smooth ball. Put it in a lightly floured 1-gallon plastic storage bag. Squeeze out the air and close with a wire twist tie, allowing space for the dough to rise. Let the dough rise in a warm place (about 80 degrees Fahrenheit) until doubled, about 1 to 1½ hours. Remove the twist tie and punch down the dough in the bag. Shape into a loaf; place it in a greased 7-cup loaf pan (about 9 × 5 × 3 inches). Cover with oiled plastic wrap and leave in a warm place until the dough rises just above the top of the pan, about 1 hour. Set the rack in the middle of the oven and preheat the oven to 375 degrees. Bake for 35 minutes, or until the loaf sounds hollow when tapped. Remove from the pan and cool on a wire rack. Makes 1 two-pound loaf.

—Jane Lyon Alderman (Mrs. Ernest A.)

🐚 *DIXIE SPOON BREAD*

    1 cup cornmeal
    2 cups boiling water
    1 tablespoon butter
    1 cup milk
    1 teaspoon salt
    1 teaspoon baking powder
    2 eggs, beaten

Pour boiling water on meal. Boil 5 minutes, stirring constantly. Remove from stove. Add butter, milk, salt, and baking powder. Mix thoroughly. Then add well-beaten eggs. Mix and pour into well-greased 1½-quart baking dish. Bake for 45 minutes at 350 degrees. Makes 5 to 6 portions.

—*Mrs. Wilber N. Davis*

🐚 *SOUTHERN SPOON BREAD*

    1 pint of milk
    ¾ cup white cornmeal
    3 tablespoons butter
    1 teaspoon salt
    3 eggs, separated

Heat milk in double boiler. Stir in meal and cook slowly until thick and smooth. Remove from fire, add butter and salt, and let cool. Beat egg yolks and add to mixture. Fold in stiffly beaten egg whites. Bake in 1½-quart casserole for 30 minutes at 350 degrees. Serves 5.

—*Miss Caroline W. Owings*

🐚 *SPOON BREAD*

    ⅔ cup white cornmeal
    2 cups scalded milk
    1 teaspoon melted butter
    1 teaspoon sugar
    1 teaspoon salt
    2 egg yolks, beaten
    2 egg whites, beaten stiff

Gradually add cornmeal to hot milk and cook 5 minutes, stirring constantly. Cool slightly and add butter, sugar, and salt. Add egg yolks, then fold in egg whites. Bake in a greased, 3-cup baking dish at 350 degrees for about 45 minutes. Serves 3.

This recipe may be increased by ⅓ , or halved.

—Elizabeth Trundle Barton (Mrs. Marvin)

❧ TEA BISCUITS

These biscuits are very short (crispy).

3 cups flour
4½ teaspoons yeast powder [baking powder]
1½ teaspoons salt
¾ cup shortening
1 cup milk

Sift dry ingredients. Add shortening and work. Add milk. Bake at 450 degrees for 12 minutes. Makes 3 dozen.

—Margaret Fesmyer Wolcott (Mrs. Milton)

❧ BREADSTICKS

Prepare one recipe of a dough of your choice—Herbed Whole Wheat is a good choice. After the first rising, punch down the dough. To get uniform sticks, first divide the dough in half and shape each into a cylinder 12-inches long; cut each cylinder into twelve 1-inch pieces. One at a time, roll up each piece between your hands and then roll it out on the work surface into an even stick about ⅓-inch in diameter. Grease a baking sheet and sprinkle it with cornmeal. Preheat the oven to 300 degrees. Place the sticks on the baking sheet. Cover them and leave to rise in a warm place for 15 minutes. Brush them with a glaze of egg and salt and sprinkle with seeds or coarse salt. Bake the sticks for 30 minutes. Then increase the heat to 350 degrees and bake until nicely browned, crisp, and dry—about 5 minutes more. Makes 24 breadsticks.

—Jane Lyon Alderman (Mrs. Ernest A.)

🍂 *MARY ELLEN'S TEA BISCUITS*

Mary Ellen for many years helped with the church suppers in the kitchen and always made these biscuits. She still does make "the undisputed best tea biscuits in Queen Anne's County," at least.

4 cups flour
3½ teaspoons baking powder
1½ teaspoons salt
2½ teaspoons sugar
¾ cup Crisco (1 cup if you want them short)
1¾ cups milk or buttermilk

Mix all ingredients except milk together with fingers or pastry cutter. When the consistency of cornmeal, add 1 cup milk. Add additional milk as needed to make a soft dough. Flour area used to roll biscuits. Roll to about 1-inch thick. Cut with a 2½-inch biscuit cutter. Bake at 450 degrees for about 20 minutes. As oven temperatures vary, check at 20 minutes. Place baked biscuits in a bowl covered with a clean tea towel. Contrary to belief, it enhances biscuits to rest under a cover while hot. Makes 3 dozen biscuits.

—Mary Ellen Roberts Smith (Mrs. Lewis G. E.)

🍂 *HERBED WHOLE WHEAT BREAD*

1 package active dry yeast
1 teaspoon sugar
¼ cup warm water (at 105 to 115 degrees)
2½ cups (7½ ounces) unbleached all-purpose flour
¾ cup (3¾ ounces) whole wheat flour
1½ teaspoons dried Italian herbs (mixture of oregano, savory, marjoram, basil, rosemary, and sage)
1 teaspoon salt
2 tablespoons olive oil
¾ cup cold water

Dissolve the yeast and sugar in the warm water and let stand until foamy, about 10 minutes. In a processor with the metal blade, put 2¼ cups of the all-purpose flour, all the whole wheat flour, the herbs and salt. Turn the machine on and off once to aerate. Add the yeast mixture and oil. Turn on the machine and pour the cold water through the feed tube in a steady stream as fast as the flour absorbs it. When the dough forms a ball, stop the machine and check the consistency. The dough should be soft but not sticky; if it feels sticky, process in the remaining flour, 2 tablespoons at a time, until the consistency feels right. Process the dough for 45 seconds to knead. With lightly floured hands, remove the dough and form it into a ball. Put it in a lightly floured 1-gallon plastic storage bag. Squeeze out the air and close the end with a wire twist tie, allowing space for the dough to rise. Leave it in a warm place (about 80 degrees) to rise until doubled, about 1 to 1½ hours. Remove the twist and punch down the dough in the bag. Shape into a loaf and place it in a greased 7-cup loaf pan (about 9 × 5 × 3-inches). Cover with oiled plastic wrap and leave it in a warm place until the dough rises just above the top of the pan, about 1 hour. Adjust the rack to the middle of the oven and preheat the oven to 375 degrees. Bake for 35 to 40 minutes, until the loaf sounds hollow when tapped. Remove from the pan and cool on a wire rack. Makes 1 two-pound loaf.

—Jane Lyon Alderman (Mrs. Ernest A.)

Shrove Tuesday, the day before Ash Wednesday, is often called Fat Tuesday, as when all household butter and lard was used up before the fasting of Lent. A traditional pancake supper is held on Shrove Tuesday at St. Paul's.

PANCAKES

These pancakes are simply delicious.

- 1 teaspoon salt
- 3 teaspoons sugar
- 1½ pints milk
- 1 tablespoon melted butter
- 2 teaspoons baking powder
  flour
- 2 eggs (separated; beat the whites)

Mix the first 5 ingredients together. Add enough flour (about 2 cups) to make a thin batter. Add egg yolks and fold in the beaten egg whites. Makes 15 to 20 pancakes.

—Reba Wright Turpin (Mrs. J. R. E.)

🐚 *ENGLISH TOMATO BREAD*

    1 8-ounce can tomatoes
    1 package active dry yeast
    2 teaspoons sugar
    1 small onion (about 1½ ounces), peeled and quartered
    3 cups (15 ounces) unbleached all-purpose flour
    2 tablespoons (¼ stick) unsalted butter at room temperature,
          cut into 4 pieces
    1 teaspoon salt
    ½ teaspoon celery seed

In a processor with the metal blade, puree the tomatoes with their juices. Empty the puree into a 1-quart saucepan and warm over low heat to 105-115 degrees. Remove from the heat and stir in the yeast and sugar; let it stand until foamy, about 10 minutes. With the metal blade, process the onion, turning the machine on and off until the onion is finely chopped. Do not remove the onion. Add the flour, butter, salt, and celery seed; process for 20 seconds. With the machine running, pour the tomato and yeast mixture through the feed tube in a steady stream as fast as the flour mixture absorbs it. Continue processing; after the dough begins to form a ball, let the machine run for 45 seconds to knead. With lightly floured hands, remove the dough and shape it into a smooth ball. Put it in a lightly floured 1-gallon plastic storage bag. Squeeze out the air and close the end with a wire twist tie, leaving space for the dough to rise. Let it rise in a warm place (about 80 degrees) until doubled, about 1 to 1½ hours. Remove the twist tie and punch down the dough in the bag. Shape into a loaf and place it in a greased 7-cup loaf pan (about 9 × 5 × 3-inches). Cover with oiled plastic wrap and leave it in a warm place until the dough rises just above the top of the pan, about 1 hour. Set the rack in the middle of the oven and preheat the oven to 375 degrees. Bake for 35 to 40 minutes, until the loaf sounds hollow when tapped. Remove from the pan and cool on a wire rack. Makes 1 two-pound loaf.

—*Jane Lyon Alderman (Mrs. Ernest A.)*

🐚 *CORN WAFERS*

    1½ cups boiling water
     2 cups yellow cornmeal (approximate)

4 tablespoons butter

1 teaspoon salt

Put the ingredients in a pan and cook to bring cornmeal to a thick consistency. Add more water if you want wafers to be thinner. Put spoonfuls on a buttered cookie sheet. Tap bottom to even out wafers. Cook at 350 to 400 degrees until brown, about 15 minutes.

You can put dough on a buttered jelly roll type pan, covering the whole sheet with the mixture and cook it at 250 to 300 degrees for about two hours. Trial and error is the best way.

—Lois S. Duffey (Mrs. Harry J., Jr.)

SUPER PANCAKE

½ stick butter or margarine

2 eggs

½ cup flour

½ cup milk

¼ teaspoon ground nutmeg (optional)

Preheat oven to 500 degrees. Melt butter in a 9-inch iron frying pan or Dutch oven. Beat together the eggs, flour, milk, and nutmeg. As the foam of the butter subsides, add batter and place pan immediately in the hot oven. Remove after 12 to 15 minutes. The pancake will have risen like a giant popover. It will subside when cut. Serve with maple syrup or any topping you like. Serves 4.

—Joan Vest Withington (Mrs. Charles F.)

In 1706, the year when Queen Anne's County officially was formed, the Vestry contracted with a Mr. Salisbury to make pews for the church at a cost of 700 pounds of tobacco for each pew. At the same time, a Mr. Mathias Pooly was paid 500 pounds of tobacco to "plaister and white lime ye breaches of the other side of the church."

❧ *BUCKWHEAT CAKES*

3 cups buckwheat flour
¼ cake of yeast, dissolved in tepid water
  a little salt
2 tablespoons molasses
¼ tablespoon baking soda

Mix flour, yeast, and salt with enough water to make an easy-to-stir batter. Set in warm place to rise overnight. In the morning, add molasses and baking soda. Cook on hot griddle. Makes 24 cakes.

—Emory recipe

❧ *SHROVE TUESDAY PANCAKES*

This recipe is used at Emmanuel Church [Chestertown] for their pancake luncheon each Shrove Tuesday and is wonderful. They must be eaten as fast as they're cooked—they do not keep when cool.

8 eggs, separated
2 cups flour
4 cups milk
4 tablespoons melted butter or margarine

Beat egg yolks until light, beat in flour and milk, and add melted butter. Fold in stiffly beaten whites. Makes 30 to 40 cakes.

—Frances Perry Metcalfe

❧ *WAFFLES*

3 eggs
1½ cups milk
6 tablespoons melted shortening (bacon fat is good)
2 cups flour
4 teaspoons baking powder
1 teaspoon salt
2 tablespoons sugar

Separate eggs. To yolks add milk and shortening, and beat well. Mix dry ingredients and add to egg mixture. Beat whites stiff but moist, and fold in gradually. Serves 5 to 6 people.

—Miss Caroline W. Owings

$\mathscr{S}$OUPS

Father, for this noonday meal,
We would speak the praise we feel.
Health and strength we have from Thee,
Help us, Lord, to faithful be. Amen.

—A noontime grace from Camp Wright

🌬 *ARTICHOKE SOUP*

  4 tablespoons butter
  2 tablespoons finely chopped onion
  2 tablespoons flour
  ½ cup milk
  2 8½-ounce cans artichoke hearts, drained, reserving juice
2¼ cups chicken broth (I use Campbell's, preferably low salt)
  1 tablespoon fresh lemon juice
  ½ teaspoon nutmeg
  ¼ teaspoon each, salt and pepper
  3 egg yolks
  ¾ cup heavy cream

Sauté onion in butter, add flour, and stir until smooth. Add milk gradually and stir to make a smooth cream sauce. Add juice from artichokes and chicken broth. Bring to a boil. Add chopped artichoke hearts, lemon juice, and seasonings. Mix egg yolks with cream and add some of the hot mixture to them. Gradually beat the rest of the soup in. Heat *without boiling* and serve. Makes 6 cups or 4 to 6 servings.

—*Miss Jenna Gadd Ashley*

🌬 *BEEF SOUP*

    1½ pounds stew beef or chuck
     1 soup bone
       salt and pepper
     2 bay leaves
     ½ cup chopped onion
     1 cup chopped celery
     1 cup chopped cabbage
4 or 5 medium carrots, sliced
       pinch of oregano
     1 20-ounce can Italian style tomatoes
     1 tablespoon Worcestershire sauce
     1 beef bouillon cube

Cover beef and soup bone with cold water in heavy 3-quart saucepan. Add salt, pepper, and bay leaves. Heat to bubbly stage. Turn heat low and add onions, celery, cabbage, carrots, and oregano. Simmer at least 2½ hours or until meat is tender. Remove bone and bay leaves and cut meat into bite size pieces. Add tomatoes, Worcestershire sauce, and beef cube. Simmer ½ hour and serve. Makes 3 quarts or 6 to 8 servings.

—Lynette Morgan Nielsen (Mrs. Orsen)

BEET SOUP

    1 dozen fresh beets
    4 cans White Rose madrilene
      sour cream

Wash beets and put through medium size knife of grinder. Put in pan, pour the madrilene over, and cook until tender. When almost done, season to taste. Strain, set aside to cool, and then put in refrigerator. It will jell. Serve either hot or cold with a teaspoon of sour cream. Makes 1½ quarts or 8 servings.

Note: I have found that, so far, White Rose is the only madrilene which makes the soup "just right."

—Eleanor Williams Miles (Mrs. Clarence W.)

CARROT SOUP

    4 tablespoons butter
    3 cups chopped onion
    2 pounds carrots, trimmed, scraped, and cut up
    4 cups chicken broth
      salt
    1 cup cream
    1 cup milk
    2 tablespoons finely chopped dill
    ¼ teaspoon cayenne

Heat butter in large pot. Add onion. Cook briefly. Add carrots and chicken broth. Bring to a boil and simmer 20 minutes or until carrots and onions are cooked. Blend in food processor until smooth. Add cream, milk, dill, cayenne, and salt and pepper to taste. Serve hot or very cold. Makes 12 servings.

—Murray Bradley Peck (Mrs. Charles R.)

❧ *TOMATO CARROT SOUP*

This will freeze well and remind one of the sunny days of summer when enjoyed by a winter fire.

3   pounds ripe red tomatoes, skinned and seeded, or 6 cups canned tomatoes, drained and seeded
1   orange
4   tablespoons butter
1   cup onions, finely chopped
1¾ cups carrots, thinly sliced
4   tablespoons flour, whole wheat preferred
6   cups chicken broth
½   cup orange juice
1   lemon
2   tablespoons sugar
    juice from 1 orange
1   bay leaf
    salt to taste
    freshly ground pepper to taste
½   cup scallions, finely chopped

Chop tomatoes coarsely. Peel the orange and julienne the peel. Set aside.

Heat butter in a soup pot. Add onions and carrots. Cook, stirring to prevent scorching, until onions are golden. Do not brown. Add flour to coat pieces. Add tomatoes, stirring. Bring to a boil and add the broth. Return to boiling. Peel the lemon in one long strip. Add the skin to the tomato mixture. (Save the peeled lemon for another dish.) Now add sugar, orange juice, and bay leaf. Salt and pepper to taste. Simmer for 40 minutes. After 40 minutes, remove and discard lemon peel and bay leaf. Ladle soup into the container of a food processor or electric blender and blend thoroughly. Do this in two or three batches. Return soup to a cleaned kettle. Bring to a boil. Stir in orange strips and scallions just before serving. Can be served hot or cold. Makes approximately 4 quarts or 16 servings.

—Committee

St. Paul's History Note: Vestry side-notes record $450 was paid in 1888 to have a cinder path made in the "Church Lane" at the request of the "Ladies." In 1890, parish members were requested not to hitch horses in the lane.

✤ CONSOMMÉ

  1 slice raw ham, about 1-inch thick
  1 good chicken fowl
    butter
  2 pounds shin beef
  1 knuckle of veal, cracked in two
3½ quarts cold water
  2 carrots, peeled
  2 leeks, split (white part only)
  2 white onions, each stuck with a whole clove
  4 stalks celery
    bouquet garni of parsley, thyme, ½ bay leaf

Soak ham for ½ hour in cold water. Put chicken in a small roasting pan with a piece of butter the size of an egg. Roast until brown, basting frequently, but only half cook through. Put shin of beef and veal knuckle in a deep soup pot and add water. Let soak until water begins to turn pink, then add roasted chicken. Put pan on hot fire and bring quickly to a boil. When it begins to get hot, but before it boils, add the ham. Skim carefully all scum on the surface when it boils. Add vegetables and bouquet garni and reduce heat. Cover pot and simmer 8 hours. When cooked, add salt if necessary and drain through a fine sieve. Cool, skim off all fat. Keep in refrigerator. When ready to serve, heat and add 1 tablespoon sherry for each plate of soup. Makes 10 servings. This may be frozen.

—*Lynette Morgan Nielsen (Mrs. Orsen)*

❧ *CAROLINA CRAB SOUP*

- 2 tablespoons butter
- 2 tablespoons flour
- 1 quart milk
- 2 cups white crabmeat
- 2 teaspoons salt
- ¼ teaspoon pepper
- ½ teaspoon Worcestershire sauce
- ¼ teaspoon curry powder
- 2 eggs, hard-boiled
- ½ cup sherry
- ½ cup heavy cream, whipped
  parsley

Melt butter in double boiler. Blend in flour, add warm milk slowly, and blend. Add crabmeat and cook 20 minutes. Add seasonings. Put egg yolks through a sieve or ricer. In bottom of each soup plate put 2 tablespoons warm sherry on one-quarter of sieved egg yolks. Add soup and top with whipped cream; garnish with parsley. Serves 4.

—Lillian Hardy (Mrs. William A.)

❧ *CRAB SOUP HELEN RIGGS*

- 1 pound backfin crabmeat with fat
- 1 tablespoon thyme
- 2 tablespoons finely chopped onion
- 3 ripe tomatoes (or equivalent canned)
- 2 teaspoons chopped parsley
- 1 quart cold water
- 1 quart milk
- ¼ teaspoon black pepper
- 1 teaspoon salt
- 6 to 8 tablespoons butter
  cayenne
  celery seed
- ½ cup cream or 1 can Pet milk

Combine first 6 ingredients and bring to a boil. Boil steadily until most of water has boiled away. Add milk, pepper, salt, butter, cayenne, and celery seed and bring to a boil again. Add cream (or Pet milk) for extra richness. Makes 3 quarts or 12 servings.

Note: Four times this recipe makes 10 quarts and 1 pint. Freezes wonderfully, but must not be boiled when reheated. Serve sherry with the soup.

—*Mrs. John G. Watson*

CELERY CONSOMMÉ

    8 cups clear beef stock (canned may be used)
    4 large ribs celery with leaves, cut in half
    2 tomatoes, cored and quartered
       salt and freshly ground pepper to taste
    ¼ cup dry sherry (optional)

Bring stock to a boil, add celery and tomatoes, simmer 40 minutes, and strain. Remove celery and slice into matchlike strips. Bring consommé to a boil again and add celery, salt, pepper, and sherry. Serve piping hot. Makes 8 servings.

—*Lynette Morgan Nielsen (Mrs. Orsen)*

CHICKEN GUMBO SOUP

    1 large stewing chicken, cooked
    3 pints chicken stock
    1 quart gumbo or okra
    4 medium tomatoes, diced, or 1 pint canned tomatoes

Take half of chicken stock and combine with tomatoes and sliced okra and cook until gumbo is tender. Add rest of chicken stock and half the chicken breast, cut fine. Season to taste. Let get cold and skim off fat. Serve hot or cold. Makes 3 quarts or 10 to 12 servings.

—*Eleanor Williams Miles (Mrs. Clarence W.)*

❧ *CORN CHOWDER I*

> 1 cup thinly sliced onions
> 2 tablespoons butter
> 1 cup diced potatoes
> 1 cup diced ham
> 2 cups fresh or 1 can creamed corn
> 1 cup condensed cream of mushroom soup
> 2½ cups milk
> ¾ teaspoon salt
>   dash of pepper
>   butter or margarine
>   parsley
>   paprika

In a large saucepan, cook onions in butter until tender but not brown. Add potatoes, ham, corn, soup, and milk. Heat until boiling. Add salt and pepper. Put a pat of butter in each bowl. Sprinkle with chopped parsley and paprika. Makes 6 to 8 servings.

—Marjorie Belt Turner (Mrs. Edward)

❧ *CORN CHOWDER II*

> 2 tablespoons butter or margarine
> 2 cups chopped onions
> 2 tablespoons flour
> 4 cups good chicken broth
> 2 large potatoes, peeled and diced
> 1 cup half-and-half
> 4 cups cooked corn; fresh is best, drain if canned
> ¾ teaspoon coarsely ground black pepper
>   salt to taste
> 1 large red bell pepper, diced
> 3 green onions, white and some green
> 1 tablespoon cilantro, chopped, for garnish

Melt butter and add onions. Cook over low heat until wilted, about 8 minutes. Add flour and cook, stirring, for about 5 minutes. Add chicken broth and potatoes. Cook over medium heat until potatoes are just tender, about 15 minutes. Add the half-and-half, corn, pepper, and salt. Cook about 5 minutes, stirring occasionally. Add red pepper and green onions, cooking for about 5 to 10 minutes. Garnish with cilantro and serve. Makes about 4 to 6 servings.

—Miss Sydney Gadd Ashley

CHEDDAR CHOWDER

- 2 cups boiling water
- 2 cups diced potatoes
- ½ cup sliced carrots
- 1 cup celery
- ½ cup chopped onion
- 1½ teaspoons salt
- ¼ teaspoon pepper
- ¼ cup margarine
- ¼ cup flour
- 2 cups milk
- 2 cups (8 ounces) shredded cheddar cheese
- ⅛ teaspoon baking soda
- 1 cup cubed cooked ham

Add water to vegetables, salt, and pepper. Cover and simmer for 10 minutes. Do not drain. Make a white sauce with margarine, flour, and milk. Add cheese and soda; stir until melted. Cool the water and vegetables to lukewarm. (Be sure vegetables are not hot. If cream sauce is added to the hot mixture, it will curdle.) Add ham and undrained vegetables to cream sauce. Heat. Do not boil. Serves 6 to 8.

Variation: Omit ham and substitute 8 slices of crumbled bacon or 1 cup of cooked shrimp.

—Janet Gadd Doehler (Mrs. William F.)

🍃 *COLD TOMATO SOUP*

Very special!

1 pint fresh tomato juice
1 tablespoon vinegar
½ tablespoon oil
1 teaspoon sugar
  few drops onion juice
  salt and pepper to taste

Mix thoroughly with an egg beater. If too thick, add a piece of ice to each bouillon cup when it is served. This will not keep. Serves 2.

—*Lois S. Duffey (Mrs. Harry J., Jr.)*

🍃 *CLEAR MUSHROOM SOUP*

Really deliciously different.

½ pound mushrooms
2 10½-ounce cans consommé
2 tablespoons butter
1 tablespoon cornstarch in ¼ cup cold water
  pepper to taste
1 tablespoon very dry French vermouth

Peel mushrooms, slice stems into a saucepan and caps into a frying pan. Pour one can consommé over stems, simmer until soft. Strain, throw stems away. Cook the caps in butter about 10 minutes with a tight lid on frying pan. Add second can of consommé and simmer 15 minutes. Put this and stem juice in a blender, blend 30 seconds. Stir in starch mixture, pepper, and vermouth. Heat to a boil. You can put a glob of salted whipped cream on top and pop under the broiler for a minute to brown. Makes a small amount, scant 3 cups serving four, but I usually double the recipe.

—*Virginia Ingles Freeland (Mrs. Samuel L.)*

🍃 *CLAM CHOWDER*

2 slices bacon, fried and diced
1½ pints clam liquor or bottled clam juice

½ pint milk
1 pint chopped clams
4 small potatoes, boiled and diced
1 onion, diced

When above ingredients are half cooked (about 20 minutes) add 1 onion, which has been diced and cooked in a small amount of water. Cook about 15 minutes longer. Salt and pepper to taste. Serves 6.

—Mabel Walls Valliant (Mrs. T. Rigby)

CROSS'S CLAM STEW

1 pound soft shell clams (maninoes), steamed, shucked,
        and snouts removed, reserving 1 cup liquor
½ cup chopped onions
½ cup chopped celery
½ cup chopped red or green pepper
1 tablespoon margarine
1 can creamed potato soup
½ cup milk
2 cloves garlic or equivalent in garlic powder
    fresh parsley

Braise onions, celery, and peppers until done (soft) in margarine. Mix remainder of ingredients into vegetable mixture, along with 1 cup of clam liquor. Stir while heating. Season with dash of soy sauce, lemon and herbs, Nature's Seasoning, pepper to taste. Makes 2 servings if hungry.

—William Cross

QUICK GAZPACHO

2 cups salsa (mild, medium, or hot to taste)
2 cups V-8 or tomato juice
1 cucumber
    lime juice to taste

Mix together in a blender or food processor. Chill for an hour or more. Serve with sour cream or a lime wedge. Makes 4 cups.

—Kathy Covert

🍃 *PAWLEY'S ISLAND CLAM CHOWDER*

½ cup (4 ounces) chopped salt pork

3 onions, minced

1 cup minced celery

4 2-pound cans tomatoes

1 quart clams, ground in meat grinder

3 potatoes, sliced very thin

Fry salt pork. Remove to kettle. Fry minced onions slowly in remaining fat and add to kettle. Add celery, cans of tomatoes, and clams. Add sliced potatoes and simmer until potatoes are tender, at least 2 hours in all. Makes 4 servings.

Pantry shelf substitutes for fresh clams: 1 bottle clam juice and 3 cans minced clams.

—*Anne Stoney Cantler (Mrs. James E.)*

🍃 *EMELIA'S SPRING SOUP*

2 pounds asparagus

½ cup butter

2 10½-ounce cans beef broth

1 16-ounce can peas

Brown asparagus in butter in frying pan. Watch, as it burns easily and cannot be used if burned. Put browned asparagus in soup pot. Pour over beef broth, diluted with water if called for on can, and one can of peas, drained. Simmer for 1½ to 2 hours. Drain through sieve: do not push on vegetable to extract juice, as your soup will be cloudy. This should make enough soup for 2 to 3 people—water can be added if necessary to bring it to the right amount.

Note: This does make rather an expensive soup, but it is wonderful for those who have an asparagus plot. I make enough, cooking it in large batches and freezing it, to last us the year. This is an excellent soup with an unusual flavor.

—*Lynette Morgan Nielsen (Mrs. Orsen)*

🍃 *ICED CUCUMBER SOUP*

2 cloves garlic, crushed

1 teaspoon salt

2 tablespoons olive oil

2 cups sour cream

1 cucumber, peeled and grated
   juice and grated rind of 1 lemon

2 cups cold water

¼ cup finely chopped mint
   salt and pepper to taste

Mix garlic, salt, and olive oil. Beat into sour cream. Add cucumber and lemon juice and rind to cold water and stir well. Add the mint and salt and pepper. Chill. Makes 4 servings.

—Mrs. John Porter

GAZPACHO

1 14-ounce can tomatoes (I prefer to use Del Monte diced
   or wedges; fresh tomatoes are too iffy in flavor
   and ripeness.)

1 green pepper, chopped (small or large, depending on your
   preference; yellow or red is nice, too.)

6 or 8 stalks celery, chopped

½ cucumber, peeled and chopped (or a whole cucumber,
   depending on your preference)

1 clove garlic, minced
   fresh parsley to taste

2 to 3 tablespoons wine vinegar

2 tablespoons light olive oil
   several dashes of Worcestershire sauce
   salt and pepper to taste

2 6-ounce containers tomato juice

6 scallions or 1 small red onion, chopped

Place all the ingredients in a food processor or blender and whirl until you have the consistency you want. Chill until ready to serve. Makes 6 to 8 servings.

—Janie Eby Ashley (Mrs. Sydney G.)

🍂 *FISH CHOWDER*

2 pounds haddock fillet (or cod)
2 cups water
4 thick slices lean salt pork (or about 4 slices country-sliced bacon)
1 onion, sliced
4 cups diced (not too small cubes) raw potato
1 quart (or less) milk (I use skim but evaporated or whole milk or light cream can be used to total 1 quart.)
   salt and pepper to taste

Cook haddock gently in water until it can be flaked with a fork. Remove haddock to cool and check for bones. Fry salt pork lightly until crisp. Remove salt pork. Add onions and sauté until limp. Remove onions (I'm particular about this). Add diced potatoes and roll in fat. Add water fish was cooked in and cook until just tender. Add fish (large chunks preferable) and milk. Salt and pepper to taste. Heat to boil but do not boil. Serve 4 to 6. To serve as main course, cut water to 1½ cups and milk to 3 cups.

—*Mary Stuart Gadd Specht (Mrs. Frederick H.)*

🍂 *OKRA SOUP*

4 pounds good knuckle of veal
2 pounds prepared okra
10 tomatoes, peeled and cut in quarters
6 sprigs parsley
4 slices bacon
1 medium onion, finely chopped
   barley
   salt and pepper
1 pound crabmeat, preferably backfin
   corn from 6 ears

Do not use an iron pot. Select young, tender, fresh pods of okra. Discard any that appear rusty or discolored. One pound of okra equals a little over a quart of pods. Cut off stems and wash carefully. Slice large pods in half lengthwise, use small pods whole. Sauté the bacon and chop fine. Use the bacon fat to sauté the onion. Put into the kettle the veal, okra, tomatoes, parsley, bacon, and onion. Add 6 quarts of water, a little barley and salt and pepper to taste. Simmer for 5 hours, skimming surface as often as necessary. One hour before serving, add the crabmeat and corn. Makes approximately 6 to 8 quarts.

—Henrietta Thompson Robertson (Mrs. John)

❧ *SPLIT PEA SOUP*

   1½ cups green split peas
    7 cups water (or broth from a ham bone)
    1 bay leaf
    1 tablespoon margarine
    2 onions, chopped
    2 carrots, chopped
    3 ribs celery, chopped
    1 teaspoon salt
    1 teaspoon garlic powder
   ½ teaspoon thyme
   ¼ teaspoon cumin
       pinch of red pepper (or to taste)
    1 tablespoon soy sauce

In a large soup pot bring peas to a boil with water or broth and bay leaf. Reduce heat and simmer for at least half an hour. Meanwhile heat margarine in a frying pan on medium heat. Add onions, carrots, then celery, adding a little salt and stirring for a minute or two after each. When peas have simmered at least half an hour, remove bay leaf and add vegetables and all other ingredients except soy sauce. Simmer until vegetables are tender, stirring occasionally to prevent sticking. Add water if necessary to thin. Add soy sauce 5 or 10 minutes before end. Serves 8.

    Note: The choice of herbs gives a special punch. Do not substitute.

—Mary Stuart Gadd Specht (Mrs. Frederick H.)

❧ OYSTER BISQUE

The bisque can be warmed over as many times as necessary, and it will still be delicious. The recipe can be stretched by increasing the amount of milk in the sauce.

1 pint oysters
  milk
2 tablespoons butter
2 tablespoons flour
  salt
  cayenne
  blade of mace
1 teaspoon chopped parsley
1 egg

Heat oysters in their own liquor to the boiling point; drain, reserve liquor, and chop oysters. Add enough milk to the liquor to make 2 cups. Add butter and flour to liquid and make a sauce. Season with salt, dash of cayenne, blade of mace, and parsley. Add oysters. Add egg, slightly beaten, and serve. Makes 4 servings.

Note: Powdered mace does not do the same thing the whole mace does.

—*Margaret Hoey Fox (Mrs. Albert C.)*

❧ VEGETABLE SOUP (St. John's Church)

This soup is better on the second day.

2 pound chuck roast with bone
4 quarts water
1 1½-pound bag frozen mixed vegetables, preferably a
    mixture for soup
½ 24-ounce-bag frozen Fordhook lima beans
2 large baking potatoes, diced
1 medium-sized green pepper, diced
1 cup diced celery (include some leaves)
1 large onion, diced
1 1-pound can of tomatoes, crushed

    1 15-ounce can tomato sauce
    1 6-ounce can tomato paste
    1 10½-ounce can beef bouillon, or 2 cubes
    1 medium rutabaga, diced (optional)
    2 cups chopped cabbage (optional)
       okra, diced (optional)
    1 teaspoon crushed thyme
    1 teaspoon crushed basil
  1½ teaspoons curry powder
    1 teaspoon ground sage
    1 teaspoon celery seeds
    1 teaspoon crushed oregano
   ¼ teaspoon fennel seeds
    2 tablespoons sugar
    1 teaspoon garlic powder
       a few red pepper flakes
    1 tablespoon salt

Cook meat in water for an hour and then add vegetables. Simmer for several hours. Add salt and other seasonings to taste. Cool and skim off fat. Makes 1½ gallons or 12 to 14 servings.

—*Thelma C. Scott, St. John's Episcopal Church, McLean, Virginia*

PEANUT SOUP

    1 quart milk
   ½ pint (1 cup) peanut butter
    1 small onion, grated
    1 cup finely chopped celery
    1 teaspoon cornstarch
    1 tablespoon cold milk
    1 teaspoon paprika

Put milk, peanut butter, onion, and celery in a double boiler and cook for 20 minutes. Moisten cornstarch with cold milk and add to hot soup. Cook and stir until smooth and thick. Strain and add paprika. Serve. Makes 1½ quarts or 4 to 6 servings.

—*Frances Neville Vest (Mrs. J. P. W.)*

🍃 *SUMMER SOUP I*

- 1 carrot
- 1 stalk celery
- 1 medium onion
- 2 fresh tomatoes, skinned
- ½ cup canned tomato juice
- 1 10½-ounce can condensed cream of celery soup
- 2 cups tomato juice
  Tabasco sauce
  salt
  cayenne
  chopped chives

Put in blender the carrot, celery, onion, tomatoes, and ½ cup tomato juice. Blend 1 minute. In a large cocktail shaker or reasonable facsimile, put the remaining ingredients and shake. Blend together. Pour into cups and put a cube of ice in each one. Makes 6 cups.

—*Lois S. Duffey (Mrs. Harry J., Jr.)*

🍃 *SUMMER PEA SOUP*

- 2 10-ounce packages frozen peas defrosted under warm running water (Reserve ½ cup for garnish.)
- 2 cups plain yogurt
- ½ cup olive oil (good grade)
- ½ cup fresh lime juice
- 4 cloves garlic smashed and chopped
- 1 tablespoon chili powder or to taste
- 2 cups chicken stock
- 1 tablespoon salt or less to taste
- ½ cup reserved peas
- ½ cup chopped tomato
- ½ cup red bell pepper
- 2 teaspoons minced jalapeno pepper
- 3 tablespoons chopped cilantro or parsley

Place peas in processor and process until smooth. Add yogurt, olive oil, lime juice, garlic, and chili powder. Process until smooth. Pour mixture into bowl and add stock and salt. Refrigerate until cool. Garnish with reserved peas and remaining ingredients. Makes 7 or 8 servings.

—*Nina DuPont Curran (Mrs. Edward A.)*

SUMMER SOUP II

    2½ cups tomato juice
    1½ cups condensed cream of celery soup
    1   medium onion, grated
        Tabasco sauce
        salt
        cayenne
        chopped chives

Blend all ingredients. Pour into cups and put a cube of ice in each one. Makes 4 cups.

—*Lois S. Duffey (Mrs. Harry J., Jr.)*

TURNIP SOUP

No one will be able to guess that you made this with turnips. Delicious!

    2   cups peeled, diced turnips
    3   cans bouillon
    ⅔   cup Pet milk or heavy cream
        salt and pepper
    1   tablespoon butter
    1   tablespoon cornstarch mixed with a little water

Cook turnips in bouillon until tender. Put through a food mill, add other ingredients, heat to boiling, and serve. Makes 14 servings (1½ quarts and 5 ounces).

—*Virginia Ingles Freeland (Mrs. Samuel L.)*

🌬 *VICHYSSOISE*

An unusual version.

2 cups diced raw potatoes
2 cups diced raw onions
1 cup canned chicken broth
1 cup sour cream
1 teaspoon Worcestershire sauce
   salt to taste

Cook potatoes and onions in very little water until soft. Put them through a food mill (or blender). Add broth and sour cream and beat well. Add seasoning and chill. Makes 6 cups or 6 to 8 servings.

—*Mrs. John Porter*

$\mathscr{S}$EAFOOD

Be present at our table, Lord,
Be here and everywhere adored;
Thy creatures bless, and grant that we
May feast in paradise with thee.
—John Wesley (1703–1791)

🍃 *BAKED CRAB SUPREME*

½ cup Miracle Whip
3 tablespoons minced green pepper
2 teaspoons minced onion
2 tablespoons minced pimiento
1½ teaspoons dry mustard
  cayenne pepper
1½ teaspoons salt
3 tablespoons flour
2 cups milk
2 egg yolks
2 teaspoons Worcestershire sauce
2 egg whites
1 pound crabmeat, lump or regular

Place Miracle Whip, green pepper, onion, pimiento, mustard, pepper, and salt in small saucepan. Cover and cook slowly for 5 minutes. Remove from heat, stir in flour, gradually add milk. Return to stove, cook until thick. Stir in beaten egg yolks, Worcestershire sauce, and crabmeat. Fold in stiffly beaten egg whites and pour into a greased casserole dish. Set dish in a pan of water. Bake at 375 degrees for 45 minutes. Makes 6 to 8 servings.

—Marjorie Belt Turner (Mrs. Edward)

🍃 *CRAB CAKES*

This recipe was used by the Corsica River Yacht Club at the Friday night regatta picnic. For the picnic, use 3½ slices of bread. At home, use 1½.

3½ slices day-old homemade-type bread
1 egg yolk
1 pound crabmeat
  red and black pepper
½ teaspoon prepared mustard
2 teaspoons chopped parsley
  mayonnaise—enough to hold cakes together

Rub bread between hands to crumble. Add egg yolk and mix well. Mix gently with rest of ingredients. Form into cakes. Brown and warm through in pan. Makes 10 cakes.

—Margaret Gadd Ashley (Mrs. John M.)

❧ CRAB DELIGHT

1 8-ounce package Velveeta cheese
2 tablespoons butter
¾ pint heavy cream
1 pound backfin crabmeat
2 cups broad noodles, cooked in salted water
½ cup crushed cornflakes

In the top of a double boiler, melt 1 package Velveeta cheese and 2 tablespoons butter. Add cream and heat. Fold in crabmeat. Mix gently and pour over cooked noodles which have been placed in a buttered casserole. Cover top with crushed corn flakes and bake at 350 degrees for about 45 minutes. Makes 6 to 8 servings.

—Mildred Lee Thompson Murray (Mrs. Gerald)

❧ IMPERIAL CRAB

4 tablespoons butter
3 tablespoons flour
1 cup milk
1 pound crabmeat
1 egg, beaten
½ cup pimiento
3 tablespoons mayonnaise
1 teaspoon dry mustard
salt and pepper
bread crumbs
butter

Make a white sauce with the butter, flour, and milk. Cool slightly. Mix the next five ingredients with the white sauce and season with salt and pepper. Put into crab shells or baking dish. Sprinkle with buttered bread crumbs, dot with butter, and brown in 350-degree oven. Freezes well. Brown after defrosting. Makes 6 servings.

—Louise Lewis Grubb (Mrs. Ernest W.)

CRABMEAT PIE

> 3   cups thick white sauce
> ½   pound grated sharp cheese
> 1   teaspoon celery salt
> 1   medium green pepper, cut very fine
> 1   small can mushrooms or equivalent in fresh
> 13   ounces fresh crabmeat or 2 6½-ounce cans

Cook sauce, stir in cheese, salt, pepper, mushrooms, and crabmeat. Put in a buttered casserole and cover top with pastry. Bake at 375 degrees for 30 minutes. Makes 6 servings, 4 if people are hungry.

—*Jennie Mae Hauser Fisher (Mrs. W. Henry)*

MARYLAND CRABMEAT À LA CASSOLETTE

From the kitchen file of Readbourne Estates.

> 3   tablespoons butter
> 2   tablespoons flour
> 1   quart light cream
> 1   pound lump crabmeat
> 1   teaspoon salt
>   white wine to taste

Melt butter in saucepan. Add flour and let simmer for 2 minutes. Heat cream. Pour hot cream slowly into the butter-flour mixture and stir until smooth. Cook slowly until it thickens, then add wine and salt. When ready to serve, add crab and let it remain over heat until it bubbles. Serve in cassolette garnished with toast points. Makes 8 to 10 servings.

—*Helen C. Marshall (Mrs. Joseph)*

IMPERIAL DEVILED CRAB

Simmer the flakes of two crabs and half a chopped onion in butter, season with salt and cayenne pepper, add two cups of thick cream sauce, a dash of Worcestershire sauce, a teaspoonful of English mustard, a little chopped chives, bring to a boil and bind with the yolks of two eggs. Add a little green and Spanish pepper chopped fine. Fill crab shells, spread a little French mustard and a sprinkle of bread crumbs over the top. Place a small piece of butter on each and bake in the oven until brown. Serve with lemon. Makes 2 servings.

—Mr. Lake, Hotel Rennert, Baltimore.
From Eat, Drink and Be Merry in Maryland

CASSEROLE OF BAKED CRAB IMPERIAL

- 4 tablespoons butter or margarine
- 4 tablespoons flour
- 2 cups milk
- 1 teaspoon salt
- ⅛ teaspoon pepper
- ½ teaspoon celery salt
  dash of cayenne
- 1 egg yolk, beaten
- 2 tablespoons sherry
- 1 cup soft bread crumbs
- 1 pound crab flakes
- 1 teaspoon minced parsley
- 1 teaspoon minced onion
- ¼ cup buttered bread crumbs
  paprika

Melt butter or margarine, add flour and blend. Gradually add milk and seasonings and cook over low heat, stirring constantly until thickened. Gradually add egg yolk and cook 2 minutes more. Remove from heat and add sherry, bread crumbs, crabmeat, parsley, and onion. Gently mix and pour into well-greased 1½-quart casserole. Top with buttered crumbs and sprinkle with paprika. Bake at 400 degrees for 20 or 25 minutes. Makes 6 servings.

—Genevieve Hall Valliant (Mrs. Edwin S., Sr.)

❧ *SCALLOPED CRAB*

    1 pound fresh crabmeat
   ¼ cup dry sherry
   ¼ cup butter
    2 tablespoons finely chopped onion
   ¼ cup sifted flour
   ½ cup milk
    1 cup light cream
    1 tablespoon Worcestershire sauce
    1 teaspoon salt
       dash of pepper
    2 egg yolks
    2 tablespoons butter, melted
   ½ cup dry bread crumbs

Drain and pick over crabmeat. Sprinkle with 2 tablespoons sherry, toss, and mix well. Sauté onion in butter in medium saucepan. Remove from heat and stir in flour. Gradually stir in milk and cream; bring to a boil, stirring. Reduce heat and simmer until thick, 8 to 10 minutes. Remove from heat, add Worcestershire sauce, salt, pepper, and rest of sherry. Stir a little of sauce into egg yolks then return to rest of sauce. Mix well. Stir in crab mixture. Place in 6 to 8 shells, or a 1-quart casserole, lightly greased. Toss bread crumbs in melted butter and sprinkle on top of crab. Bake at 350 degrees for 20 minutes for the shells, 25 minutes for a casserole. Makes 6 to 8 servings.

—Janie Eby Ashley (Mrs. Sydney G.)

❧ *CRAB SOUP OR CREAMED CRAB*

   ¼ pound butter
    2 tablespoons flour
    1 pint milk
    1 pound lump crabmeat
    1 large pinch salt
    1 pinch red pepper
   ½ pint cream
    1 glass sherry

Melt half of the butter in a saucepan. Add flour and make cream sauce with heated milk. Keep this hot. Melt balance of butter in another saucepan and fry crabmeat a little. Add salt, pepper, cream sauce, and cream. Let boil 2 or 3 minutes. Remove from heat and add sherry. Mix well. Be sure it does not boil after wine is added. Makes 8 to 10 servings.

—From the collection of Mrs. Luther Gadd

A LEMON FISH

3   pounds fresh fish
1   tablespoon olive oil
1   clove garlic
1   lemon

Put fish in a shallow baking pan, pour oil over it, squeeze garlic over it with a garlic press, and then completely cover fish with thin slices of lemon. Bake at 350 degrees for 30 to 35 minutes. Serve with parsley potatoes. Makes 4 servings.

—Isa Louise Byers Blaney (Mrs. Arthur J.)

FISH STUFFED WITH CRABMEAT

1   tablespoon minced onion
1   tablespoon minced parsley
2   tablespoons butter
4   slices white bread, broken into small crumbs
1   pound crabmeat
2   eggs
    pinch cayenne pepper
1   tablespoon lemon juice
8   small, dressed whole rockfish, bluefish, or baby flounder

Sauté onion and parsley in butter. Add bread. Add crabmeat along with raw eggs and seasonings. The mixture will be dry and crumbly. Pack stuffing into body cavities of fish. Brush fish with butter and bake at 350 degrees about 30 minutes or until skins are brown and fish flakes to touch of fork. Serve with lemon wedges. Makes 6 to 8 servings.

This stuffing may also be spread on fish fillets which are then rolled and secured with toothpicks or skewers. Brush with butter and bake on a foil-lined pan for 10 to 15 minutes at 350 degrees.

—Sara Warren Kidd (Mrs. A. L.)

SEAFOOD

❧ BILL'S ESCARGOT

            1 can French snails
            2 dozen snail shells
            2 sticks butter
          ¼ cup finely chopped fresh parsley
   1 or 2 cloves garlic, minced (depending on how well you like garlic)
            1 teaspoon salt
            2 tablespoons minced shallots or green onions
          ½ teaspoon pepper

Drain can of French snails. There should be 2 dozen. Wash and dry snail
shells. Pack snails into shells. Combine remaining ingredients. Pack
butter sauce in shells over snails. Place snails on sheet of foil in broiler.
Broil until butter is bubbly. Remove and serve immediately with plenty
of French bread (for dipping up the sauce) and a good rosé or light red
wine. Makes 4 servings.

—Brigadier General W. F. Doehler, USMC (Ret.)

❧ STEPHEN LYLE'S STEAMED SALMON WITH BASIL AND TOMATO

            2 medium tomatoes, excellent and ripe
            2 shallots
            1 small clove garlic
          ½ cup excellent full flavored olive oil
          ¼ cup red wine vinegar
            1 teaspoon fresh thyme, chopped
          ½ teaspoon salt or more
               lots of black pepper from the mill
          20 fresh basil leaves
            1 24-ounce salmon filet
   6 or 7 teaspoons olive paste (see below)

Peel the tomatoes by plunging them for 20 seconds in boiling water and
then pulling off the skin. Cut them in half and squeeze gently to remove
seeds. Cut into small dice, sprinkle with a little salt, and drain. Dice the
shallot very small, put the garlic through a press and mix them with the
oil, vinegar, thyme, salt, and pepper. It should be highly seasoned. Slice

94

four of the basil leaves thinly and add. Add tomato (should be about ½ cup), mix, and let sit for at least one hour.

Slice the salmon on an angle with a very sharp, thin knife into eight 3-ounce slices. Put them between large sheets of plastic wrap and pound lightly with the side of a cleaver till about an eighth of an inch thick. Brush four large, heavy dinner plates lightly with olive oil. Heat them at 425 degrees for 2 or 3 minutes, so they are too hot to touch but just barely. Season the salmon with a little salt and pepper and place slices on plates, not overlapping. They will probably fill the plate. Put the plates back in the oven immediately, and cook salmon till just opaque but medium inside (check by pulling a piece slightly apart). Do not overcook—the dish's success depends on it. And remember: the fish will continue to cook a little after it is removed from the oven. Spread 2 or 3 tablespoons of tomato mixture over each salmon. Dot with five or six tiny dabs of olive paste. Slice the basil leaves into strips at the last minute and sprinkle generously over salmon. Serve immediately, with a chilled Chardonnay. Makes 4 servings.

Olive Paste

Pit and process in a food processor Niçoise olives with a dash of red wine vinegar, pepper, and enough olive oil to give it a thick but slightly liquid consistency.

—*Stephen Kirk Lyle*

❧ POACHED SALMON

3 to 4	pounds salmon
	water
½	cup white wine
1	tablespoon salt
1	onion studded with 2 cloves
2	bay leaves

Wrap fish in wet cheesecloth. Bring enough water to cover fish to boiling in fish steamer. Add remaining ingredients. Place wrapped fish on rack in steamer. Simmer 30 minutes. Drain. Cool enough to peel skin, first one side and then the other. Cool thoroughly. Cover and refrigerate. Makes 6 to 8 servings.

—*Committee*

❦ *CREAMED FINNAN HADDIE*

 1 pound smoked fish (try to get a thick piece)

 2 cups milk

 1 green pepper

 4 hard-boiled eggs

   salt and pepper to taste

 4 tablespoons butter

 4 tablespoons flour

Set fish in pan, cover with milk, and simmer 15 to 20 minutes until meat flakes off smoked skin. If fish is too thick to cover, start skin side down and turn it over after half the cooking time has elapsed. Seed and chop green pepper and simmer a few minutes in a little water. Drain and reserve water for sauce. Chop hard-boiled eggs into large pieces. When fish is done, drain, reserve milk, and flake off meat from skin in as large pieces as you can. Make a cream sauce of flour and butter using the milk the fish was cooked in. If the fish was very salty, you may have to use some fresh milk to avoid too salty a sauce. Use as much of the water the peppers were cooked in as you like. When sauce is a good consistency, taste for seasoning and add flaked fish, chopped peppers, and eggs. Keep hot over hot water about 15 minutes to blend flavors, and serve. Makes 4 servings.

—*Lynette Morgan Nielsen (Mrs. Orsen)*

Many of the ecclesiastical articles at St. Paul's bear evidence of the historical influence of England upon the settlement of the Eastern Shore. The 1716 chalice and 1717 flagon, gifts of Major John Hawkins, have been in continuous use.

❦ *OYSTERS CLARENCE (Not Named for C.W.M.)*

 2 quarts oysters

 2 tablespoons flour

 ¼ pound butter

 2 cups cream

2½ pounds mushrooms, cut up
3 red pimientos, cut in strips
1 dessert spoon Worcestershire sauce
3 tablespoons sherry
salt
pepper
½ cup chicken stock

Drain oysters, being sure they are well drained. Make sauce of flour, butter, oyster liquid, and cream. Cut out the hearts of oysters and brown in butter. Add salt and pepper to taste. Broil mushrooms in 2 tablespoons butter and remaining chicken stock separately from oysters. Mix oysters and mushrooms and keep hot in a double boiler along with pimiento, Worcestershire, and sherry until ready to serve. Serves 10 to 12 persons.

—*Eleanor Williams Miles (Mrs. Clarence W.)*

DEVILED OYSTERS

1 pint oysters
1 tablespoon butter
2 tablespoons flour
¾ cup rich milk (½ milk, ¼ cream)
½ teaspoon salt
¼ teaspoon nutmeg
few grains cayenne
¼ teaspoon mustard
½ tablespoon Worcestershire sauce
1 egg yolk
buttered bread crumbs
paprika

Cook oysters in their own liquor for a few minutes (until edges curl), then pour in colander to drain. Cut oysters with knife and fork. Make paste with butter and flour. Add milk, then seasoning. Cook until it thickens, about 12 minutes. Add slowly to egg yolk; then add oysters. Pour into ramekins. Top with buttered bread crumbs and sprinkle with paprika. Bake at 400 degrees for 10 or 15 minutes. These can be prepared early in the morning and baked when ready to serve hot. Makes about 5 ramekins.

—*Mackey Perry Beck (Mrs. S. Scott)*

❧ *PANNED OYSTERS À LA GUN CLUB*

> 1 cup butter
> 1 tablespoon chopped bacon which has been crisply
>   cooked and drained
> 1 tablespoon lemon juice
> 2 teaspoons chopped parsley
>   salt, black and red pepper to taste
>   enough oysters for 4 people

Prepare sauce by melting butter. Add bacon, lemon juice and parsley and seasoning. Mix well, keep hot, but do not cook further. Pan oysters in their own liquor. They are done when their edges begin to curl. When oysters are done, mix in sauce and serve immediately. The oysters may be transferred to ramekins for individual service and a tablespoon of sauce spread upon each portion.

—*Mr. and Mrs. Orsen Nielsen*
From The Gun Club Cook Book

❧ *SCALLOPED OYSTERS AND CORN*

> 1 pint oysters, reserve liquid
> ¼ cup butter or margarine
> 2 cups coarsely crumbled crackers
> 1 12-ounce can whole kernel corn, drained
>   salt and pepper
> 6 tablespoons cream

Drain oysters, reserve liquid. Remove all bits of shell. In skillet, melt butter or margarine; add crackers and stir until mixed. Grease casserole, 12 × 8 × 2 inches. Spread one-third of buttered crumbs over bottom. Arrange half of drained oysters and half of can of corn over these; season very lightly with salt and pepper. Scatter third of remaining crumbs on top. Add remaining oysters and corn; sprinkle with salt and pepper. Mix ¾ cup oyster liquid with cream; dribble over all. Chill. About 30 minutes before dinner, heat oven to 425 degrees. Top oyster mixture with remaining crumbs. Bake about 20 minutes until done or crumbs are browned. Serve with tossed salad. Makes 6 servings.

—*Isa Louise Byers Blaney (Mrs. Arthur J.)*

❦ *SKILLET OYSTERS*

    1 pint oysters with some liquid
    2 tablespoons butter
  ½ cup milk
      salt and pepper to taste
    1 loaf party rye bread

Heat oysters with butter and milk in skillet until oysters' edges curl. Do not boil. Toast party rye in oven. Butter one side. Spoon oysters with some liquid on toast and serve. Makes 4 servings.

—Dorothy Young Turner (Mrs. B. Hackett)

❦ *MUSHROOM OYSTER RAREBIT*

      Buttermilk Corn Bread
    4 tablespoons butter
  ½ pound fresh mushrooms, sliced
    1 pint oysters
    2 tablespoons flour
 1½ cups light cream
    3 cups grated cheddar cheese
    2 teaspoons Worcestershire sauce
      dash liquid hot pepper sauce
    2 eggs

Prepare one recipe of Buttermilk Corn Bread in Breads chapter. Melt 2 tablespoons butter in a medium skillet. Sauté mushrooms until tender. Remove from skillet and set aside. In same skillet heat oysters until edges curl; remove from skillet. Meanwhile, melt 2 tablespoons butter in top of double boiler. Blend in 2 tablespoons flour. Stir in light cream. Continue stirring until mixture thickens. Add cheddar cheese, Worcestershire sauce, and hot pepper sauce. Stir until cheese melts. Beat eggs until light; stir into cheese sauce. Fold in the mushrooms and oysters. Heat 4 or 5 minutes. Serve over corn bread. Makes 4 servings.

—Nancy Insley Gribbon (Mrs. Robert T.)

The Reverend Robert T. Gribbon is the current rector at St. Paul's Parish.

SCALLOPED OYSTERS *(Mother's Recipe)*

    2 dozen oysters
    ¼ pound butter
    1 large tablespoon flour
    ¾ cup cream
       salt
       Worcestershire sauce
       bread crumbs
       grated cheese

Put oysters in a pan in their own juice. Heat to a boil and drain. Save oyster liquid. In another pan, put butter and flour and mix until butter is melted. Add cream and ¾ cup oyster liquid to butter and flour. Stir and cook until thick. Add oysters to which salt (to taste) and a few drops of Worcestershire sauce have been added. Put in individual baking dishes and sprinkle with bread crumbs and grated cheese. Bake 10 minutes in hot oven and serve at once. Makes 8 servings.

—Mrs. Wilbur N. Davis

OYSTER STEW

    1 quart oysters
    ½ cup milk and a little cream
    2 tablespoons butter
    2 tablespoons flour
       a little finely chopped celery with tops
       salt
       pepper to taste

Drain oysters through a colander for an hour or more. Then hold colander under cold water spigot and run the water, washing the oysters in the hands. Drain for a few minutes so that they will be free of water. Put the oysters in a saucepan and add the clear liquor that has been drained from the oysters. Put on stove with milk, salt, pepper, and celery and cook until the oysters' gills curl, then add butter and flour which has been mixed by melting the butter and stirring the flour in it. Lastly add cream, the more the richer.

—From Eat, Drink and Be Merry in Maryland

Mr. Richard Tilghman of "The Hermitage" contracted with the Vestry in 1697 to build up the walls of St. Paul's and make bricks for a new building 40 feet in length by 25 feet in breadth and to procure five windows, two to be on each side of the church and a window at the chancel. This was the second St. Paul's Church used until 1720.

❧ SCALLOPS EN COQUILLE

  1 pound fresh sea scallops
½ cup white wine
  2 tablespoons butter
  2 tablespoons flour
  1 cup milk
½ teaspoon salt
     pinch of cayenne pepper or 2 drops Tabasco sauce
  1 tablespoon finely minced onion
  2 teaspoons finely cut parsley
     dry breadcrumbs
     butter

Cut each scallop in 4 to 6 pieces and cook in wine over low heat 4 minutes. Make cream sauce of butter, flour, and milk and add seasonings and vegetables when sauce is smooth. Add cooked scallops with wine and divide mixture into 8 ceramic or foil shells. Sprinkle with fine dry bread crumbs and dot with butter. Place shells on baking sheet and bake at 350 degrees for 10 to 12 minutes until crumbs are brown. Makes 6 servings.

—*Sara Warren Kidd (Mrs. A. L.)*

The scallop shell is the traditional symbol for Holy Baptism.

❧ *SCALLOP CASSEROLE*

 2 tablespoons butter
 2 pounds scallops
 1 pound whole small mushrooms
    salt
    pepper
 ½ stick butter
 4 tablespoons flour
 1 cup white wine (sauterne)
 1 12-fluid-ounce can evaporated milk or cream
    nutmeg

Butter large baking dish with 2 tablespoons butter. Layer mushrooms in bottom with scallops on top. Sprinkle with salt and pepper. Melt ½ stick butter and stir in flour. Gradually stir in wine and cook until sauce is thick. Gradually stir in evaporated milk. Season with pepper and a pinch of nutmeg. Pour sauce over casserole. Cover and bake at 350 degrees for 35 minutes. Makes 8 to 10 servings.

—*Katharine Nicols Grove (Mrs. J. Robert)*

❧ *SHRIMP CREOLE*

 2½ cups water
  1 pound shrimp (30-40 count)
  1 tablespoon salt
  1 bay leaf
  1 teaspoon pickling spices
  1 tablespoon vinegar
     bacon drippings
  1 cup chopped onion
 ¾ cup chopped celery
 ¾ cup chopped green pepper
 ½ cup water
  1 cup undiluted tomato soup
  1 6-ounce can tomato paste
  1 tablespoon catsup
  1 tablespoon Worcestershire sauce
 ½ tablespoon Louisiana hot sauce

½ tablespoon soy sauce

1 tablespoon sugar

Steam shrimp in water, salt, spices, and vinegar until pink. Remove shells and devein. Sauté onion, celery, and green pepper in bacon drippings. Heat remaining ingredients thoroughly. About 10 minutes before serving, add shrimp to sauce. Do not cook. Serve over rice. Makes 4 servings.

—Jennie Mae Hauser Fisher (Mrs. W. Henry)

SCALLOPS ON SKEWERS

1 cup dry white wine

3 sprigs parsley

1 bay leaf

½ teaspoon salt

⅛ teaspoon pepper

½ pound scallops, washed, drained, quartered

3 strips bacon, partially cooked

Bring to boil the wine, parsley, bay leaf, salt, and pepper. Add the scallops and simmer for 5 minutes. Drain. Alternate squares of bacon and scallops on skewers. Place skewers on lightly buttered baking pan and bake at 325 degrees until bacon is crisp.

May be prepared in advance and put in oven at the last minute. Makes 3 or 4 servings.

—Janet Gadd Doehler (Mrs. William F.)

SHAD BAKED IN CREAM

1 3-pound boned shad

butter

salt and pepper

1 cup heavy cream

chopped parsley

Oil a baking dish and place shad on it. Dot with butter and sprinkle with salt and pepper. Bake at 400 degrees for 20 minutes. Add cream and bake 10 minutes longer, basting occasionally with cream. Sprinkle with chopped parsley and serve. Makes 6 servings.

—Lynette Morgan Nielsen (Mrs. Orsen)

🍃 *FRESH CURRIED SHRIMP*

    1 pound fresh or frozen shrimp
    3 tablespoons butter
    2 medium onions, chopped
    2 cloves garlic, crushed and chopped
    2 tablespoons flour
    2 teaspoons curry powder
    1 cup milk
    1 teaspoon lemon juice
       salt and pepper
    1 stick cinnamon

Shell shrimp and sauté in butter until lightly brown. Remove from pan (omit this step if using frozen shrimp). Brown onions with crushed and chopped garlic. Add flour and curry powder. Stir well; add milk gradually. Stir until thickened. Add lemon juice. Season sauce to taste. Add shrimp. Break cinnamon stick and add. Stir, then cover tightly and simmer gently about ½ hour. Stir occasionally to prevent sticking. Add more milk if necessary. Serve over rice, with usual curry accompaniments. Makes 4 servings.

—Mollie Eaton Hallowell

🍃 *SALMON MOUSSE*

    1 10¾-ounce can tomato soup
       salt to taste
       pepper and red pepper flakes
    9 ounces cream cheese
    2 tablespoons gelatin
   ½ cup cold water
       celery, green pepper, onion cut up fine to make ½ cup in all
    1 cup mayonnaise
    1 14¾-ounce can red salmon, drained

Warm tomato soup, seasonings, and cheese over low heat. Beat until smooth. Dissolve gelatin in cold water. Pour into heated soup. Cool slightly and add other ingredients. Pour into quart-mold and chill. Serve with Caper Sauce, below. Makes 4 servings.

Caper Sauce

½ cup chopped capers, drained
1 cup mayonnaise

Mix together.

—*Elizabeth Trundle Barton (Mrs. Marvin)*

❧ MIXED SEAFOOD CASSEROLE

2 quarts water
2 tablespoons salt
1 pound medium shrimp, shelled and deveined
1 pound scallops
1 pound fillet of sole
½ pound crabmeat
¾ pound butter or margarine
3 tablespoons flour
5 cups half-and-half
2 tablespoons sherry
1 tablespoon Worcestershire sauce
1 tablespoon capers
2 tablespoons Parmesan cheese
1½ teaspoons salt (optional)
1 teaspoon paprika
¼ cup Parmesan cheese
½ cup fine bread crumbs

Heat water and salt in large saucepan. Add shrimp and scallops and boil for 2 minutes. Then add sole and boil for 3 minutes longer. Drain, saving liquid in case you need to thin the cream sauce. Flake scallops and sole and cut shrimp in small pieces. Melt butter in saucepan and blend in flour. Gradually add half-and-half. Cook over low heat, stirring constantly until thickened. Add sherry, Worcestershire sauce, capers, 2 tablespoons Parmesan cheese, 1½ teaspoons salt and 1 teaspoon paprika. Fold in all of the seafoods and pour into a greased 3-quart casserole. Mix together ¼ cup Parmesan cheese and bread crumbs and sprinkle over top of casserole. Preheat oven to 300 degrees and bake for 40 minutes. Very rich. Serves 8 to 10.

—*Julia Browne Sause (Mrs. John W., Jr.)*

❧ *SEAFOOD À LA VOISEU*

   6 mushrooms
      butter
      pinch finely chopped garlic
  24 scallops
  12 opened oysters
  ½ cup white wine
  12 shrimp, cooked and peeled
   2 egg yolks
  ¼ cup heavy cream
      cayenne pepper
      chopped chives
      wild rice

Cut mushrooms into pieces. Sauté in butter and add a pinch of finely chopped garlic. Add scallops, oysters, and white wine. Cook together for 8 minutes. Add shrimp. Thicken sauce with 2 egg yolks and heavy cream. Season with a little cayenne pepper and chopped chives. Serve with wild rice. Makes 8 servings.

—Eleanor Williams Miles (Mrs. Clarence W.)

❧ *SEAFOOD CASSEROLE*

  1 pound cooked shrimp
  1 pound lobster meat
  ½ pound crabmeat, cut up
  ½ pound mushrooms, sauteed
  1 stick butter (¼ pound)
  ½ cup flour
  4 cups milk
     salt
     pepper
     paprika
     chives
     parsley
  ¼ cup dry white wine (optional)
  ½ cup grated Parmesan cheese

Mix seafood gently and add mushrooms. Make a cream sauce with butter, flour, and milk. Season to taste with salt, pepper, paprika, chives, and parsley. Add white wine if desired. Place seafood in a 2-quart casserole and pour sauce to cover. Sprinkle with Parmesan cheese. Bake at 350 degrees for 20 minutes. Place under broiler for 1 minute and serve immediately. Makes 8 to 10 servings.

—Mildred Smith Thompson (Mrs. Philemon Hopper)

❧ SMOTHERED SHAD ROE

¼ pound butter
3 pairs shad roe
   salt and pepper to taste
   chopped parsley
   lemon slices
   crisp bacon

In an iron skillet, melt butter. (If same pan bacon was fried in, be sure all bacon fat is drained from pan beforehand.) When butter is hot, add the roe. Cover and cook 10 to 15 minutes, depending on size. Turn once. Season with salt and pepper and sprinkle with chopped parsley. Serve with lemon slices and crisp bacon. Makes 3 servings.

—Maria McKenney

❧ BONELESS SHAD

1 3-pound fish, cleaned (allow ½ to ¾ pound per serving)
3 quarts of cold water
1 tablespoon vinegar
6 strips of bacon

Grease a heavy roasting pan that has a tightly fitting lid. Place shad in pan and add water to almost cover fish. Add vinegar. Place strips of bacon inside and over shad. Bring to a boil on stove. Remove to 250 degree oven and cover. Bake 5 hours. Last 30 minutes, pour off any remaining water and leave uncovered.

Note: You may run the fish under the broiler at the end of the 5 hours to brown the bacon.

—Anne Stoney Cantler (Mrs. James E.)

The Reverend James E. Cantler was rector at St. Paul's from 1965 to 1976.

🦐 SHRIMP AND CHEESE CASSEROLE

  6 slices bread
  ½ pound sliced Old English cheese
  1 pound prepared shrimp (ready to eat)
  ¼ cup margarine, melted
  3 whole eggs
  ½ teaspoon dry mustard
  ½ teaspoon salt
  1 pint milk

Break bread in pieces the size of a quarter. Break cheese in bite size pieces. Arrange shrimp, bread, and cheese in several layers in greased casserole. Pour melted butter over this mixture. Beat eggs and add mustard and salt to eggs. Add milk and mix. Pour over mixture in casserole. Let stand a minimum of 3 hours, preferably overnight, in refrigerator, covered. Bake, covered, at 350 degrees for 1 hour. Before removing from oven, remove cover and brown slightly.

An increased amount of shrimp will improve the dish but it's good as is. When I double the recipe, I use 3 pounds of shrimp. Makes 6 to 8 servings.

—*Madeline Harris Bartlett*

When the second church was completed, before 1700, pews were sold for 600 pounds of tobacco each. Thirteen pews were sold at this price.

🦐 BAKED TROUT IN CHAMPAGNE

This was adapted from a recipe served at a Waldorf Astoria dinner to honor Lafayette on April 11, 1957.

  1 8- to 10-inch trout (2 pounds)
  2 cups bread crumbs
  1 teaspoon chopped onion
  1 teaspoon chopped shallots

2 teaspoons chopped mushrooms
2 teaspoons chopped parsley
1 egg, beaten (reserve 1 tablespoon of egg for sauce)
   salt and pepper
   a little nutmeg to taste
   milk
   shallots
   champagne, or white wine, about 1 cup
   some fresh shrimp (optional)
1 teaspoon butter
   flour
1 teaspoon whipped cream

Prepare trout and split from head to tail for stuffing. Mix well the bread crumbs, chopped vegetables, ¾ beaten egg, and seasonings. Add just a little milk to make it slightly pasty. Stuff fish and roll in foil. Grease a pan and sprinkle with shallots. Put fish in pan with shrimp. Pour in champagne. Cover pan well with cover or foil and cook 30 minutes in moderate oven. Take fish out and remove skin. Take out shrimp. Add to the wine in the pan the butter and a very little flour (¼ teaspoon), rest of egg, and whipped cream and cook gently, stirring to thicken. Return fish to pan or preheated casserole, surround with shrimp, pour over sauce, and return to oven to just brown slightly. Makes 4 servings.

—*Louise McFeely Perry (Mrs. John W.)*

EASIEST WAY TO COOK FISH

Spread fillet with a touch of mayonnaise. Bake at 400 degrees for 20 minutes or until fillet flakes. Makes 1 serving.

—*Lois S. Duffey (Mrs. Harry J., Jr.)*

POULTRY AND GAME

The eyes of all wait upon thee, O Lord;
And thou givest them their meat in due season,
Thou openest thy hand,
And fillest all things living with plenteousness.
—Psalm 104

❧ *BRUNSWICK STEW*

This stew is most popular in Virginia and the Carolinas and is an old, old recipe.

6 slices boiling bacon (fatback)
1 2-pound frying chicken, cut up
1 32-ounce can tomatoes
1 quart cold water
2 medium onions, chopped fine
2 medium white potatoes, peeled and cut up
    (not too fine)
2 cups chopped cabbage
1½ cups lima beans
    salt and red pepper
1½ cups fresh corn

Cut bacon in small pieces and fry in the pot. If bacon yields too much fat, remove some. Add chicken and let brown in bacon grease. (Don't use the backs and wings of chicken.) Add tomatoes, water, chopped onions, potatoes, cabbage, and lima beans. Season with salt and red pepper (not cayenne) to taste. Let this cook over low heat for 4 to 5 hours, stirring frequently, as it sticks and burns easily. Then pick out all the bones from the stew. Ten minutes before serving, add corn and watch carefully as corn sinks to bottom and burns if not stirred often. Success depends on long, slow cooking.

When perfect, it should not be soupy. This stew is also very nice served cold but usually is served hot. It can be warmed over and when frozen in deep freeze seems to keep indefinitely. Serves 12.

—*Eleanor Williams Miles (Mrs. Clarence W.)*

In 1809, St. Paul's counted only 14 communicants.

❧ *FRIED CHICKEN*

    1 frying chicken, cut up
       salt and pepper
       flour
       paprika
       oil or Crisco

Wash and drain pieces of chicken. Place chicken on cookie sheet. Sprinkle with salt, then pepper, on both sides. Then cover all with flour. Sprinkle lightly with paprika. Remove from cookie sheet and place in frying pan in which about 2 inches of oil or Crisco has been heated to hot. Use a long-handled fork or tongs to put chicken in skillet. Brown on both sides, being careful not to burn. Turn heat down and cover to cook slowly for about half an hour; larger pieces may take a little longer. Peek once in a while to turn pieces so that they brown evenly. About ten minutes before end of cooking time, remove lid. Try to get pieces of equal sizes together in skillet such as breasts together or legs and thighs together. Place cooked chicken on heat-proof platter lined with paper towels to absorb grease. Serves 6.

—Mary Ellen Roberts Smith (Mrs. Lewis G. E.)

❧ *BREAST OF CHICKEN AND DRIED BEEF CASSEROLE*

    1 10¾-ounce can mushroom soup and equal amount sour cream
    1 package dried chipped beef
  12 half-breasts of chicken, boned
    6 strips bacon, cut in half, making 12 pieces

Bone chicken and let it drain thoroughly. Make sauce by combining soup and sour cream. Line greased casserole with chipped beef. Place chicken on this, then place piece of bacon on each piece of chicken. Cover with prepared sauce. Do not use additional salt. Cook at 350 degrees until done. Reduce heat to 325 degrees if necessary. Do not cover. Serves 12.

—Ruth Willis Draper (Mrs. Frank W., Jr.)

❧ *BREASTS OF CHICKEN STUFFED*

        3   chicken breasts, split (6 pieces)
            salt and pepper
            paprika
      ¼   pound butter
        4   cups bread crumbs
        1   onion, minced
        2   stalks celery, minced
      ¼   teaspoon salt
      ¼   teaspoon pepper
      ½   teaspoon sage

Season chicken breasts with salt, pepper, and paprika. Brush on both sides with butter. Mix bread crumbs and seasonings with remaining butter and pack firmly into hollow of chicken. Place chicken skin side down, stuffing side up, in baking dish. Place a pat of butter on stuffing and sprinkle with paprika. Bake at 350 degrees for 1 hour. Serves 6.

—Genevieve Hall Valliant (Mrs. Edwin S., Sr.)

❧ *BREASTS OF CHICKEN WITH WILD RICE*

        3   whole chicken breasts, split
      ½   tablespoon salt
            black pepper
      ½   cup butter
        1   pound mushrooms, sliced
        1   tablespoon grated onion
        2   cups heavy cream
        4   tablespoons brandy
        4   tablespoons dry sherry
        8   ounces wild rice, cooked

Bone and skin chicken breasts. Season with salt and pepper. Sauté in butter over low heat for 20 minutes or until rich brown. Remove chicken and keep hot. Add mushrooms and onion to butter remaining in pan and cook for 5 minutes, stirring constantly. Reduce heat and add cream slowly, stirring constantly. Simmer for 5 minutes. Add brandy and sherry and simmer for 5 minutes. Arrange chicken on wild rice, pour sauce over. Serves 6.

Note: One of the best ways to cook wild rice is to cover the rice three times with boiling water, a method that takes 1½ hours. First wash the rice thoroughly in cold water. Put rice in a saucepan. Cover rice with 4 cups rapidly boiling water, put lid on pan, and let the rice stand 30 minutes. Drain. Repeat this twice, adding salt to the last 4 cups of water.

—*Virginia Potter (Mrs. Holland)*

CHICKEN BURGUNDY

Chicken Burgundy is especially good served with giblet rice (mix cooked, minced giblets with rice), broccoli, and Indian pudding (see Desserts and Sauces chapter). Using cornstarch in place of flour gives a glossiness to the gravy.

1 3½ to 4 pound roasting chicken
   salt and pepper
2 tablespoons salad or olive oil
2 tablespoons minced onion
1 tablespoon minced celery
1 clove garlic, minced
1 tablespoon minced parsley
¼ cup water
1 bouillon cube
½ cup red cooking wine
1 bay leaf
¼ teaspoon rosemary
1 tablespoon cornstarch
2 tablespoons cold water
   salt and pepper

Cut up chicken for frying. Reserve wings and backs for chicken pie later in the week. Salt and pepper remaining pieces and lightly brown in oil. Place in casserole. Add minced onion, celery, garlic, and parsley with ¼ cup of water and a bouillon cube to frying pan and simmer for a few minutes, stirring up browned particles at the bottom of the frying pan. Pour over chicken. Add wine, bay leaf, and rosemary. Cover and cook in oven at 325 degrees for about 45 minutes, or until chicken is tender. Remove chicken from pan and keep hot on serving platter. Make a paste of cornstarch and water. Stir paste into the gravy, cover, and cook about 5 minutes more. Salt and pepper to taste. Before serving, spoon gravy over chicken. Makes 8 servings.

—*Isa Louise Byers Blaney (Mrs. Arthur J.)*

🐾 *BREAST OF CHICKEN SUPREME*

       4 ready-to-cook chicken breasts
      ¼ cup fat or salad oil
      ½ cup minced onion
       1 teaspoon paprika
       1 teaspoon salt
       2 tablespoons hot water
       1 tablespoon flour
     1½ tablespoons cold water
      ¼ teaspoon lemon juice
           grated lemon rind
       1 cup sour cream

Brown chicken breasts lightly on all sides in hot fat in skillet. Add onion, saute until tender. Add paprika, salt, hot water. Cover and simmer 30 minutes or until tender. Remove to heated platter; keep hot. Into liquid remaining in skillet stir flour blended with cold water. When thickened, stir in lemon juice and a little grated lemon rind. Just before serving, stir in sour cream. Heat, but do not boil; pour over chicken. Serves 4.

—*Isa Louise Byers Blaney (Mrs. Arthur J.)*

🐾 *CHICKEN CASSEROLE*

       6 chicken breast halves
      ⅓ cup flour
       2 teaspoons salt
       1 teaspoon paprika
      ¼ cup butter
       6 slices cooked ham
       1 teaspoon dried savory, crumbled
           celery leaves
       1 cup (½ pint) sour cream
       1 cup sliced fresh mushrooms
       2 tablespoons butter
      ½ cup sauterne (or ½ cup water)

Wipe off chicken breasts with damp paper towel. Combine flour, salt, and paprika in paper bag; shake chicken breasts in bag, one at a time, until well floured. Brown lightly in butter in heavy iron skillet. Place ham slices in a casserole with a little savory and a few celery leaves on each. Cover with chicken. Add remainder of seasoned flour to sour cream (this keeps it from curdling during baking time), then blend with drippings. Sauté mushrooms in remaining butter. Add to sauce. Pour over chicken. Cover and bake at 350 degrees for 1 hour. If you like more gravy, increase the liquids. This recipe can be made a few hours ahead and baked later. Serve chicken with spiced fruit (see Pickles and Jams chapter). Serves 6.

—*Margaret Gadd Ashley (Mrs. John M.)*

🍂 *CURRIED CHICKEN OR LAMB*

This dish is good for a buffet dinner.

¼ cup butter
½ cup unpeeled, chopped apples
½ cup chopped onion
1 large canned whole chicken, or 2 to 3 cups cooked lamb, or 1 stewing chicken, cooked and boned
1 cup chicken stock or canned chicken broth
1 or 2 tablespoons curry powder
salt to taste
¼ teaspoon pepper
1 cup milk
2 tablespoons currant jelly
small amount chutney juice and pieces of chutney
1 wine glass sherry

Melt butter in frying pan and add apples and onions. Simmer until apples are soft and yellow. Mash with a spoon. Add meat, stock, and curry powder, salt and pepper. Bring to a boil. Simmer 15 minutes, add milk and currant jelly, and simmer 15 minutes longer. Add chutney and juice and sherry just before serving. Serve with rice and small dishes of chopped egg yolks and whites, chutney, grated coconut, and chopped onion. Serves 6.

—*Elizabeth Lea Ferguson (Mrs. Spencer)*

🌿 CHICKEN AND CORN WITH DUMPLINGS

Pennsylvania Dutch recipe.

 1 fat chicken
    frozen or fresh corn
    hard boiled eggs
 1 cup flour
 1 whole egg
    milk (enough to make a fairly thick batter)

Cook chicken until soft. Cool and debone. Add chicken to broth and add
as much corn as desired. Make a batter with the flour, egg, and milk.
Have soup boiling; add batter and hard-boiled eggs, sliced. Let boil only
until dumplings are done. Serves 8 to 10.

—G. Myron Latshaw

*Latshaw was a jeweler and photographer with great interest in local
history. He and his partner, Katy Everett, were strong supporters of
the first two editions of this cookbook. They sold many copies from
their shop on Commerce Street where the money was carefully kept
in a cigar box under the counter.*

🌿 BREAST OF CHICKEN WITH WHITE WINE SAUCE

 ¼ pound butter, melted
 ¼ cup flour
  1 pint chicken stock
 ½ pint heavy cream
 ⅔ cup light sherry (you may add more)
    salt and pepper
 10 chicken breast halves
 10 slices ham (preferably Smithfield)

Cream butter and flour in saucepan and add slowly the stock and cream.
Then add wine and seasonings. Broil chicken breasts and place each on
a slice of hot baked ham. Pour on wine sauce at the very last moment.
Makes 10 servings.

—Mildred Smith Thompson (Mrs. Philemon Hopper)

❧ *EASY CHICKEN DIVAN*

    2   10-ounce packages frozen broccoli
    2   cups sliced cooked chicken
    2   10½-ounce cans cream of chicken soup
    1   cup mayonnaise
    1   teaspoon lemon juice
    ½   teaspoon curry powder
    ½   cup shredded sharp cheese
    ½   cup soft bread crumbs
    1   tablespoon margarine, melted
        pimiento strips

Cook broccoli according to directions on package. Arrange stalks in a greased rectangular baking dish with flowerets along the long sides. Place chicken slices lengthwise across the broccoli stalks. Combine soup, mayonnaise, lemon juice, and curry powder; pour over the chicken. Sprinkle with cheese. Combine bread crumbs and butter; sprinkle over all. Bake at 350 degrees for 30 minutes. Trim with pimiento strips. Serves 8.

—*Katherine Maybeck Draper (Mrs. Frank W., III)*

❧ *CHICKEN PAPRIKASH*

    2   cut-up chickens
        flour
        salt and pepper
        paprika
    ½   stick or more butter, melted
    ½   cup water
    1   cup sour cream

Shake chicken in paper bag with flour, salt, pepper, and paprika. Arrange in baking pan and cover with melted butter. Bake at 400 degrees for an hour or more until brown and tender. Pour off all but a couple of tablespoons of drippings, to which add 2 tablespoons of flour. Stir in water and cook until thickened. Blend in sour cream and serve over rice. Serves 8.

—*Harriet Willcox Gearhart (Mrs. David F.)*

🦅 *CHICKEN AND SAUSAGE WITH MARINARA SAUCE*

    2 garlic cloves, minced
    1 small onion, chopped
    1 tablespoon olive oil
    1 16-ounce can tomatoes
    1 6-ounce can tomato paste
    1 tablespoon sugar
    2 teaspoons basil
    1 teaspoon salt
    1 whole chicken breast fillet
    ½ cup flour
    ½ teaspoon black pepper
    1 teaspoon salt
       oil
    1 pound sweet sausage (Italian)
    1 green pepper
    1 red pepper
    1 yellow pepper
    2 ounces mozzarella cheese
    2 tablespoons Parmesan cheese

Warm a two-quart saucepan over medium heat, add the oil, swish it around, then add the garlic and onions. Cook for several minutes until tender. Stir in the tomatoes with their liquid; then add the tomato paste, sugar, and seasonings. Reduce heat to low, cover the saucepan, and cook for 20 minutes, stirring occasionally. Cut the boneless chicken breast in half and coat or dust with the mixture of flour, salt, and black pepper. Sauté the chicken breast in moderately hot oil for about 4 or 5 minutes on each side. Remove, drain, and set aside. If you are using bulk sausage, roll into small balls. If you are using link sausage, cut into 1-inch lengths. Sauté the sausage in the same oil, then remove, drain, and set aside. Cut the peppers into long slivers, sauté, drain, and set aside. (If the marinara sauce is prepared in advance, the sauce, drained chicken, sausage, and peppers can be layered directly into the casserole.) Ladle some marinara sauce into the bottom of a medium size casserole dish and place the chicken on the sauce. Layer the sausage over the chicken and cover this with more marinara sauce. Spread the sautéed peppers around on top of the dish. Sprinkle the shredded mozzarella cheese and the Parmesan cheese over top of the dish. Bake, uncovered, at 375 degrees for approximately 35 to 40 minutes. The dish can be served nicely on a bed of linguini or other appropriate pasta.

To simplify matters, the dish can be prepared earlier up to the point of putting it in the oven. Then, while the dish is in the oven, the pasta can be cooked. Also note that the ingredient amounts suggested are not critical.

—Lynda Eby Jordan (Mrs. Harold)

❧ SAVORY CHICKEN

This recipe should be made a day in advance and allowed to mellow in icebox. It is even better after a few weeks in the freezer.

1 large frying chicken
2 cups water
  butter
1 can celery soup
1 teaspoon savory

Set aside breast and legs of chicken and simmer rest to make broth. (If there is not enough time, canned broth or water can be used.) Cut chicken legs in two pieces. Brown breasts and legs in a generous amount of butter in a heavy iron skillet. Heat celery soup diluted with ¼ cup broth, add savory, and stir well. Place browned chicken in casserole with a cover. Pour soup into frying pan to absorb butter, scrape pan to dislodge bits sticking to the bottom, and pour over chicken. Bake casserole, covered, at 300 to 400 degrees for about 40 minutes or until chicken is tender. Sauce should not boil. Before serving, thicken sauce if necessary with flour, or if you have a blender, pour sauce in, add flour or unsalted soda crackers, and blend. Put in saucepan to cook about 5 minutes, and pour over chicken.

—Lynette Morgan Nielsen (Mrs. Orsen)

🍂 CHICKEN SOUFFLÉ

Serve with a green salad for a nice luncheon dish. This recipe came from my aunt in Lexington, Kentucky, and we all think it is an excellent one.

5 slices trimmed, buttered, cubed bread (2 for bottom of dish, 1½ for middle, 1½ for top)
2 whole poached and cubed chicken breasts
½ pound grated cheddar cheese (2 cups)
3 eggs
2 cups milk
½ teaspoon dry mustard
½ teaspoon salt
¼ teaspoon poultry seasoning
¼ teaspoon paprika
   dash of Tabasco sauce

Arrange layers of bread, chicken, 1½ cups of cheese in greased 2-quart casserole. Beat eggs with milk and seasonings, pour over chicken. Place pan in hot water. Bake at 325 degrees for 45 minutes. Sprinkle on remaining cheese, bake 40 minutes more. 6 to 8 servings.

—*Virginia Ingles Freeland (Mrs.Samuel L.)*

🍂 CHICKEN DELIGHT

1 3- to 4-pound chicken
1 8-ounce package Velveeta cheese
2 tablespoons butter
1 10¾-ounce can mushroom soup
½ cup chicken broth
2 cups broad noodles, uncooked
2 cups cornflakes, crushed

Boil the chicken; skin and bone it and break it into bite size pieces. In the top of a double boiler, put the Velveeta cheese and the butter. Melt and then add mushroom soup and ½ cup chicken broth. Cook noodles in salted water until tender. Drain well, mix all ingredients together, and put in a buttered baking dish. Cover top with crushed cornflakes and bake at 350 degrees for about 45 minutes. Serves 4 to 6.

— *Mildred Lee Thompson Murray (Mrs. Gerald)*

CHEESY CHICKEN CASSEROLE

  1 4-pound stewing chicken or 6 chicken breasts
  2 10-ounce packages frozen broccoli spears
  2 cups milk
  2 8-ounce packages cream cheese
  1 teaspoon garlic salt
1½ cups shredded Parmesan cheese

Early in the day, gently simmer chicken or chicken breasts until tender in seasoned boiling water to just cover. Remove chicken from water and let cool, then remove skin and slice thinly. Cover with wax paper and refrigerate. About an hour before serving, preheat oven to 350 degrees. Lightly grease a 2-quart oblong casserole. Cook broccoli as label directs. Cut each broccoli spear into bite size pieces and arrange in bottom of casserole. In double boiler, blend milk, cream cheese, and garlic salt until smooth and hot. Stir in ¾ cup shredded cheese until smooth. Pour 1 cup of this sauce over broccoli then add all the chicken, cover with rest of sauce, and sprinkle top with ¼ cup shredded cheese. Bake for 25 to 30 minutes or until piping hot. Remove from oven and let stand 5 to 10 minutes. Serve with rest of cheese. Makes 6 to 8 servings. If using half the recipe, use a 1½-quart casserole.

—Mary Davy Pippin (Mrs. James O., Jr.)

SHERRIED CHICKEN LIVERS

  1 pound chicken livers
¼ cup butter or margarine
¼ cup flour
  2 cups hot water
  1 teaspoon salt
     sherry to taste

Cut each liver in half. Sauté in butter in a skillet over low heat until light brown, about 5 minutes, turning often. Remove livers; stir flour into fat. Stir in water gradually; heat until thickened, stirring. Add salt and sherry, then livers. Serve on toast, toasted English muffins, boiled noodles, or buckwheat griddle cakes, or with an omelet. Serves 6.

—Isa Louise Byers Blaney (Mrs. Arthur J.)

❧ *CHICKEN WITH ROSEMARY*

1 2½- to 3-pound broiler (or chicken breasts)
1 small onion
1 clove garlic
  few sprigs parsley
1 stalk celery
2 tablespoons salad or olive oil
½ teaspoon basil
1 teaspoon rosemary
¼ cup sherry
1 tablespoon vinegar
  a little salt

Split chicken in half or use chicken breasts. Chop onion, garlic, parsley, and celery quite fine. Heat oil in a skillet; add chicken and all the chopped vegetables. Cook over medium heat until chicken is brown on both sides (takes 10 to 15 minutes).

Now add basil, rosemary, sherry, vinegar, and salt, and cook gently for 20 to 30 minutes until tender. Serves 2.

—*Louise Albers Gambrill (Mrs. William)*

❧ *CHICKEN SUPREME*

8 or 10 chicken breast halves or legs
        salt and pepper
        flour
     ¼ cup butter
     1 cup sour cream
     ½ cup white wine
     1 4-ounce can mushrooms with liquid
        pinch of chervil, rosemary, or tarragon

Salt, pepper, and flour chicken. Brown quickly in the butter (other fat may be substituted) in a frying pan. Remove to baking dish. Pour the other ingredients into the frying pan. Mix thoroughly and pour over the chicken. Bake at 350 to 400 degrees for 45 minutes to 1 hour, according to size of pieces. Serves 8.

—*Ruth Branner Gadd (Mrs. A. Sydney, Jr.)*

❧ GARLIC CHICKEN

    1 cup fine, dry bread crumbs
    ⅓ cup Parmesan or Romano cheese
    ¼ cup minced parsley
    2 teaspoons salt
    ⅛ teaspoon ground pepper
  1½ sticks melted butter or margarine
    1 small clove garlic, crushed
    1 broiler-fryer, 2½ to 3 pounds, cut up
       paprika

Blend bread crumbs, cheese, parsley, salt, and pepper. Combine melted butter and garlic. Dip chicken in butter mixture, coating thoroughly. Roll chicken in crumb mixture and arrange in a single layer in shallow baking pan. Drizzle remaining butter over, and sprinkle with paprika. Bake at 350 degrees for 1 hour. Makes 4 to 5 servings.

—Shirley Tuttle Freestate (Mrs. William M.)

❧ PINEAPPLE CHICKEN FROM THE DOMINICAN REPUBLIC

  2 frying chickens, cut up
     flour seasoned with salt and pepper
  1 cup oil
  1 cup pineapple juice
  2 tablespoons fresh lemon juice
  2 tablespoons soy sauce
  1 bay leaf
  1 cup pineapple tidbits (optional)

Dip pieces of chicken in seasoned flour. Put oil in heavy pan and heat in oven at 500 degrees. Quickly brown the coated chicken in the oven, turning once. Drain oil from pan. Mix pineapple juice, lemon juice, and soy sauce, and pour over chicken. Add bay leaf. Cover and bake at 350 degrees for 1 hour. Ten minutes before finish, uncover and add pineapple tidbits, if desired. Serves 8.

—Janet Gadd Doehler (Mrs. William F.)

🍂 *SHERRIED CHICKEN*

    1 whole chicken, cut up, or 6 chicken breast halves
       flour
       salt and pepper
       paprika
  ¼ pound butter
  ½ cup sherry
    1 can mushrooms

Roll chicken pieces in flour, salt, pepper, and paprika. Melt butter in covered pan; add chicken. Bake, covered, at 400 degrees for 1 hour. Remove from oven, add sherry and mushrooms. Return to oven, uncovered, for ½ to 1 hour, until done. Serves 4 to 6.

—*S. Ethel Chance*

🍂 *CHICKEN SPECIALTY*

From Charleston Receipts *cookbook.*

    1 large chicken, or 2 frying chickens, disjointed
          (4 to 5 pounds)
       seasoned flour
    1 cup salad oil
    3 large onions, sliced
    1 clove garlic, minced
    1 green pepper, diced
    1 16-ounce can tomatoes
    1 cup beer
    1 tablespoon salt
  ½ cup seedless raisins
    4 cups cooked rice

Dust chicken with flour; brown in oil. Remove. Add onions, garlic, and green pepper. Cook until soft but not brown. Return chicken to pan, add tomatoes, beer, and salt. Cover. Simmer 1 hour or until tender. Add raisins; cook 10 minutes. Serve with rice. Makes 6 to 8 servings. Freezes well.

—*Mary Ashley Long (Mrs. Paul M.)*

❧ SMOKED TURKEY

  1 large heavy-walled pot with cover and rack (I improvise
        with expendable pie plates with holes punched in them.)
  1 smallish turkey (8 to 11 pounds)
     boiling water
  1 tablespoon tea
  1 tablespoon brown sugar
     plenty of aluminum foil
     salt to taste

Steam the turkey over about 1-inch of boiling water until it is done, about 45 minutes. It is wise to keep boiling water in the tea kettle in case the water in the pot boils away, but with a tight-fitting cover this may not be necessary. Dry everything off, including the turkey. Line the pot and its cover with foil and put the tea and sugar on the bottom of the lined pot under the rack. Put the turkey back, cover and place the whole thing over medium-high flame on the stove. Keep an eye on things and when the tea/sugar starts burning, smoke for about ten minutes or until the turkey has browned to a lovely color. Slice thin and serve with brown bread and whipped butter in dainty cocktail bite sizes.

—*Miss Virginia Withington*

❧ HOT TURKEY SALAD

  2 cups cubed cooked turkey
  2 cups diced celery
  ½ cup chopped pecans
  ½ teaspoon salt
  2 teaspoons grated onion
  2 tablespoons lemon juice
  ¾ cup mayonnaise
  ½ cup grated American cheese
  1 cup crushed potato chips

Combine all ingredients except cheese and chips. Put in casserole and sprinkle chips and cheese over top. Bake at 450 degrees, covered, for 10 minutes. Uncover and continue cooking for 5 minutes. Makes 6 to 8 servings.

—*Mrs. Louis G. Michael*

❧ *TURKEY TETRAZZINI*

         8 ounces spaghetti, broken in 2-inch pieces (2½ cups dry)
      1½ quarts boiling salted water
         ¾ cup sliced mushrooms (4-ounce can)
         4 tablespoons butter
         3 tablespoons chopped onion
         ½ teaspoon celery salt
             few grains cayenne pepper
         ¼ teaspoon marjoram
         1 can cream of chicken soup
         1 tall can (1⅔ cups) evaporated milk
         2 tablespoons chopped pimiento
         2 cups cubed cooked turkey or chicken
         ½ cup shredded sharp cheddar cheese (processed
                 or natural)
         ¼ cup grated Parmesan cheese

Cook spaghetti until tender in boiling water. Drain. Rinse with hot water. Drain mushrooms, saving liquid. Melt butter in saucepan. Sauté onion. Add seasonings and mushroom liquid. Blend in soup. Stir until smooth. Gradually add evaporated milk, stirring constantly, until smooth and thickened. In buttered 2-quart casserole, mix spaghetti, mushrooms, pimiento, and turkey. Pour sauce over and mix well. Top with cheddar and Parmesan cheeses. Bake at 350 degrees for about 30 minutes or until lightly browned on top. Makes 8 servings.

—Margaret Gadd Ashley (Mrs. John M.)

❧ *HOT CHICKEN SALAD*

         3 cups diced chicken
         ½ cup walnuts or pecans
      1½ cups chopped celery
         1 small, crisp apple, cored and chopped
         2 tablespoons lemon juice
         ¼ cup white raisins, or more
         1 cup mayonnaise
         2 tablespoons sour cream

½ teaspoon salt

½ teaspoon pepper

dash of nutmeg

1 cup homemade béchamel sauce prepared with chicken stock or cream (or 1 undiluted 10½-ounce can cream of chicken soup)

2 tablespoons dry sherry

½ package Pepperidge Farm seasoned stuffing, finely crushed

3 tablespoons melted butter

1 sliced hard-boiled egg (optional)

paprika and parsley for garnish

Mix first six ingredients in bowl. Combine mayonnaise, sour cream, salt, and pepper in another bowl and toss lightly with ingredients in first bowl. Turn mixture into a 2-quart shallow baking dish. Add sherry to sauce or soup. Spread over all. Add melted butter to stuffing mix. Sprinkle evenly over casserole. Place in preheated 325-degree oven for 30 minutes or until golden. Garnish with eggs, paprika, and parsley. Makes 6 generous servings.

—Shirley Tuttle Freestate (Mrs. William M.)

SHERRY ROASTED QUAIL

2 quail

¼ apple

2 tablespoons butter

salt and pepper

paprika

½ cup sherry

Clean quail thoroughly. Place apple quarter and 1 tablespoon butter in cavity (this is very important, as it helps to keep quail moist). Butter the outside of quail thoroughly and dust with salt and pepper and paprika. Place quail in baking pan and cook, uncovered, at 325 degrees for 1¼ hours, basting *very* frequently with ½ cup sherry, and with juices from the pan. Makes 1 serving.

—Mary Ingram

❦ *CHICKEN ENCHILADAS*

    4 large chicken breast halves, boned
    1 4-ounce can green chilies, drained
    4 scallions
    4 ounces sliced black olives (½ cup), drained
    2 10-ounce cans medium hot enchilada sauce
    1 package large flour tortillas (preferably whole wheat)
    1 cup shredded Monterey Jack cheese
    ½ cup sliced almonds, roasted
    1 cup sour cream
    1 16-ounce jar picante sauce, mild

Broil or fry chicken breasts. Skin and slice meat in strips. Set aside. Chop chilies, scallions, and olives. Heat enchilada sauce in large frying pan. Dip flour tortillas in warmed sauce, covering both sides. Lay in large baking dish and sprinkle chicken, a bit of chopped ingredients, almonds, and sour cream on middle of tortilla. Roll up and place in baking dish, seam side down. Repeat until chicken is used up. Pour leftover sauce in frying pan over enchiladas. Sprinkle shredded cheese over top and sprinkle liberally with picante sauce and a few olive slices. Bake in 350 degree oven until bubbly and heated through, approximately 25 minutes. Serves 8.

—Miss Sydney Gadd Doehler

❦ *STUFFED CHICKEN BREASTS SAVANNAH*

    4 whole chicken breasts, skinned, boned, and halved
    4 thin slices boiled ham, cut in half
    4 thin slices Swiss cheese, cut in half
    ½ cup all-purpose flour, divided
    1 egg, slightly beaten
    ⅔ cup fine dry breadcrumbs
    ½ cup plus 2 tablespoons melted butter or margarine
    1 cup dry white wine
    ¼ cup finely chopped onion
    ½ teaspoon salt
       pepper to taste

    1 cup milk
    1 cup half-and-half
       chopped fresh parsley
       hot cooked rice or noodles

Flatten chicken breasts with meat mallet. Place a slice of ham and cheese on each chicken breast; roll up and secure with toothpicks. Dredge each roll in ¼ cup flour, and dip in egg; coat well with breadcrumbs. Lightly brown on all sides in ¼ cup butter. Add wine; simmer, covered, for 20 minutes. Place rolls in a shallow baking dish, reserving drippings. Sauté onion in 6 tablespoons butter until tender, stirring occasionally; blend in ¼ cup flour, salt, and pepper. Gradually add milk and half-and-half, stirring constantly, until smooth. Add reserved drippings; simmer, stirring constantly, until smooth and thickened. Pour sauce over rolls; bake, uncovered, at 325 degrees for 20 minutes. Garnish with parsley. Serve over rice. Makes 8 servings.

—Marybelle Weatherford Henry (Mrs. Elmer T.)

OPOSSUM

    1 opossum
       bacon fat
       salt and pepper
    4 slices bacon
    1 large onion, sliced
       orange slices, halved
       fried sweet potatoes

Skin the opossum and wash it thoroughly; wipe dry. Grease inside and out with bacon fat; season with salt and pepper. Put in roasting pan and lay 3 or 4 slices of bacon across opossum. Put the onion slices and the opossum's liver, finely chopped, in the pan. Bake at 350 degrees, basting every 15 minutes, for about ½ hour or until tender. Garnish with half slices of orange and fried sweet potatoes placed around the edge of platter. The opossum may be stuffed with a bread stuffing as for poultry, in which case the animal should be tied up like a suckling pig. Makes 6 to 8 servings.

—Isabel Atkinson Lieber (Mrs. Albert C.)

✺ *CHICKEN LOCUST HILL*

Receives rave notices!

½ cup white vinegar

½ cup ketchup

½ cup apricot nectar

1 cup brown sugar

1 tablespoon Worcestershire sauce

1 dash soy sauce

¼ cup cornstarch

4 tablespoons pineapple juice (reserved from can of pineapple below)

1 whole chicken breast

1 tablespoon cooking oil

2 stalks celery, sliced crosswise

2 carrots, sliced crosswise

1 6½-ounce can pineapple chunks

1 8-ounce can water chestnuts (optional)

Combine first 6 ingredients and simmer for 30 minutes. Mix cornstarch and pineapple juice and add to sauce; cook until it thickens. Cut whole chicken breast into ½-inch cubes. Sauté in oil until white on outside. Add celery, carrots, and pineapple cubes to pan with chicken and cook for 10 minutes. Add the above sweet and sour sauce. Simmer until everyone is ready, or it can be reheated later. For a classier dish, add a can of water chestnuts. Serve with rice, string beans almondine, salad, and rolls. Enjoy with white or rosé wine. Makes 4 servings.

—*William P. Turpin IV*

The chancel was erected in 1892 in honor of the 200th anniversary of St. Paul's Parish in memory of the Hon. Richard Tilghman Earle (1765-1843), "Through whose Exertion This Church was Erected in 1835," and of Mary Tilghman Earle, his wife (1782-1836).

❧ *MUSKRAT*

1 muskrat
flour
salt and pepper
oil for frying
1 onion

Drain muskrat well and pat dry with towel. Mix flour, salt, and pepper as for fried chicken. Dredge cut-up muskrat with seasoned flour. Put in skillet with about an inch of hot grease and brown on all sides. Pour off grease and add cut-up onion and about an inch of water and simmer slowly, adding water from time to time to keep meat from getting dry. Muskrat is done when meat starts to fall from bones. Thicken the gravy if it is too thin. Makes 4 servings.

—Ruth Gray

❧ *CODDLED CONEEN (Rabbit)*

1 rabbit, dressed
½ cup vinegar
½ cup water
¼ cup flour
½ teaspoon salt
⅛ teaspoon pepper
4 tablespoons butter
4 slices bacon, diced
1 tablespoon parsley, minced
2 onions, finely chopped
1 cup scalded milk

Cut dressed rabbit in pieces and marinate for 2 hours in vinegar and water. Remove rabbit from marinade; dry and roll in flour seasoned with salt and pepper. Melt butter in hot frying pan and brown rabbit pieces. Arrange in casserole; add bacon, parsley, onions, and scalded milk. Cover and bake for 1 hour at 300 degrees. Makes 4 servings.

—Ethel H. Green (Mrs. Clifton)

❧ LEE'S EASTERN SHORE MUSKRAT

meat of two muskrats
flour
salt and pepper
½ stick margarine
several onions, sliced
1 32-ounce can V-8

Cut muskrat into pieces. Dredge pieces in mixture of flour, salt, and pepper. Fry in margarine as you would fry chicken. When browned, cover meat with onion slices. Cook 5 minutes. Cover with V-8. Simmer at least an hour until meat falls from the bones.

—*Frank W. Draper III*

❧ ROAST PARTRIDGE

4 partridge
4 slices bacon
salt and pepper
1 cup water
1 cup sour cream
toast
baked oranges

Carefully clean partridge inside and out. Pin over each breast a long strip of bacon. Rub salt and pepper on the inside of each. Put in a roasting pan with 1 cup water. Roast at 450 degrees for 30 minutes, basting every 5 minutes. When birds and gravy are a rich golden brown, pour over them 1 cup sour cream. Let the cream bubble up in the pan for a minute, baste once more, and serve on toast with gravy poured over. Garnish with baked oranges. Serves 4.

—*Isabel Atkinson Lieber (Mrs. Albert C.)*

❧ SKINNED QUAIL

This quail is wonderful cold and a delight for a picnic.

2 quail
butter
½ cup sherry

Remove skin from quail—the birds need not be plucked. Melt ample amount of butter in skillet. Sauté quail very slightly, turning frequently for a few minutes, then add sherry. Cover tightly and simmer very gently for about 45 minutes or until tender. Makes 1 serving.

—Mary Ingram

ROASTED QUAIL

> 2 quail
> butter
> salt and pepper
> 2 slices bacon
> grape leaves
> chicken stock (optional)
> grape jelly

Wash quail in cold water. Butter and salt the inside of the birds. Salt the outsides and wrap a bacon strip over breastbone of each bird (use 2 or more if strips are small). Wrap birds in well-washed grape leaves. Bake at 350 degrees for about 30 minutes. When done, remove from pan and keep hot while making gravy from pan drippings. Add a little butter to gravy in pan, or some chicken stock if there is not enough gravy. Salt and pepper to taste and cook on top of stove a few minutes. Serve with a good, tart grape jelly. Makes 1 serving.

—Lynette Morgan Nielsen (Mrs. Orsen)

MOCK DIAMONDBACK TERRAPIN

Cover young muskrat with salted water and boil until tender. Prepare meat as in Diamondback Terrapin I recipe and season accordingly. Meat is dark and makes a perfect substitute. (Use 3 or 4 hard-boiled chicken eggs to take the place of the terrapin eggs.) Chop the yolks and add the sliced whites if you are not too serious about the deception. Add sherry to taste.

—Mrs. Emerson C. Harrington, Sr.

🌾 RABBIT PIE

>   1   dressed rabbit
>   3   tablespoons flour
>   water
>   salt
>   2   tablespoons finely chopped onion
>   2   tablespoons minced parsley
>   flour
>   Tabasco sauce
>   unbaked pastry crust

Cut the rabbit into 2 or 3 pieces, place in a saucepan, and barely cover with water. Cover the pan and simmer until tender. Add salt to season when partially cooked. Drain and measure the liquid. Remove all meat from the bones, keeping it in large pieces. Melt butter in skillet, add chopped onion and minced parsley. Cook about 5 minutes, stirring constantly. Use 1½ tablespoons flour for each cup of liquid and mix well in pan with butter and onion. Add liquid and stir until thick. Season to taste, adding a little Tabasco sauce. Mix well with rabbit meat and pour into baking dish. Cover with pastry and bake at 350 degrees for 35 minutes. Makes 4 servings.

—Isabel Atkinson Lieber (Mrs. Albert C.)

🌾 DIAMONDBACK TERRAPIN I

> *This recipe is from my uncle, Thomas Deford of Baltimore, who later lived in Luray, Virginia.*

>   2   diamondback terrapin
>   water
>   unsalted butter
>   salt and pepper
>   cayenne
>   sherry

Plunge terrapin headfirst into boiling water. Cook 8 minutes. (Best to do two at a time.) Then skin head, tail, feet, and upper layer of shell skin with a rough cloth. Put back in fresh water and cook until feet are tender and squashy (about 45 minutes to an hour, depending on size of terrapin). The best terrapin is a diamondback of about 7 inches. Take out and lay on back in large vessel so as not to lose essence. Let cool until you can handle comfortably. Remove lower shell, leaving meat, etc., in top shell. Have vessel ready for meat and essence from top shell. Remove entrails and windpipe. Take out liver and put aside. You will see the terrapin eggs. Place in a cup separately, as they are cooked enough. Remove and save all the meat from the head, leaving only the skull. Pull toenails from feet and put feet and tail with rest of meat. Cut rest of meat with scissors. Now start on liver. Look inside for green gallbladder or sac. Very carefully break liver from gallbladder. If there is a tinge of green, cut it out, and break liver into medium pieces or smaller.

To 1 quart of terrapin add ¼ pound of unsalted butter. Put the meat and essence in double boiler but not the eggs. Season with salt, pepper, and cayenne, and cook for 10 minutes or until good and hot. Allow to simmer, not come to boil. Do not stir. Shake the boiler from time to time. Add about 1 wine glass of sherry to a quart of terrapin; add the terrapin eggs just before serving. Some do not add the tail or feet, using only the meat and liver. Also, some like a few tiny bones; others do not.

—*Eleanor Williams Miles (Mrs. Clarence W.)*

🐢 *DIAMONDBACK TERRAPIN II*

This dish was served at the home of Colonel Staunton Brown, Chestertown, at a luncheon on October 31, 1933, honoring President Franklin Delano Roosevelt. The occasion was the conferring of an honorary degree upon the president at Washington College's homecoming exercises. The president, seated beside Mrs. Beck at the luncheon, laughingly remarked, when the terrapin was passed for the fifth time, "I have had four servings already and were it not a breach of etiquette, I would ask for another."

  1 hard-boiled egg to each terrapin
     butter, the size of 2 eggs
  ½ pint cream (could use evaporated milk)

Put hard-boiled egg yolks through potato ricer and while hot add butter and cream well. Season to taste with a little mustard, vinegar, salt, and red pepper. Cook in double boiler until very hot and then add the cooked terrapin meat. Must be very hot to be at its best. Do not stir too often, as it makes the mixture stringy. For preparation of terrapin meat for above, see Standard Method as given in preceding recipe. To serve 30 people, use 3 quarts terrapin, 2 quarts cream, 1 pound butter, and 2½ dozen eggs.

—*Mackey Perry Beck (Mrs. S. Scott)*

🦢 *CURRIED DUCK*

    3   cups shredded duck
    1   pound mushrooms
    ¼   cup butter
    ⅓   cup grated onion
    1   cup peeled, diced apples
    3   tablespoons butter
    2   tablespoons flour
    ½   teaspoon salt
        few grains black pepper
    1   tablespoon curry powder
    1   cup sweet cream
    3   tablespoons Madeira wine
        generous ½ cup duck stock

Sauté duck and mushrooms in butter over low flame until mushrooms are tender and duck slightly browned, stirring often with wooden spoon. Remove pan from heat. Cut grated onions with apples. Cook in butter until apples become soft. Remove pan from heat; sprinkle with flour, salt, pepper, and curry powder. Blend thoroughly. Mix cream, wine, and stock. Return pan to fire and stir in the cream mixture. Cook this mixture over low heat, stirring constantly, until thick and creamy. Stir in duck and mushroom mixture. Heat well, taste, and adjust seasonings. Serve at once with hot rice which has been mixed with 1 cup of diced ripe bananas heated in double boiler. Makes 6 to 8 servings.

—*Helen Keith Peck*

🦢 *GRILLED WILD DUCK*

Pick duck, removing all pin feathers. Split down back and clean. Chop lightly with cleaver to break breastbone and open duck fairly flat. Brush with drawn butter and salt fairly well. Sear back side first, about 3 or 4 minutes over hot charcoal; then turn and sear breast side. Raise grill 4 or 5 inches and cook 18 minutes each side, or less if you like them very pink. Baste with butter while cooking. The birds will be juicier than when cooked in an oven. Don't kill the natural flavor by adding any other seasoning.

—*Charles R. Humphreys*

❧ WILD DUCK

Broadbill, Goldeneye, Redhead

Roast duck for 8 minutes at 475 to 500 degrees. Carve breasts. Place in a shallow pan (a jigger of red wine may be used—no more), skin down, and sear under preheated broiler for 1½ minutes. By this method duck comes to table piping hot.

Canvasback, Black Duck, Green Mallard

Follow directions above, except roast for 10 minutes in oven, and 1½ minutes under broiler.

Place 2 carcasses, with half an orange and 4 ounces of rye whiskey in each, in a duck press (or whatever you have that resembles one—some people use a lard renderer). Heat gravy boat to blood temperature and maintain to prevent clotting of essence. Two carcasses will produce sufficient essence for 6 breasts. Pepper and salt to taste. Serve with hominy and sweet butter with old-fashioned corn sticks. Pour essence over hominy. Follow with a green salad, cheese or fruit, and demitasse.

Serve a good claret or Burgundy with the duck.

—Maria McKenney

❧ WILD DUCK II

This was a favorite of Mr. and Mrs. William Fahnestock and was served frequently at Readbourne during the ducking season.

1 wild duck
  red wine
1 teaspoon red currant jelly
¼ cup pâté de foie gras
  cognac

Place duck in a shallow pan and cook 10 minutes (5 minutes on each side) at 500 degrees. Cut off the breast and remove skin; set aside. Press out the blood from the carcass by placing the carcass in a lard press or by using a very heavy iron. (This may be done ahead of time.) For the sauce, use equal amounts of duck blood and red wine. Add red currant jelly, and about ¼ cup pâté de foie gras. Cook for 5 minutes and pour over the hot duck breasts; put a dash of cognac over each serving and serve at once.

—Helen C. Marshall (Mrs. Joseph)

🐚 *WILD GOOSE, WELL DONE*

   1 wild goose
   2 tablespoons sherry
   1 teaspoon celery salt
   1 teaspoon onion salt
   1 teaspoon celery seed
   ½ teaspoon curry
   2 teaspoons salt
   ½ teaspoon pepper
   2 small onions, chopped
   2 stalks celery, chopped
      water
   2 tablespoons flour

Place goose in pan, breast side up. Sprinkle with sherry and seasonings. Leave in pan at least an hour; overnight is not too long. Place onions and celery in pan. Add ½ inch of water. Bake at 500 degrees until breast is brown. Reduce heat to 300 degrees and cook, covered, until well done and tender—at least 2 hours. Thicken sauce in pan with flour; strain and serve with goose. Duck may be done the same way using half the quantity of each ingredient and a shorter cooking time.

🐚 *JELLY WINE SAUCE FOR WILD DUCK, GOOSE, OR VENISON*

   1 cup currant jelly
   1 cup red wine
   1 pinch of ginger
      a few cloves
   1 tablespoon lemon juice
   1 tablespoon cognac
      flour to thicken gravy

Slowly melt jelly in saucepan; add red wine; mix and simmer gently while adding ginger, cloves, and lemon juice. Thicken with equal parts of game gravy from roasting pan and flour worked smooth. Just before serving, add cognac.

Cook goose very rare (35 minutes in a 500 degree oven). Then slice it very thin, put it in the hot sauce and simmer until meat is done as you like it. It will not take more than a minute or two.

If need be, this can all be done the day before and reheated just before serving. Simmering as above is also a good way to reheat and use leftover game.

—Isabel Atkinson Lieber (Mrs. Albert C.)

SADDLE OF VENISON

1	6- to 8-pound saddle of venison, well larded
1	pint sour cream
1	onion, sliced
1	bay leaf
	a little powdered thyme
2	carrots, sliced
1	tablespoon lemon juice
12	whole black peppercorns
2	cloves garlic, minced
	salt
	flour
1	cup butter
1	cup water
1	cup port
	flour

Make a sauce of sour cream, onion, herbs, carrots, lemon juice, peppercorns, and garlic. Soak venison in sauce, turning at intervals, for 24 hours. Wipe, salt, dredge with flour, and brown in hot butter. After browning, add water and bake at 350 degrees for 2 to 3 hours, basting with the drippings from the pan. Thirty minutes before serving, pour over the strained sauce that the meat was marinated in and continue basting. Remove the meat to a heated platter. Strain the sauce, thicken it with flour and add 1 cup port. Boil up and serve from a gravy boat. Makes 10 to 12 servings.

—Thomas L. Hale, Jr.

🎇 *BITTERSWEET ORANGE SAUCE FOR WILD DUCK*

    4 teaspoons grated orange peel (zest only)

    3 tablespoons sour juice of any kind (lime, lemon, etc.)

    1 dash Worcestershire sauce

    1 tablespoon Curaçao

    6 large tablespoons bitter orange marmalade

       salt and cayenne to taste

    2 tablespoons brandy

Melt all ingredients in a pan. Pour a little over duck breasts and serve the rest in a boat.

—Isabel Atkinson Lieber (Mrs. Albert C.)

🎇 *MY BARBECUE SAUCE*

Good for barbecued or rotisseried wild duck especially.

  ½ bottle Kraft oil and vinegar salad dressing

    1 tablespoon Worcestershire sauce

    1 tablespoon soy sauce

    1 teaspoon dry mustard

    1 tablespoon Old Bay Seasoning

    3 dashes chili powder

    3 tablespoons dry red wine

Mix all ingredients.

—Mary Harrington Truitt (Mrs. Reginald)

🎇 *GRILLED DOVES*

Pick doves. Split down back and clean. Break open and brush with drawn butter. Salt liberally and put on hot charcoal grill to sear back of dove for 2 minutes. Turn and sear breast side. Then raise grill from charcoal about 4 inches higher and cook each side 10 minutes. Birds should be well done but juicy.

—Charles R. Humphreys

🌿 BAKED WILD GOOSE

    1 wild goose
       salt and pepper
       canned consommé
       sherry

Wash and wipe goose well. Salt and pepper. Turn breast side down on rack. Pour 1 or 2 cans consommé and equal amounts of water in the pan. Add 1 or 2 cans sherry. Cook, uncovered, at 350 degrees for 1½ hours or longer. Baste every 15 minutes. If unable to baste that often, then cover the bird. The open pan method is better, however.

—Catherine Forman Thompson (Mrs. W. Stuart)

🌿 TURKEY MARSALA

    ½ cup flour
    ½ cup Parmesan cheese
       salt and pepper
       paprika to taste
       garlic salt (optional)
    1 pound turkey cutlets
    2 tablespoons butter
    2 tablespoons olive oil
    ½ cup dry Marsala
    2 tablespoons lemon juice
       lemon wedges

Combine first five ingredients and roll turkey cutlets in mixture. Heat butter and olive oil in skillet and sauté cutlets until they are lightly browned. Make a sauce with the Marsala and lemon juice; pour over cutlets and simmer lightly (don't overcook cutlets). Garnish with lemon wedges. Serves 4.

—Lou Snyder Eby (Mrs. J. Walter)

MEATS

Some hae meat and canna eat,
And some wad eat that want it;
But we hae meat, and we can eat,
And sae the Lord be thankit.

—Robert Burns (1759–1796)

🌿 *BOEUF BOURGUIGNONNE*

2	pounds cubed beef
3 or 4	carrots, cut up
1	cup chopped celery
2	onions, sliced
½	cup Burgundy
2	cups canned tomatoes
1	cup tomato sauce
1	clove garlic
3	tablespoons minute tapioca
1	tablespoon sugar
1	8-ounce can mushrooms
2	1-pound cans small Irish potatoes
1	8-ounce can sliced water chestnuts (optional)

Combine all ingredients except the last three in a large casserole. Bake, covered, at 250 degrees for 5 hours. During last hour, add mushrooms, potatoes, and water chestnuts. This may be refrigerated or frozen. It reheats in the oven beautifully. A perfect dish when you are planning to be away during the afternoon—supper will be "ready and waiting" when you get home.

—*Janie Eby Ashley (Mrs. Sydney G.)*

🌿 *BURGUNDIAN BEEF*

¼	pound salt pork
2	tablespoons fat
	butter
3	pounds rump beef
2	cups chopped onions
1	clove garlic, minced
2	small shallots, minced
2	carrots, sliced
2	tablespoons parsley, minced
2	tablespoons chervil, minced
6	peppercorns
2	bay leaves
1	tablespoon tarragon vinegar

⅛ teaspoon thyme
2 cups red wine
salt

Dice salt pork and sauté in butter. Cut beef into 2-inch cubes. Sear thoroughly in hot fat. Lift out. Simmer onion, garlic, shallots, and carrots in the fat until onion is light yellow. Add remaining ingredients and beef. Cook this in an iron skillet, covered, over low heat for about 3 hours. Remove excess grease and make a thick gravy from the liquid. This may be reheated to advantage. May also be frozen. Serves 8.

—*Lois S. Duffey (Mrs. Harry J., Jr.)*

🍂 BEEF STROGANOFF I

2 cloves garlic
¼ pound butter
2 pounds shredded sirloin or sirloin strips
3 tablespoons flour
2 large onions, diced
1 8-ounce can mushrooms
1½ cups tomato juice
4 tablespoons sherry
salt and pepper
paprika
oregano
basil
allspice
1 bay leaf
2 teaspoons soy sauce
2 tablespoons Worcestershire sauce
1 pint sour cream

Rub a large skillet with garlic and put over heat. When hot, add half the butter and sauté the beef. When beef is brown and rendered, pour off juice into a large saucepan. Dredge the beef with 1½ tablespoons flour and add it to beef juices along with onions, mushrooms, tomato juice, and sherry. Add seasonings and sauces. Heat, and when the mixture bubbles, add sour cream. Serve over steamed rice. Serves 6.

—*Janet Gadd Doehler (Mrs. William F.)*

🍂 *BEEF STROGANOFF II*

 2 pounds lean strips beef, cut in ¼ × 3 × 1-inch strips
   flour
 ¼ cup butter
 ½ cup minced onion
 1 clove garlic, minced
 1 pound mushrooms or 1 8-ounce can
 ¼ cup sherry
 2 cups beef stock or water
 1 teaspoon salt
 ¼ teaspoon pepper
 1 cup sour cream

Flour meat and fry in butter until brown. Remove to baking dish. Fry onion, garlic, and mushrooms in same pan. Add to meat. Then add sherry and stock, cover, and bake at 300 to 325 degrees until tender. Stir in sour cream. Serve with rice. Serves 6.

Note: Hamburger can be used; then simmer on top of stove instead of baking.

—*Harriet Willcox Gearhart (Mrs. David F.)*

🍂 *BEEF BURGUNDY*

 4 pounds chuck cubes (fat removed)
   oil for frying
 2 10½-ounce cans (not boxes) onion soup
 1 clove garlic
 1 pound mushrooms, whole or sliced as desired
 1½ cups Burgundy

Brown beef in a little oil. Place in casserole. Add remaining ingredients. Cover very tightly (foil is very helpful). Bake at 325 degrees for 3 hours. Serve on rice. Makes 8 servings.

—*Anne Stoney Cantler (Mrs. James E.)*

🍂 *BARBECUED HOT DOGS*

 ¼ cup chopped onion
 2 tablespoons salad oil

  2 teaspoons sugar
  ¾ teaspoon dry mustard
  ¼ teaspoon salt
  ⅛ teaspoon pepper
  ¾ teaspoon paprika
  6 tablespoons catsup
  3 tablespoons vinegar
  6 tablespoons water
  2 teaspoons Worcestershire sauce
  2 drops Tabasco sauce (optional)
  8 hot dogs

Sauté the chopped onion in the salad oil. Add remaining ingredients except hot dogs and simmer for 15 minutes. Split hot dogs and place in a baking dish. Pour the sauce over them. Bake at 375 degrees for ½ hour. Baste several times while cooking. Serves 8.

—Henrietta Holton Dallum (Mrs. John)

ULTRA EASY BAR-B-QUE

This is a speedy dish for Little League suppers, sleep-overs, and end of season get-togethers.

  2 12-ounce cans corned beef (*not* corned beef hash!), chopped up
  1 onion, chopped
  ½ cup chopped celery
  1 cup catsup
  2 tablespoons brown sugar
  2 tablespoons vinegar
  2 tablespoons butter
  3 tablespoons fresh lemon juice
  3 tablespoons Worcestershire sauce
  ½ teaspoon prepared mustard
  ½ cup water

Mix all ingredients together and simmer for 1 hour. Serve on toasted hamburger rolls. Makes enough for 8 to 10 sandwiches.

—Janie Eby Ashley (Mrs. Sydney G.)

🍲 *HAMBURG CASSEROLE*

A confidence-building casserole that has been served at first dinner parties for three generations. French bread, a green salad, and perhaps a bottle of wine guarantee a fine evening.

1½ pounds ground beef (use 2 pounds beef to serve 10)
 1 clove garlic
 1 teaspoon salt
    pepper to taste
 1 teaspoon sugar
 2 8-ounce cans tomato sauce
 6 scallions, chopped, including tops
 1 8-ounce package noodles, cooked and drained
 1 8-ounce package cream cheese
 1 cup sour cream
½ cup cheddar cheese (optional)

Brown beef and clove of garlic. Add salt, pepper, sugar, and tomato sauce. Cover and cook slowly for 15 to 20 minutes. In separate bowl, mix scallions, cream cheese, and sour cream. Use a 3-quart casserole. Put in 1 layer of noodles, 1 of sour cream mixture, 1 of meat mixture. Repeat. Top with ½ cup cheddar cheese. Bake at 350 degrees for 30 minutes, until bubbly and slightly brown. Makes 8 to 10 servings.

—*Frances Freestate DeJonge (Mrs. Carl)*

🍲 *HAMBURGER PIE*

This is a great favorite with Gunston School girls.

 3 cups flour
½ teaspoon salt
2½ teaspoons sugar
½ teaspoon baking soda
 1 cup lard
 1 egg
 2 tablespoons lemon or orange juice
 2 tablespoons cold water
 1 medium onion
 1 clove garlic, minced
 2 pounds ground chuck steak

1 tablespoon butter

2 teaspoons soy sauce

½ teaspoon Worcestershire sauce

1 teaspoon salt

¼ teaspoon freshly ground pepper

3 eggs, beaten

1 pound cottage cheese

⅛ teaspoon salt

⅛ teaspoon paprika

Sift flour, salt, sugar, soda together; cut in lard until pieces the size of peas. In separate bowl, beat egg, lemon or orange juice, and water; add this to flour mixture. Roll out to ¼-inch thickness and line two 10-inch pie pans. Bake at 425 degrees for 4 to 5 minutes. Freeze one piecrust for future use or double the filling and sauce recipes. Cook onion, garlic, and chuck in butter until brown, pouring off excess fat. Add seasonings and put in pie shell.

Mix eggs, cottage cheese, salt, and paprika together in a bowl and pour on top of meat filling. Bake at 375 degrees for 30 minutes or until brown.

—*Mary Ashley Long (Mrs. Paul M.)*

HAMBURGERS DIANE

1 pound good ground beef

2 tablespoons freshly ground pepper
   butter

2 tablespoons cognac
   chives or dried onion pieces

Shape beef lightly into cakes, sprinkle with pepper and, with heel of hand, press pepper into cakes. Let stand 30 minutes. Sprinkle a light layer of salt over bottom of a heavy frying pan. Turn heat to high, and when salt begins to brown, add hamburgers. Cook until well browned on one side, turn and brown other side; reduce heat and cook until done to suit (best if on the rare side). Place a tablespoon of butter on each cake, pour over cognac, and set ablaze. Sprinkle cakes with chives or dried onions, and serve with pan gravy.

—*Lynette Morgan Nielsen (Mrs. Orsen)*

🌾 *SPRING GARDEN COUNTRY HAM*

Curing Method I

2 pounds brown sugar

¼ pound (less 1 level tablespoon) saltpetre

2 teaspoons (level) red pepper

2 quarts (level) salt

1 tablespoon (rounded) ground cloves

¼ pound black pepper

100 pounds meat

Combine seasonings and rub thoroughly into meat, especially hock end. Pack extra in this area and around butt end. Lay meat on boards, first sprinkling a little seasoning where each ham is to lie.

About January 21st, or 6 to 8 weeks after curing, wash hams in weak borax water (1 pound borax to 1 gallon water). Select warm, sunny day, and let meat dry in sun; or wipe dry before sprinkling lightly with dry borax (fill hock end with extra to prevent greenfly and at bone at butt end. *Note:* Too much borax makes meat hard). Hang hams in cold place to dry for a few days, then wrap tightly in brown paper bags and seal tight in muslin bags. Hang in very cold place. For best flavor, do not use for at least 12 months or longer. Flavor increases with age.

Curing Method II

2 quarts (level) salt

   black molasses

¼ pound (less 1 level tablespoon) saltpetre

2 teaspoons (level) red pepper

1 tablespoon (rounded) ground cloves

¼ pound black pepper

100 pounds meat

Follow directions for Method I.

Cooking Method

1 cup Po-t-rik molasses

   brown sugar

⅛ teaspoon allspice

⅛ teaspoon cloves

⅛ teaspoon cinnamon
bourbon, wine, or vinegar

If your country ham has cured less than a year, do *not* soak overnight. Three days before serving, weigh and wash meat thoroughly. Cover in cold water and let stand overnight. Next morning, pour off water and cover with fresh cold water, keeping skin side down. Add molasses, bring to a boil and let boil hard for 15 to 20 minutes. (Do not pierce with fork during cooking.) Lower heat until just bubbling and cook, allowing in all 20 minutes to the pound. One half hour before time is up, remove from heat. Open kettle top halfway and leave overnight until cold. Remove skin, dot fat with whole cloves, and pack brown sugar over top of ham. Drop a few drops of bourbon in sugar. Brown in oven at 350 degrees about 20 minutes, basting several times with a paste made by combining 1 cup brown sugar, spices, and ham drippings.

—*Louise McFeely Perry (Mrs. John W.)*

❧ MORE

Especially recommended for large informal buffet suppers of young and old, and may be cooked without worry during the cocktail hour. I try to concoct the whole thing in the morning and then put it in the oven an hour before serving. The name derives from the usual comment heard when the first plates are emptied: "May I have some more, please?"

1   large onion, sliced
1   green pepper, sliced
4   tablespoons butter
1½ pounds ground round steak
½   cup rice, uncooked
1   15-ounce can tomatoes
    salt and pepper to taste

Sauté onion and green pepper in hot butter in skillet for about 5 minutes. Add meat all at once, turning often to brown well, then add rice, tomatoes, and salt and pepper. Place all in a casserole and bake at 350 degrees, tightly covered, for 1 hour. This should serve 4. It may be stretched to serve 6 by adding more meat, ½ cup more rice, and a cup of tomato juice.

—*Frances Neville Vest (Mrs. J. P. W.)*

❧ *PAUPER'S FILET*

2 pounds ground chuck
2 beaten eggs
2 tablespoons Worcestershire sauce
3 tablespoons catsup
1 cup grated sharp cheese
8 slices bacon
  salt and pepper

Mix all ingredients except bacon (using your hands works best). Divide into 8 portions. Form into 1½-inch patties. Wrap with bacon and secure with picks. Broil about 5 minutes on each side. Makes 8 servings.

—Anne Stoney Cantler (Mrs. James E.)

❧ *STEAK AND KIDNEY PIE*

1 pound lean stewing beef, cut up
1 beef kidney, cut up
1 cup canned beef consommé, undiluted
1 tablespoon flour
1 teaspoon salt
½ teaspoon pepper
  pie pastry
1 beaten egg

Roll beef and kidney pieces in seasoned flour. Alternate in shallow casserole. Add consommé and cover with pastry, rolled ⅓-inch thick, reserving enough pastry to make narrow strip 1-inch wide to place on rim of casserole. Flute with fingers or fork. Cut 2 slashes in piecrust to allow steam to escape. Brush pastry with beaten egg. Bake 15 minutes at 450 degrees; reduce heat to 350 degrees and cook 1 hour and 45 minutes or until done. Freezes well, but add more consommé when reheating. Serves 4.

—Jean Wetzel (Mrs. Frank)

❧ *GLAZED HAM LOAF*

This is an ideal main dish for a party.

2 pounds lean fresh pork
2 pounds lean smoked ham

1½ cups rolled fresh cracker crumbs

½ cup chopped onion

4 well-beaten eggs

1¼ teaspoons salt

2 cups milk

2 tablespoons chopped parsley

½ cup brown sugar

½ cup cider vinegar

1½ teaspoons dry mustard

Mix rolled crackers with meat. Do not use fine cracker meal. Add chopped onions, eggs, salt, milk, and parsley. Work well together until blended. Shape into 2 loaves in 9 × 5 × 5-inch bread pan and bake at 350 degrees for 30 minutes. While loaves are baking, make glaze. Combine brown sugar, cider vinegar, and dry mustard. Mix and boil 1 minute. Remove ham loaves from oven, baste with glaze; then set pans on metal tray to catch drippings, and bake 1 hour longer. If there is any sauce left, baste again after loaves have baked 30 minutes. Remove from pans while warm. Cool, wrap, and freeze. On day of the party, remove loaves from freezer 1½ hours before serving, if serving cold; longer if you wish to reheat them. Heat for 20 minutes at 325 degrees. Serve with Zippy Sauce or Mustard Sauce. Makes 16 servings.

Zippy Sauce

½ cup mayonnaise

½ cup sour cream

¼ cup prepared mustard

1 tablespoon minced chives

2 tablespoons prepared horseradish
   salt and lemon juice to taste

Combine all ingredients. Do not freeze.

Mustard Sauce

1 cup damson preserves

3 tablespoons mustard

Combine all ingredients and serve with Ham Loaf.

—*Janet Gadd Doehler (Mrs. William F.)*

❧ *HAM IN SHERRY*

> 1 slice ham, ¾-inch thick
> 2 tablespoons brown sugar
> ½ teaspoon ground cloves
> ½ teaspoon cinnamon
> 2 ounces sherry

Mix together brown sugar, cloves, and cinnamon. Rub mixture well into each side of ham. Place in frying pan and cook slowly until slightly browned on both sides. Add sherry, cover, and cook over low heat until done—about 10 minutes.

—Louise C. Layton (Mrs. C. Rodney)

❧ *OLD-FASHIONED WAY TO COOK HOME-CURED, SUGAR-CURED HAMS*

> 1 whole sugar-cured ham
> 3½ cups cider vinegar
> 1½ pounds brown sugar
> 2 tablespoons Colman's dry mustard
> ½ teaspoon ground cloves
> 1½ cups brown sugar
> ham drippings to make a thick paste

First, scrub the ham very thoroughly. Then put it to soak. It needs to be well covered with water to which the vinegar and brown sugar have been added. Leave to soak 36 hours. Put to boil in same water for one hour then reduce heat to a simmer. (Never let it boil again). This needs watching and is important for perfect results. Simmer 5½ hours. As scum comes to top, remove it and add more water if necessary to keep ham covered. Remove pot from heat and cool a bit before removing ham from liquid. (The ham will handle much better if cool.) Then remove skin and excess fat (according to taste), and coat with a mixture of dry mustard, cloves, brown sugar, and ham drippings, and brown nicely in the oven.

—Hedwig Moser Oertel (Mrs. William K.)

❧ *HOPPING JOHN*

> 1 smoked ham hock
> 1 large onion, chopped

2 carrots, chopped
3 ribs of celery, chopped
1 cup dried black-eyed peas
1 cup chopped onion
1 tablespoon Puritan oil
⅛ teaspoon McCormick Hot Shot pepper
1 cup cooked, chopped honey ham
1 clove garlic, put through garlic press
1 6-ounce box Uncle Ben's Long Grain and Wild Rice
    Original Recipe
Pam or butter

Place ham hock in pan and cover with water. Add onion, carrots, and celery. Cook hock until meat comes off bone easily. Remove hock from pan. To ham stock add black-eyed peas, which have been washed and sorted. Soak peas overnight in stock. Next day, pour ham stock off black-eyed peas. In separate pan, sauté chopped onion in oil. Add pepper and honey ham. Add pressed garlic. Cook together about 5 minutes. Add peas. Cook until tender, about 20 minutes. Prepare rice according to directions on box. Add cooked rice to pea mixture and stir to mix. Spray 10-inch casserole dish with Pam, or grease with butter. Fill with above mixture. Cover and refrigerate. Reheat next day in oven or microwave until heated through. Makes 6 to 8 servings.

—Jean Blackman Todd (Mrs. Ben)

CABBAGE PIE

Pastry for double-crust 9-inch pie
3 ounces cream cheese
3 tablespoons margarine
1 small cabbage, chopped
1 onion, chopped
4 ounces mushrooms, sliced
½ pound ground beef
salt and pepper to taste

Bake pie shell at 375 degrees. Cool. Spread cream cheese on inside. Sauté vegetables in margarine. Brown ground beef. Add to vegetables. Put in shell. Top with crust. Cut vents. Bake 20 to 30 minutes at 350 degrees. Serves 6.

—Nancy Insley Gribbon (Mrs. Robert T.)

BELMOST SAUCE FOR GRILLED HAMBURGERS

    4 tablespoons (½ stick) butter
    ½ cup chili sauce
    1 teaspoon sugar
    ¼ cup orange juice
    1 teaspoon prepared mustard
    1 tablespoon wine vinegar

Melt butter in a small saucepan, add remaining ingredients. Heat, stirring once or twice, just until bubbly. Spoon over grilled hamburgers. Makes 1 cup.

—*Margaret Gadd Ashley (Mrs. John M.)*

CHAFING DISH MEATBALLS

    2 pounds ground beef, ground twice
    1 pound pork tenderloin, ground
3 or 4 eggs, beaten
    2 teaspoons salt
    ¼ teaspoon pepper
    ½ cup flour
    ½ cup salad oil or shortening
    3 tablespoons flour
    2 cans condensed beef consommé
    1 tablespoon bottled sauce for gravy
¾ to 1 cup sherry

Mix first six ingredients. Shape with teaspoon into balls ¾-inch in diameter. Heat oil in skillet. Brown a few meatballs at a time. Put in pans the size and shape of your chafing dish. Add 3 tablespoons flour to fat left in skillet and stir until smooth. Add consommé and bottled sauce; cook, stirring until thickened. Pour sherry over meatballs. Cool, freeze, and wrap. To serve, slip into skillet or chafing dish, cover, and heat 25 minutes. Makes 24 meatballs.

—*Mary Ashley Long (Mrs. Paul M.)*

SWEET-SOUR MEATBALLS

    2 pounds ground chuck
    ½ pound sausage

1 medium onion, chopped fine
1 clove garlic, minced
  salt and pepper to taste
2 teaspoons Worcestershire sauce
3 teaspoons chopped parsley
½ teaspoon nutmeg
  cayenne and paprika to taste
2 cups soft bread crumbs
4 eggs, beaten
  flour
2 tablespoons cornstarch
½ cup cool chicken stock
2 tablespoons soy sauce

Mix meats, onion, seasonings, bread crumbs, and eggs. Form into balls and roll in flour. Bake at 375 degrees for 15 minutes. Drain. Make a paste of cornstarch, stock, and soy sauce. Melt butter in a heavy pan. Add broth, green pepper, and pineapple. Cover and simmer 3 to 5 minutes, add cornstarch paste and the vinegar, pineapple juice, sugar, and flavorings. Simmer, stirring constantly, until mixture thickens. Meatballs may be put in plastic bag and frozen. Sauce can also be frozen.

Sweet-Sour Sauce

2 tablespoons butter
1 cup chicken broth
¾ to 1 cup diced green pepper
6 slices canned pineapple, diced
½ cup vinegar
¾ cup pineapple juice
½ cup sugar
½ teaspoon salt
¼ teaspoon ginger

—*Janet Gadd Doehler (Mrs. William F.)*

This sauce is wonderful with Vienna sausages for a cocktail treat. Cut sausages in thirds, heat in sauce, then serve on toothpicks with chunks of pineapple. Great!

—*Janie Eby Ashley (Mrs. Sydney G.)*

❦ *STIR-FRY BROCCOLI AND BEEF*

  1 pound boneless round steak
  ⅓ cup soy sauce
  ¼ cup water
  2 tablespoons brown sugar
  1 clove garlic, crushed
  1 teaspoon ground ginger
  1 teaspoon cornstarch
  3 tablespoons vegetable oil
  4 cups fresh broccoli flowerets
  1 large onion cut into 8 wedges
  ¼ cup water, scant
   hot cooked rice

Partially freeze steak; slice across grain in 3 × ¼-inch strips and set aside. Combine next 6 ingredients, mix well, add steak. Cover and refrigerate 1 hour. Drain steak and reserve marinade. Pour oil around top of electric preheated wok or skillet, coating sides; allow to heat to medium high (325 degrees) for 1 minute. Add steak, stir-fry 2 to 3 minutes, remove, and set aside. Add broccoli and onion and ¼ cup water to wok. Cover and reduce heat to 225 degrees; cook 3 to 5 minutes. Stir in steak and marinade and cook 1 minute, stirring constantly until thick. Serve over hot cooked rice. Makes 6 to 8 servings.

—*Barbara Seaman Efland (Mrs. Herman)*

❦ *PICADILLO*

A Cuban recipe given to me by Mrs. D. A. Clement. This is especially piquant in the summer when vegetables are fresh from the garden. Accompany with a dry white wine.

  2 tablespoons vegetable oil
  2 large garlic cloves, minced
  1 large onion, chopped coarsely
   salt and pepper
  1 pound lean ground beef
  ⅓ cup dry white wine
  2 large ripe tomatoes, peeled and chopped
  ½ cup raisins, plumped up in hot water

⅓ cup stuffed olives, sliced
1 seeded green pepper, chopped in ½-inch squares
hot cooked rice

In the oil, fry the garlic and onion for 5 minutes, stirring frequently. Add the seasoning, meat, and wine, and stir again. Add the tomatoes, raisins, and olives, and stir. Add the green pepper pieces and cook only long enough to heat them (they should retain crispness and color). The chopping and slicing can be done in advance, the cooking requiring only 10 minutes. Serve on or with white rice. Serves 3 to 5.

—Janet Gadd Doehler (Mrs. William F.)

SKILLET BEEF AND BEANS

½ to 1 pound lean, tender beef
2 tablespoons Wesson oil
1 chopped onion
2 cups French-cut string beans (fresh or frozen)
1 cup diced celery
1 tablespoon cornstarch
1 tablespoon soy sauce
¾ cup liquid (juice from mushrooms and water)
1 8-ounce can mushrooms
pimiento

Cut beef in strips, brown in oil. Add onion, beans, and celery. Cook 4 to 6 minutes, stir. Combine cornstarch and soy sauce with liquid. Add to skillet with mushrooms and stir, cooking until liquid is shiny. Cover, cook until beans are tender. Garnish with pimiento. Serve with rice. Serves 4 or 5.

—Anna Grace Keith (Mrs. Ronald L.)

STEAK CHATEAUBRIAND

Trim most of the fat off a 3-inch-thick steak. Brush lightly with olive oil and sprinkle with pepper. Brown quickly on all sides in a heavy, very hot iron frying pan on top of stove, pouring off extra fat as it melts. Remove meat from skillet. Salt the steak, and bake at 350 degrees for 20 to 25 minutes (for rare or medium rare). This is very good cold, sliced thin.

—Maria McKenney

🍃 *CORNED BEEF IN GINGER ALE*

>   corned beef (preferably Mash's)
>   ginger ale (use a cheap brand)

Rinse well and place fat side up in cooking bag. Place in microwave-safe casserole, add ginger ale to bag to cover meat. Tie bag loosely with 1-inch opening. Cover casserole with lid and place in microwave oven. Cook at high for 10 minutes. Turn microwave to low and cook for 30 minutes. Remove from oven and turn meat over in bag so fat side is down. Return to microwave. Cook on low for 1 hour more. Let cool in bag. Remove and weight down for about 1 hour. Serve cold. Makes 8 to 10 servings.

—David Williamson, Jr.

🍃 *CORNED BEEF PASTRIES*

>   2 cups flour
>   1 teaspoon baking powder
>   ½ teaspoon salt
>   6 tablespoons shortening
>   1 egg yolk
>   ⅓ cup milk
>   2 tablespoons butter
>   ½ cup onion, chopped
>   2 tablespoons flour
>   1½ cups corned beef or 1 12-ounce can
>   1½ cups tomatoes

Mix flour, baking powder, and salt; cut in shortening. Add egg yolk and milk and stir. Roll out dough and cut in 3-inch squares. Sauté onions in butter till soft. Stir in flour; add corned beef and tomatoes. Cook 10 minutes. Line muffin tins with pastry. Fill with hot tomato filling. Fold the four corners of the pastry over the top. Bake at 425 degrees for 20 minutes. Makes 10 or 12 pastries.

—Margaret Gadd Ashley (Mrs. John M.)

🍃 *OXTAIL STEW*

>   2 oxtails
>   oil or fat

salt and pepper to taste
beef broth (canned may be used)
½ cup sweet vermouth or sherry
potatoes, peeled
carrots, peeled
onions, peeled
canned beef gravy (or butter-flour roux or
cornstarch in a little water)
Worcestershire sauce (or Tabasco)

Disjoint oxtails. Brown well in fat or oil, using heavy iron pot. Add salt and pepper, and enough beef broth (diluted, if desired) to cover oxtails. Add ½ cup sweet vermouth or sherry. Cover pot or place oxtails in casserole. Bake at 300 degrees for 3 to 4 hours. Turn oven down if liquid is boiling furiously. Add warmed water or broth if necessary. About 1 hour before serving, check oxtails. Meat should be almost falling off bones. Add potatoes, carrots, celery, onions, cut into bite size pieces. (Other vegetables, such as tomatoes, squash, or peppers may also be added.) About 10 minutes before serving, add canned beef gravy, roux, or cornstarch and water, enough to thicken the dish moderately. You may also add Worcestershire sauce, Tabasco, or any favorite seasoning. This dish may be cooked on top of stove, but baking gives a richer, glazed quality to the meat. Oxtails are especially good when prepared a day ahead. Vegetables may be added either then or on the serving day. Makes 6 to 8 servings.

—Pamela Wahl Kramer (Mrs. Egon)

SAUSAGE

24 pounds pork (lean and fat as desired)
8 heaping tablespoons sage
8 rounded tablespoons black pepper
2 tablespoons brown sugar
1 teaspoon red pepper
10 tablespoons salt

Mix seasoning and sprinkle through meat before grinding. Grind twice.

—Ruth Branner Gadd (Mrs. A. Sydney, Jr.)

❧ *WHARF HOUSE PARTY BEEF*

> *This won first prize in a* Queen Anne's Record-Observer *cooking competition. It may be halved.*

6 pounds of lean beef, cut into 2-inch chunks
    several tablespoons of margarine (sufficient to brown meat)
2 cups of dry red wine
4 cups Italian style tomatoes, drained, juice reserved
4 cloves garlic, chopped
1 tablespoon salt
1 teaspoon cinnamon
1 teaspoon allspice
    pepper to taste
2 pounds whole small yellow onions
1 pound fresh sliced mushrooms
1 12-ounce can tomato paste
½ cup chopped parsley

Trim the meat and brown thoroughly on all sides in hot skillet, a few pieces at a time. When done, remove to lidded, flame-proof casseroles. For this recipe, which makes about six quarts, you will need a four-quart and a three-quart casserole. Turn heat on very low under casseroles, add wine gradually, cover, and simmer 10 minutes. Stir in tomatoes. The reserved tomato juice may be used in case stew becomes too dry. Mash together the chopped garlic and salt. Stir into the stew with the other seasonings. Sauté onions in skillet, slowly, stirring to coat them with fat until lightly browned. Sauté mushrooms and add them to the stew with the onions, tomato paste, and parsley. At this point, the cooking is to be completed in the oven. Because I have been guessing up till now on the division of the ingredients between the two casseroles, I now empty the meat and onion-mushroom mixtures into an eight-quart mixing bowl and stir well before redistributing the casseroles. Start baking at 325 degrees. When the sauce begins to bubble, reduce heat to as low as 250 degrees or as low as possible to maintain a simmer. Total cooking time is about 2½ hours. A good feature of this recipe is that it can be done mostly the day ahead. It is best to refrigerate this dish before completing the cooking, for then the grease can be skimmed off before reheating. Serves 12 to 16 and freezes well.

—Mary Payne Franklin (Mrs. William)

❧ SPRING GARDEN LIQUID PICKLE FOR PORK

    100 pounds meat (use middlings, spareribs, shoulders, chine,
           and backbone)
      8 pounds salt
      2 pounds brown sugar
      1 ounce saltpetre
    1½ ounces pearl ash
      2 ounces ground allspice
      1 level ounce red pepper
      4 gallons water

Soak backbone and chine in water for a day and drain before putting into pickle. Let rest of meat cool for 24 hours, then cover with a brine made of above ingredients. Pack meat loosely in tight barrels, then weigh meat down with board and rock. If this is insufficient brine to cover meat, make extra brine with enough salt to float an egg. Let meat remain in brine 4 to 6 weeks, according to size of pieces and the weather. Shoulder meat could be sprinkled lightly with borax and kept in brine longer. Wash in fresh water, hang to dry. Use before warm weather.

—Louise McFeely Perry (Mrs. John W.)

❧ PORK CHOPS WITH SAUERKRAUT

      4 slices bacon
      4 thick center-cut pork chops
      2 tablespoons bacon drippings
      1 onion, sliced
    1½ pounds sauerkraut
      1 teaspoon pepper
      2 cans beer

In a large skillet fry bacon, then drain. Brown pork chops in bacon drippings. Return bacon to skillet, add onion and sauerkraut. Add pepper and enough beer to barely cover all. Cover skillet, bring to boil, lower heat, and simmer for 30 minutes. Serve with boiled potatoes. Makes 4 servings.

—Susan McFadden Miller (Mrs. Mark)

🍃 *BARBECUED PORK LOIN OR FRESH PORK SHOULDER*

3 to 5 pounds pork (loin or shoulder)
    1 can tomato soup
  ⅓ cup chopped onion
    1 tablespoon brown sugar
    1 tablespoon Worcestershire sauce
  ⅓ cup chopped celery
    1 clove garlic, minced
    2 teaspoons prepared mustard
    4 drops Tabasco sauce
    1 tablespoon lemon juice

Bake meat in shallow roasting pan at 325 degrees, allowing 45 minutes to the pound. Combine rest of ingredients to make sauce. One hour before meat is done, pour off drippings and pour barbecue sauce over meat. Continue cooking, spooning sauce over meat often.

—*Anna Grace Keith (Mrs. Ronald L.)*

🍃 *ROAST SUCKLING PIG*

For roast suckling pig, use only a young pig under 6 weeks old. Scald the butchered pig by immersing in very hot water (not boiling) for 1 minute. Remove from water and use a very dull knife to scrape off hair in order that skin will not be broken. Cut a slit from the bottom of the throat to the hind legs and remove organs and entrails, being careful not to break the brains. Wash thoroughly in cold water and chill. Fill with any desired poultry stuffing and sew opening. Roast at 350 degrees for 3 to 4 hours. When serving, place a red apple in the mouth and red cherries in the eyes. Serve with candied sweet potatoes and applesauce. Makes 6 to 8 servings.

—*Isabel Atkinson Lieber (Mrs. Albert C.)*

❧ *ZUCCHINI SAUSAGE PIE*

      2 pounds zucchini
      ½ pound sausage
      ¼ cup chopped onion
      ½ cup crumbs
      2 eggs, slightly beaten
      ¼ cup Parmesan cheese
         pinch dried thyme
         pinch dried rosemary
         garlic salt
         salt and pepper

Cook zucchini whole in boiling water for 15 minutes. Drain and chop coarsely. Cook sausage and onion together until sausage begins to brown. Combine with rest of ingredients, saving 2 tablespoons cheese for top. Put in greased 9-inch pie plate. Sprinkle with cheese. Bake at 350 degrees until firm and slightly brown, about 20 minutes. Serves 4.

—Suzanne Cartier James (Mrs. Oliver)

❧ *FILET OF BEEF*

      1 beef filet, about 4 pounds, trimmed, at room temperature

Preheat oven to 475 degrees. Rub beef with salt, pepper, and 1 clove garlic, sliced, and set in a shallow roasting pan. Place in preheated oven and immediately reduce temperature to 350 degrees. Bake for 1 hour for rare (120 degrees on a meat thermometer), or 15 minutes more for medium (130 degrees on a meat thermometer). Remove filet from oven and rest for 10 minutes before serving.

—Committee

🦢 *VEAL CASSEROLE WITH DUMPLINGS*

>   2 pounds veal cut from leg, sliced ½-inch thick
> ⅓ cup flour
>   paprika
>   salt and pepper
>   vegetable oil
>   2 cups chicken broth
> 36 small white onions (canned)
>   1 10½-ounce can condensed cream of chicken soup
>   1 recipe dumplings

Slice veal in strips ¼-inch thick and drop in bag with flour seasoned with salt and pepper and a generous amount of paprika. Shake until strips are well coated. Pour enough oil in large skillet to make a film. Put over medium heat and sauté veal on all sides, a few pieces at a time. Put browned veal in a greased 2-quart casserole. Heat chicken broth, onions, and cream of chicken soup together to boiling and pour over veal. Top with dumplings and bake at 425 degrees for 20 to 30 minutes. Serve with Sour Cream Sauce. Makes 14 servings.

Dumplings for Veal Casserole

>   2 cups sifted all-purpose flour
>   2 teaspoons baking powder
>   salt
> ½ tablespoon poultry seasoning
> ½ teaspoon celery seed
> ½ tablespoon onion juice
>   2 tablespoons vegetable oil
> ½ cup milk
> ½ cup butter, melted
>   fine bread crumbs

Mix all together except butter and bread crumbs until just moistened. Drop by tablespoonfuls into melted butter, then roll in bread crumbs. Arrange on top of casserole and bake. Serve with Sour Cream Sauce.

Sour Cream Sauce

1 cup sour cream

1 10½-ounce can condensed cream of chicken soup

Mix together and heat to boiling point. Serve with veal and dumplings.

—Lynda Eby Jordan (Mrs. Harold)

VEAL CHOPS IN MUSTARD SAUCE

4 tablespoons finely chopped onions

1 stick butter

4 veal chops, ¾-inch thick

   flour

   salt and pepper

½ cup dry white wine

4 tablespoons thick cream

1 heaping teaspoon or more prepared mustard

Cook chopped onions slowly in ¼ stick of butter until soft, without browning. Remove from pan and reserve. Sprinkle chops lightly with flour. Heat rest of butter in heavy iron frying pan, and when sizzling hot, add chops and sauté quickly until golden brown. Salt and pepper chops well and place in hot covered baking dish. Add wine to the drippings and butter in the skillet. Stir and cook until it is reduced to syrupy consistency. Pour over chops and place onions around chops. Cover well and cook slowly at 320 degrees for about 20 minutes, or until chops are tender. Remove chops, add warm cream to juices in baking dish. Bring to boil and add prepared mustard and stir well, but do not boil. Pour over chops and serve. If there is not enough gravy in dish, hot water may be added. Use the same directions to achieve quite a new sauce, by substituting red wine for white (must be good wine) and omitting mustard.

—Lynette Morgan Nielsen (Mrs. Orsen)

🍃 *LAMB SHANKS IN SWEET VERMOUTH*

- 5 tablespoons salt-free margarine
- 4 trimmed lamb shanks or 3 pounds boneless lamb shoulder cut in 1½-inch cubes
- 3 tablespoons cognac, warmed
- 1 tablespoon Wondra flour (or any other quick-mixing flour)
- 3 tablespoons tomato sauce
- 3 cups chicken soup
- 1 cup sweet vermouth
- 1 bay leaf
  freshly ground pepper (no salt)
- 2 large baking type potatoes, peeled and cut in 1-inch cubes
- 2 large carrots, scraped and cut in 1-inch lengths
- 1 dozen small white onions
- 1 package frozen peas, defrosted
- 2 tomatoes in season (otherwise do not bother)
  chopped parsley

Preheat oven to 350 degrees. Melt 2 tablespoons of margarine in heavy ovenproof pan such as a Dutch oven. Brown the lamb shanks. Pour over warmed cognac and ignite. After the flames die out remove shanks to a warm plate. Pour off any excess fat and melt the remaining 3 tablespoons of margarine. Off the heat, mix in the flour and tomato sauce then add the soup, vermouth, bay leaf, pepper, and lamb shanks. Return to fire, bring to boil, cover, and put in the oven. Cook for 1½ hours. After 30 minutes remove cover, and after another 30 minutes add all the vegetables except peas and tomatoes (if used). Five minutes before serving, add peas and tomatoes. Garnish with chopped parsley. Makes 4 servings.

—*Joan Vest Withington (Mrs. Charles F.)*

🍃 *TONGUE IN WHITE WINE ASPIC*

Very good and easily prepared!

- 1½ pounds sliced cooked tongue
  stuffed olives
- 2 envelopes unflavored gelatin

2 cans condensed consommé

1 cup dry white wine

Arrange overlapping slices of tongue in two rows along either side of a shallow serving dish. Arrange a row of stuffed olives in center. Soften gelatin in ½ cup cold water. Bring 1 can of consommé to a boil and add it to the gelatin, stirring until the gelatin is dissolved. Stir in the wine and remaining can of cold consommé. Cool for 30 minutes until the wine and gelatin mixture is slightly syrupy. Pour over the tongue and chill in the refrigerator for at least 2 hours or until the wine aspic has set. Serves 6.

—*Virginia Potter (Mrs. Holland)*

FRENCH TONGUE

1 fresh beef tongue

1 teaspoon dry mustard

1 teaspoon ginger

bacon fat

½ cup finely chopped onions

¾ cup finely chopped parsley

1 cup finely chopped celery and leaves

1 cup finely chopped carrots

1 clove garlic, chopped

1 bay leaf

½ teaspoon thyme

1 tablespoon Worcestershire sauce

1 8-ounce can tomato sauce

1 cup sliced mushrooms

salt and pepper to taste

Wash tongue and cook slowly for 2 hours in water to cover. Skin tongue and rub with mustard and ginger. Brown in bacon fat. Place in covered casserole with vegetables, seasonings, and Worcestershire sauce. Cover tightly and cook slowly about 2 hours in a moderate oven Add tomato sauce and mushrooms and heat thoroughly; adjust seasonings. Serve immediately, or can be made beforehand and reheated. If fresh mushrooms are used, they should be cooked until tender in tomato sauce before adding to meat. Makes 8 servings.

—*Miss Caroline Wilson*

❧ *VEAL SCALLOPINI*

1	pound veal, cut on diagonal in scallops (8 to 10 slices)
	flour
	salt and pepper
1	green pepper, diced
3	tablespoons olive oil
1	pound fresh small mushrooms
1	can drained whole tomatoes
¾	cup white wine or Marsala
8 to 10	slices mozzarella cheese

Flour meat lightly, salt and pepper, and pound until quite thin. Cook green pepper until tender in the olive oil, then add to mushrooms which have been cooked in the tomatoes. Put everything together and add the wine. Cook all ingredients slowly for ½ hour with top on, or until meat is tender. Place mozzarella cheese on top of each serving and continue heating untill it melts. Makes 8 to 10 servings.

—*Katharine Nicols Grove (Mrs. J. Robert)*

❧ *CHILLED STEAK FOR A HOT SUMMER NIGHT*

1	large clove garlic, minced
1	teaspoon salt
½	teaspoon pepper
½	teaspoon dry mustard
1½	tablespoons blue cheese
2	tablespoons dry vermouth
½	cup olive oil
3 to 4	pounds sirloin steak, 2 inches thick

Make a marinade by combining garlic, seasonings, cheese, vermouth, and olive oil. Whisk until you have a smooth paste. Rub on both sides of steak and then marinate several hours, turning often. Broil steak rare; cool 30 minutes. Wrap and refrigerate overnight.

—*Amelia Dell Booze (Mrs. Robert)*

❧ *MANDARIN PORK AND VEGETABLES*

4	tablespoons corn oil
1	pound boneless pork

    2 cloves garlic, minced

    2 cups broccoli flowerets and sliced stems (about ½ pound)

    2 onions, cut in thin wedges

    1 carrot, cut in 2-inch julienne strips

    ½ pound mushrooms, sliced

    2 tablespoons cornstarch

  1¼ cups water

    ⅓ cup soy sauce

    ½ cup Karo (light or dark)

¼ to ½ teaspoon of crushed, dried red pepper

In a large skillet or wok, heat 2 tablespoons of corn oil over medium high heat. Add pork, cut in thin strips. Add garlic. Stir fry 5 minutes or until tender. Remove from pan. Heat 2 tablespoons of corn oil. Add broccolli, onions, and carrot. Stir-fry 2 minutes. Add mushrooms. Stir-fry 1 minute or until vegetables are crisp-tender. Return pork to pan. Whisk sauce mix a bit and add to skillet, stirring constantly. Bring to boil over medium heat and boil 1 minute. Serve over rice.

Sauce for Mandarin Stir-Fry

In bowl mix cornstarch with water until smooth. Stir in soy sauce, Karo syrup, and red pepper.

    Note: As a substitute for pork use 1 pound boned, skinned chicken cut into thin strips (stir-fry 2 to 3 minutes). Or substitute beef for pork: 1 pound tender, boneless beef cut in thin strips (stir-fry 1 to 2 minutes).

—Barbara Seaman Efland (Mrs. Herman)

❧ *ALOHA SAUCE FOR GRILLED HAMBURGERS*

    1 can (about 9 ounces) crushed pineapple

    ¾ cup catsup

    ¼ cup firmly packed brown sugar

    1 teaspoon Worcestershire sauce

Simmer all ingredients for 20 minutes or until slightly thick. Spoon hot over grilled hamburgers. Makes 1⅔ cups.

—Margaret Gadd Ashley (Mrs. John M.)

🍃 *LASAGNA*

          1 pound sweet or hot Italian sausage (5 links)
          ½ pound ground beef
          ½ cup finely chopped onion
          2 cloves garlic, crushed
          1 tablespoon sugar
          ½ tablespoon salt
       1½ teaspoons dried basil leaves
          ½ teaspoon fennel seed
          ¼ teaspoon pepper
          ¼ cup chopped parsley
          4 cups canned tomatoes, undrained (or 1 2-pound 3-ounce can)
                  Italian style tomatoes
          2 6-ounce cans tomato paste
          ½ cup water
        12 curly lasagna noodles (three-fourths of a 1-pound package)
          1 15-ounce container ricotta or cottage cheese, drained
          1 egg
          ½ teaspoon salt
          ¾ pound mozzarella cheese, thinly sliced
          1 3-ounce jar grated Parmesan cheese (¾ cup)

Remove sausage meat from casings; chop the meat. In a 5-quart Dutch oven over medium heat sauté sausage, beef, onion, and garlic, stirring frequently, until well browned, about 20 minutes. Add sugar, salt, basil, fennel, pepper and half of parsley; mix well. Add tomatoes, tomato paste, and ½ cup water, mashing tomatoes with wooden spoon. Bring to a boil; reduce heat; simmer, covered and stirring occasionally, until thick, 1½ hours. In an 8-quart kettle, cook the lasagna noodles according to the package directions. Drain in colander; rinse under cold water. Dry lasagna on paper towels. Preheat oven to 375 degrees. In medium bowl, combine ricotta, egg, remaining parsley, and salt; mix well. In bottom of 13 × 9 × 2-inch baking dish, spoon 1½ cups sauce. Layer lengthwise with 6 lasagna noodles, overlapping to cover. Spread with half of ricotta mixture; top with third of mozzarella. Spoon 1½ cups sauce over cheese; sprinkle with ¼ cup Parmesan. Repeat layering, starting with 6 lasagna and ending with 1½ cups sauce. Top with rest of mozzarella and Parmesan. Cover with foil, tucking around edge. Bake 25 minutes; remove foil; bake uncovered 25 minutes longer, or until bubbly. Cool 15 minutes before serving. With a sharp knife, cut in squares. Use a wide spatula to serve. Makes 8 servings.

—Stephanie Michalec Thompson (Mrs. Robert B.)

SPAGHETTI PIE

    6 ounces spaghetti
    2 tablespoons butter
    ⅓ cup Parmesan cheese
    2 eggs, beaten
    1 pound ground beef
    1 teaspoon onion powder
    1 8-ounce can tomato sauce
    1 6-ounce can tomato paste
    1 teaspoon sugar
    1 teaspoon oregano
    ½ teaspoon garlic salt
    1 cup cottage cheese
    ½ cup shredded Mozzarella cheese

Cook spaghetti, drain. Stir butter into hot spaghetti, add Parmesan cheese and eggs. Form mixture into a "crust" in a buttered 10-inch pie plate. Cook ground beef, stir in next 6 ingredients. Heat through. Spread cottage cheese over spaghetti "crust." Add tomato/beef mixure. Bake uncovered at 350 degrees for 20 minutes. Sprinkle mozzarella cheese on top. Bake 5 minutes longer or until cheese melts. Serves 6.

—Beth Strong (Mrs. Harlan)

MUSTARD SAUCE

    1 cup dry mustard
    1 cup cider or white vinegar
    1 cup sugar
    2 eggs, beaten

Combine dry mustard and vinegar. Let stand for several hours or overnight. Place in double boiler. Stir in sugar and cook over low heat until sugar is dissolved. Next slowly stir in eggs and continue cooking and stirring until thickened. Cool and keep refrigerated.

—Jane Corey (Mrs. R. Reece)

🍃 *VEAL IN CREAM*

veal, cut in pieces suitable for single helping, or chops
flour
cooking oil
1 tablespoon Kirsch per piece of veal
¼ cup whipping cream per piece of veal, set on stove to warm
1 tablespoon chopped parsley (very fine) to each piece veal

Flour veal very lightly. Heat cooking oil (be sure it is very fresh) in heavy iron frying pan. Quickly brown veal in pan, turn down heat, and cook until done. Just before veal is done, add Kirsch to pan, heat, and flambé. Remove veal immediately to hot platter and keep warm. Pour warm cream into same frying pan, loosen drippings in pan, and stir well into cream. Add parsley and heat slowly 5 minutes. Do not let sauce boil. Pour over veal and serve. Makes 1 serving.

—*Lynette Morgan Nielsen (Mrs. Orsen)*

🍃 *EASY SPAGHETTI SAUCE*

1 pound ground beef or combination of ground beef and fresh Italian sausage
2 or 3 onions, chopped
2 cloves garlic
olive oil
1 cup wine
2 or 3 #1 cans Del Monte stewed tomatoes, traditional or pasta or Italian type
salt
pepper
2 teaspoons basil
1 teaspoon fennel seeds
a little oregano, rosemary, or whatever
pinch of sugar
2 tablespoons tomato paste

Brown meat and sauté onions until transparent with garlic in about 2 tablespoons olive oil. Add wine (red or white), tomatoes, seasonings, and tomato paste (preferably the tube kind). Simmer for an hour or two.

—*Joann W. Valliant (Mrs. James W.)*

✢ SAUCE ROBERT FOR GRILLED PORK CHOPS

2 onions, chopped fine
1 tablespoon butter
1 cup stock
1 teaspoon chopped parsley
salt and pepper
1 teaspoon vinegar
1 teaspoon dry mustard

Brown onions slowly in the butter. Add the stock and chopped parsley. Simmer for 10 minutes, until reduced by half. Add salt and freshly ground pepper to taste. Add vinegar and mustard. Bring to boiling point and serve with chops. Makes 1 serving.

—*Lynette Morgan Nielsen (Mrs. Orsen)*

✢ ENGLISH SAUCE FOR COLD MEAT, GAME, OR TURKEY

peel from 2 oranges
1 heaping teaspoon Dijon mustard (Or make your own using Colman's dry mustard. It must be hot and bright yellow.)
4 tablespoons red currant jelly
4 tablespoons port wine
salt and pepper

Cut orange peel in 2-inch strips and blanch in boiling water for 5 minutes. Drain and combine with other ingredients in top of double boiler. Cook, stirring constantly, over hot water until the jelly is melted (about 10 to 15 minutes). Taste for seasoning and serve cold. This sauce will keep well in the refrigerator for a week or so. Makes four servings.

—*Jean Wetzel (Mrs. Frank)*

In 1881, subscriptions were being solicited to purchase a bronze cross to surmount the St. Paul's church spire, one half to be collected to defray the cost of freight and putting the cross in place.

EGGS AND CHEESE

Thank you, Father, for this food,
Which you gave to do us good;
Help us to remember you
All day long, in all we do.

❧ BAKED EGGS

> 1 slice bacon
> 6 chicken livers
>   butter
>   cayenne pepper
>   dry mustard
> 6 tablespoons heavy cream
> 6 eggs
>   salt
>   black pepper

Cut bacon into 6 pieces and sauté until crisp. Drain and save bacon, discard fat. Sauté chicken livers in 2 tablespoons butter for 5 minutes, or until lightly browned. Put 1 liver in each of 6 buttered individual baking dishes. Add a few grains of cayenne and pinch of mustard to cream and stir well. Put 1 tablespoon cream into each dish and break 1 egg in on top of the cream. Season with salt and pepper. Put a piece of bacon on top of each egg. Cover the baking dishes and bake eggs at 375 degrees for 10 minutes, or until eggs are set.

Custard cups covered with foil may be used instead of individual china baking dishes.

—Virginia Potter (Mrs. Holland)

❧ EGGS IN CREAM SAUCE

> 4 tablespoons butter or fat
> 4 small onions, chopped fine
> 1 tablespoon flour, or less if you use all cream
> 1 cup cream (or milk, but best when at least ¾ cup
>   cream is used)
> 4 eggs
>   salt and pepper to taste

Sauté onions in butter, but do not let them brown. Sprinkle with flour and mix thoroughly. Add cream and allow to thicken to consistency of thick cream, adding more milk if necessary. Drop eggs into sauce and poach until white is cooked—about 15 minutes. Serve on toast with sauce, or in deep soup plate. Serves 2.

—Lynette Morgan Nielsen (Mrs. Orsen)

❧ SWISS FONDUE

  ¼ pound Swiss cheese
  ¼ pound Gruyère cheese
  1 heaping teaspoon cornstarch
  2 jiggers white wine
  ¼ cup kirschwasser
     toasted squares French bread

Melt cheeses together in wine. Dissolve cornstarch in kirsch and add to cheese. Cook until thickened. Serve in fondue pot kept hot over flame. Use toasted squares to dip. Serves 4 to 6.

                                    —*Isabel Atkinson Lieber (Mrs. Albert C.)*

❧ BREAKFAST STRATA

This freezes well and is wonderful if you're having company overnight.

  8 slices French bread
  ¾ pound Monterey Jack cheese, shredded
  ½ pound sausage
  4 eggs
1½ cups milk
  ½ teaspoon salt
  1 teaspoon Dijon mustard
     pinch cayenne
  ½ teaspoon Worcestershire sauce
  3 tablespoons melted butter

In 13 × 9-inch baking dish, layer one-third bread, one-third cheese, all sausage, one-third bread, one-third cheese, one-third bread. Press down. Whisk all other ingredients and pour over layers. Top with last third of cheese. Refrigerate overnight. Bake uncovered at 350 degrees for 45 minutes. Easily serves 6.

                                  —*Arline Goodwin Mayer (Mrs. Charles E.)*

At Eastertide the egg symbolizes the miracle of new life in the Resurrection.

❧ CURRIED EGGS

Serve this with a choice of accompaniments: pickle relish, chopped peanuts, flaked coconut, chutney, pickled onion, crisp crumbled bacon.

2 tablespoons minced onion
2 tablespoons butter
2 tablespoons flour
1 teaspoon curry powder
2 cups milk
1 teaspoon salt
1 teaspoon pepper
2 teaspoons grated orange rind
¼ cup orange juice
6 quartered hard-cooked eggs
3 cups fluffy rice
  parsley

Sauté onion in butter; stir in flour and curry powder and cook until bubbly. Add milk. Cook until thickened. Add salt, pepper, and orange rind and juice. Add eggs; serve over rice. Garnish with parsley. Serves 4.

—*Louise Albers Gambrill (Mrs. William)*

❧ SPANISH OMELET

Filling for the omelet can be fixed the day before and reheated. This is Grace Berry's receipt and is not only most attractive and impressive but delicious.

6 eggs, separated
  cold water
  salt and pepper
7 tablespoons butter
1 large onion, cut
1 green pepper, cut
1 stalk celery, cut
1 quart canned tomatoes, drained
  salt and pepper
  sugar

Mix egg yolks, cold water, and salt and pepper to taste. Beat until well mixed. In a separate bowl, beat egg whites until stiff but not dry. Fold yolks into whites. While preparing the eggs, heat 3½ tablespoons butter in frying pan until it is sizzling hot. Add egg mixture. Cook over low heat until well puffed, then place in preheated oven for 10 minutes at 350 degrees.

Sauté vegetables in remaining butter. Cook until soft, not brown. Drain a quart of tomatoes and add salt and pepper to taste. Add small amount of sugar for flavor. Arrange vegetables over omelet. Fold in half and slide from pan onto plate. Garnish with watercress.

—Catherine Forman Thompson (Mrs. W. Stuart)

CHEESE SOUFFLÉ I

½ cup unsalted butter or unsalted margarine
½ cup cake flour
1 teaspoon paprika
½ teaspoon Tabasco
2 cups 2% milk
½ pound (1 cup) diced sharp cheddar cheese
8 eggs at room temperature, separated
grated Parmesan

In a double boiler, melt butter or margarine over hot (not boiling) water. (You may add a pinch of salt. I omit it because of the salt already in the cheese.) Then add cake flour and paprika. Mix well and cook for several minutes, until the flour froths. Be sure not to brown! Gradually stir in milk and Tabasco. Cook, whisking constantly until sauce is thickened. Add cheese and stir constantly, until melted. Remove from heat and allow to cool. (Sauce may be prepared ahead; refrigerate at this point.) Preheat oven to 475 degrees. Beat yolks until light and fold into cooled cheese sauce. In a separate bowl, beat egg whites until stiff but not dry. Fold a large spoonful of whites into the sauce, then gently fold the sauce into the egg whites. Pour mixture into a 2-quart soufflé dish that has been buttered and dusted with grated Parmesan. Bake for 10 minutes at 475 degrees. Reduce heat to 400 degrees and bake 25 minutes longer. Serve immediately! Makes 4 to 6 servings.

—Hallie Rogers Rugg (Mrs. Daniel M., III)

🐝 *MACARONI AND CHEESE*

Very cheesy and rich. The onion makes it more flavorful than the usual baked macaroni. With baked ham and a tossed salad, this provides the makings of an easy and festive supper.

     1 cup evaporated milk .
    ¼ cup water
    ¾ cup soft bread crumbs
     3 tablespoons butter
     1 cup cooked macaroni
     1 teaspoon chopped onion
     1 teaspoon salt
     3 cups grated cheese
     2 eggs, beaten

Scald milk and water and pour over bread crumbs and butter. Add macaroni, onion, salt, cheese, and eggs. Mix well and put in a buttered casserole. Set in pan of hot water and bake at 375 degrees for 45 minutes. Serves 6 to 8.

—*Virginia Ingles Freeland (Mrs. Samuel L.)*

🐝 *WELSH RAREBIT*

    1½ tablespoons butter
    1½ tablespoons flour
    1½ cups milk
     2 cups cut up sharp cheese
    ½ teaspoon dry mustard
    ½ teaspoon Worcestershire sauce

Make a white sauce of butter, flour, and milk. Add cheese and let melt slowly; then add the other seasonings. This should be made in a double boiler and then poured into a chafing dish when ready to serve. Serve over Uneeda biscuits, English muffins, or toast. Makes 4 to 6 servings.

—*Margaret Gadd Ashley (Mrs. John M.)*

🐝 *CHEESE ONION PIE*

     1 10-inch pie shell (see Pastry recipe below)
    ½ pound Swiss cheese
     2 tablespoons flour

1 large onion, sliced
4 eggs, lightly beaten
1 cup heavy cream
1 cup milk
½ teaspoon curry powder
¼ teaspoon nutmeg
  Tabasco
1 teaspoon salt
  freshly ground black pepper

Mix cheese with flour and spread over crust. Separate onion slices into rings and cover cheese mixture. Beat eggs lightly. Beat in cream, milk, curry powder, nutmeg, 2 drops of Tabasco, salt, and pepper. Pour over cheese and onion rings. Bake at 350 degrees for 45 minutes. Serves 8.

Pastry

1 large egg, lightly beaten
2 teaspoons vinegar
3 cups flour
1 cup shortening
1 teaspoon salt
4 tablespoons ice water

Blend egg and vinegar together. Blend flour, shortening, and salt until the consistency of coarse meal. Toss two mixtures together lightly. Add ice water until pastry holds together. Form into ball, wrap in plastic, and chill. Use half of crust for onion pie and freeze half. Roll pie crust and line 10-inch pie tin. Flute edges.

— *Committee*

Old Chester Church was torn down in the spring of 1834, and some of the ancient bricks from the old church were removed and placed in the new church building erected in the town of Centreville. The cornerstone of St. Paul's was laid by the Rev. Robert Goldsborough, current rector in 1834, and consecrated in 1835 by the Rt. Rev. Wm. Stone, Bishop of Maryland.

❧ *CHEESE SOUFFLÉ II*

>   1 cup scalding milk
>   1 cup soft bread crumbs
>   ½ pound cheese, cut in small pieces
>   1 tablespoon butter
>   ½ teaspoon salt
>   3 egg yolks
>   3 egg whites

Mix first five ingredients. Add egg yolks beaten very well. Then cut in stiffly beaten egg whites. Pour into buttered baking dish. Cook 40 minutes at 375 degrees. Will not fall. Makes 4 to 6 servings.

—Katharine Nicols Grove (Mrs. W. Robert)

❧ *HAM AND EGGS AU GRATIN*

>   4 tablespoons butter
>   4 tablespoons flour
>   2 cups milk
>   1½ teaspoons prepared mustard
>   1½ teaspoons Worcestershire sauce
>   1 cup grated cheese
>   ½ pound cooked ham, cut into ½ inch cubes (1¼ cups)
>   6 hard-cooked eggs, halved
>   buttered crumbs

Melt butter and flour to make a roux in saucepan. Add milk slowly, stirring constantly. Simmer 3 minutes. Add mustard, Worcestershire, and cheese. Heat until cheese melts. Add ham and eggs, heat through. Place on a serving dish, garnish with buttered crumbs. Makes 6 servings.

—Frances Freestate DeJonge (Mrs. Carl)

VEGETABLES

O Thou who art Lord of the Harvest,
The Giver who gladdens our days,
Our hearts are for ever repeating
Thanksgiving and honour and praise.

❧ SWEET POTATO AND APPLE SCALLOP

    2 cups cooked, peeled, and sliced sweet potatoes
    2 cups thinly sliced cooking apples
    ½ cup fine, dry bread crumbs
    1 cup maple syrup
    ¼ cup butter
        chopped black walnuts

Arrange sweet potatoes, apples, and crumbs in alternate layers in buttered baking dish. Add syrup, dot with butter, sprinkle with nuts and bake, covered, at 400 degrees until apples are tender. Serves 6 to 8.

—Mary Davy Pippin (Mrs. James O., Jr.)

❧ ASPARAGUS AND PIMIENTO CASSEROLE

    3 tablespoons butter
    4 tablespoons flour
    ½ teaspoon salt
    ⅛ teaspoon pepper
    1 cup light cream
    1 14-ounce can asparagus tips
    2 whole pimientos, cut up (1 4-ounce jar)
    ½ cup buttered bread crumbs

Melt butter over low heat; add flour, salt, and pepper; stir until well blended. Slowly whisk in cream, stirring constantly, until thick and smooth. Remove from heat. Add asparagus and pimiento to sauce. Pour into buttered casserole. Cover with bread crumbs. Bake uncovered at 350 degrees until browned. Serve hot. Makes 6 servings.

—Mabel Walls Valliant (Mrs. T. Rigby)

❧ BAKED ASPARAGUS WITH CHEESE

    1 bunch asparagus, cooked
        butter
        lemon juice

finely grated cheese (Gruyère, Swiss, or Parmesan)
bread crumbs (optional)

In a buttered casserole, arrange a layer of asparagus spears, dot with butter, and sprinkle with lemon juice. Sprinkle generously with cheese. Repeat twice more, so as to have three layers of asparagus, ending with cheese. Dot with butter. A few bread crumbs may be used to make more topping. Bake at 400 degrees for about 10 to 12 minutes, so dish is well heated through and top is somewhat crusty. Serves 6.

—*Lynette Morgan Nielsen (Mrs. Orsen)*

❧ ARTICHOKES AU GRATIN

A delicious dish; someone always asks for the recipe. I usually use Gruyère cheese but believe Swiss would add a completely different zest.

3   10-ounce packages frozen artichoke hearts
6   tablespoons butter
4   tablespoons flour
1½ cups milk
    several dashes Tabasco sauce
½   cup grated Gruyère or Swiss cheese
½   cup heavy whipping cream
    salt and pepper
½   cup grated Parmesan cheese

Preheat oven to 400 degrees. Cook artichokes according to package directions. Drain very well. Melt 4 tablespoons butter in heavy saucepan and stir in flour. Cook over low heat 2 or 3 minutes. Heat milk to just below boiling, add to roux all at once, stirring vigorously. Simmer 5 minutes. Add Tabasco sauce, cheese, cream, and seasoning. Stir until cheese is melted. (You may make sauce ahead, add to artichokes when ready to use.) Pour over artichoke hearts. Melt remaining 2 tablespoons butter and brush it on tops of artichokes. Sprinkle with Parmesan cheese. Bake 10 to 12 minutes. Serves 12.

—*Janie Eby Ashley (Mrs. Sydney G.)*

🌿 *ARTICHOKE HEARTS*

    4 6-ounce or 2 14-ounce cans artichokes
    1 pint sour cream
    2 tablespoons good mayonnaise
    3 tablespoons Worcestershire sauce
       dash salt
    1 tablespoon wine vinegar

Rinse artichokes and stack closely, leaves up, in greased baking dish. Mix all other ingredients and beat. Pour sauce over artichokes and heat at 350 degrees until bubbling. Serves 6.

—*June Mitchell LaMotte (Mrs. Ferdinand, III)*

🌿 *BROCCOLI AND CAULIFLOWER WITH SALSA*

    1 bunch broccoli
    1 head cauliflower
    ½ cup parsley
    ⅓ cup pimiento
    ⅓ cup black olives
    4 anchovies, rinsed, dried, and minced
    1 tablespoon capers, crushed
    ⅓ cup lemon juice
    1 cup olive oil
       salt and pepper
    2 hard-boiled eggs, chopped

Trim broccoli and cauliflower and separate into flowerets. Cook in salted water until tender. Pat dry. Into a 1-quart bowl put large cauliflower flowerets upside down. Form a circle of broccoli flowerets with stems toward center. Arrange rest in same manner (tightly). Weigh down thirty minutes. Drain off any liquid and chill two to four hours or overnight. Mix next 5 ingredients, then stir in lemon juice and olive oil *slowly*. Beat and then add salt and pepper to taste. Add chopped eggs last. Invert broccoli and cauliflower "mold" on platter and serve with sauce. Makes 12 servings.

—*Amelia Dell Booze (Mrs. Robert)*

❧ PICNIC BAKED BEANS

This recipe was served at the Corsica River Yacht Club's annual regatta each summer as the sailors arrived on Friday evening.

1 cup brown sugar
1 teaspoon dry mustard
1 teaspoon Worcestershire sauce
½ cup catsup
2 3-pound, 5¼-ounce cans baked beans
6 slices bacon

Mix brown sugar, mustard, Worcestershire sauce, and catsup with beans. Pour into casserole and lay slices of bacon on top. Bake, covered, for 1 hour at 375 degrees. Remove cover and continue cooking for ½ hour. Serves 12 to 15.

—*Marguerite Marshall Thomas (Mrs. William T.)*

❧ GREEN BEANS

1 10-ounce package frozen green beans, cut or Frenched
2 chicken bouillon cubes
2 tablespoons butter or margarine
1 tablespoon sugar
  dash of pepper
1 tablespoon cornstarch
1 tablespoon cold water
3 to 4 tablespoons vinegar
2 cups chopped cabbage

Cook beans according to package directions. Drain liquid from beans into saucepan. Add bouillon cubes, butter, sugar, and pepper. Heat to boiling, stirring constantly. Stir in cornstarch, which has been mixed with water. Cook, stirring until mixture thickens and is clear. Add vinegar. Stir in cabbage. Bring to a boil. Simmer, covered, about 5 minutes or until cabbage is tender. Add beans and reheat. Makes 4 servings.

—*June Mitchell LaMotte (Mrs. Ferdinand, III)*

❧ STRING BEAN CASSEROLE

Quick, but impressive.

3 10-ounce boxes French style frozen green beans
3 teaspoons butter
   salt
2 10¾-ounce cans cream of mushroom soup, undiluted
   dash of cayenne pepper
   dash of nutmeg
2 3½-ounce cans French-fried onions

Prepare beans as directed on box. Drain well, and add butter, salt, pepper, and nutmeg to taste. Add soup and mix well. Top with onions (fresh onions can be used). Heat at 325 degrees until heated through and onions brown. Makes 10 to 12 servings.

—*Elizabeth Bland Nesbit (Mrs. Thorpe)*

❧ CHINESE BEANS

1 stick margarine (or butter)
1 medium onion, chopped
¼ cup flour
2 cups milk
1 teaspoon salt
1 teaspoon soy sauce
   dash of Tabasco sauce
½ teaspoon pepper
½ pound grated sharp cheese
3 16-ounce cans French style green beans
   sliced water chestnuts (optional)
½ cup slivered almonds

In a large frying pan, sauté onions until brown in margarine or butter. Add flour and milk and cook until it thickens. Add salt, soy sauce, Tabasco sauce, pepper, and cheese. Put beans and water chestnuts in flat-bottomed well-greased casserole. Pour over sauce from frying pan and sprinkle almonds on top. Bake at 350 degrees for 45 minutes. Serve hot. This can be made the day before and heated. Serves 12.

—*Louise Lewis Grubb (Mrs. Ernest W.)*

❧ *BOSTON BAKED BEANS*

      bacon
1 onion, cut up
1 tablespoon brown sugar
1 teaspoon dry mustard
1 tablespoon molasses
1 tablespoon vinegar
3 tablespoons water
    salt and pepper
1 16-ounce jar B and M beans

Line casserole with bacon. Mix remaining ingredients and put in casserole. Bake at 250 to 300 degrees for 2 to 3 hours. Baste occasionally. Serves 4 to 6.

—Joan Davidson Knapp (Mrs. Halsey)

❧ *PARTY BROCCOLI*

2 10-ounce packages frozen broccoli
2 tablespoons grated onion
1½ cups sour cream
1 teaspoon vinegar
2 teaspoons sugar
½ teaspoon poppy seeds
½ teaspoon paprika
¼ teaspoon salt
    dash of pepper
½ cup cashew nuts, chopped

Cook broccoli until tender. Drain. Make a sauce of remaining ingredients, except nuts. Then pour sauce over broccoli and sprinkle with nuts. This may be served as is or used as a casserole. Makes 8 servings.

—Henrietta Thompson Robertson (Mrs. John)

🌿 *CASSEROLE OF VEGETABLES AU GRATIN*

    ¼ cup butter
    ¾ cup green pepper, cut in large pieces
    1 clove garlic, crushed
    ¼ cup flour
    ⅔ cup milk
    ¾ teaspoon salt
    ⅛ teaspoon pepper
    ⅛ teaspoon basil
    ⅛ teaspoon oregano
    ¼ teaspoon sugar
    1 cup grated cheese
    1 cup strained solid-pack tomatoes
    1 9-ounce package frozen corn, thawed
    1 1-pound can small whole onions

Melt butter in saucepan, add green pepper and garlic. Cook until pepper is tender. Stir in flour, milk, and seasonings. Heat until mixture begins to thicken; then add ½ cup grated cheese and drained tomatoes. Heat until mixture is thickened and turn into 8-cup casserole. Add thawed corn and onions and stir into sauce mixture. Sprinkle ½ cup cheese on top. Bake, uncovered, at 350 degrees for 50 minutes. Makes 8 servings.

—Susie Harris Jones (Mrs. Oliver C.)

🌿 *CAULIFLOWER SCALLOP*

       1 small head cauliflower
    2 or 3 carrots, sliced
       8 small white onions
       3 tablespoons butter or margarine
       3 tablespoons flour
      1½ teaspoons salt
       ¼ teaspoon pepper
       3 cups milk, less vegetable liquid used
       ½ cup grated cheese, Parmesan or cheddar

Separate cauliflower into flowerets and cook in boiling salted water. Cook carrots and onions. (Do not overcook.) Drain vegetables and reserve part of liquid to use in white sauce for part of milk. Melt butter over low heat; add flour, salt, and pepper; stir until well blended. Remove from heat. Gradually stir in milk and return to heat. Cook, stirring constantly, until thick and smooth. Butter baking dish and arrange vegetables. Pour sauce over, top with grated cheese, and bake at 375 degrees until heated through and cheese is browned. Serves 8.

—*Miss Pearle E. Bishop*

CELERY SAUTERNE

> 3   cups cut up celery
> 2   tablespoons butter, melted
> ½   cup whipping cream
> ½   teaspoon instant onion (or 1½ teaspoons finely chopped raw onion sautéed in butter until soft but not brown)
> ½   cup dry sauterne
>   salt and pepper to taste

Cut up celery as desired. Cook in boiling water until tender and drain off water. Add to celery the melted butter, cream, onion, sauterne, and salt and pepper to taste. Heat slowly. *Do not let boil.* Keep warm until ready to serve. Sauce may be thickened with flour if desired. Makes 4 servings.

—*Lynette Morgan Nielsen (Mrs. Orsen)*

CORN PUDDING

> 1   16½-ounce can cream style corn
> 2   eggs
> 3   heaping tablespoons sugar
> 1   small can evaporated milk (or ½ cup to ⅓ cup milk)
>   pinch salt
> 1   level tablespoon flour
>   butter

Mix in order of ingredients. Butter a 1½-quart casserole. Dot with butter and bake 1 hour at 375 degrees. Serves 4.

—*Janie Eby Ashley (Mrs. Sydney G.)*

✿ CORN FRITTERS DELUXE

        1 egg
      ½ cup milk
        1 8¾-ounce can cream style corn
      ½ cup flour
      ½ cup white cornmeal
        1 teaspoon baking powder
      ½ teaspoon salt
        1 teaspoon sugar
        3 tablespoons melted butter
          fat for frying

Beat together egg and milk; add corn. Sift dry ingredients and add to corn mixture. Drop by spoonfuls into shallow hot fat. Test fat with a few drops of water. Serve with ham, bacon, or sausage; top with apple butter or syrup. Serves 4 to 6.

—Virginia Ingles Freeland (Mrs. Samuel L.)

✿ CORN FRITTERS

        6 ears corn
        1 well-beaten egg
        1 tablespoon melted butter
        2 tablespoons (rounded) flour
        2 tablespoons milk
        1 teaspoon baking powder
        1 teaspoon sugar
          salt to taste

Cut raw kernels from the cob. Scrape the cobs well and to this add remaining ingredients. Stir. Drop by spoonfuls into hot fat. Serve immediately. Serves 4.

—Mildred Smith Thompson (Mrs. Philemon Hopper)

✿ HOMINY CHAFING DISH

        3 pints cold cooked hominy 1 pint cream, ¼ pound butter,
          2 teaspoons sugar, ½ teaspoon salt.

Place hominy, butter, salt and pepper in chafing dish with gill of cream, keep stirring and as hominy begins to thicken add balance of cream. Makes 8 servings.

—Hotel Rennert, Baltimore.
From Eat, Drink and Be Merry in Maryland

❧ *EGGPLANT WITH MUSHROOMS*

This can be made ahead up to the point of baking. Nice addition to beef, grilled fish, or lamb.

- 1 medium eggplant, peeled and cut into 1-inch cubes
- 1 small onion, chopped
- 2 tablespoons butter
- 1½ cups sliced mushrooms
- 1 tablespoon sugar
- 1 teaspoon salt
- ½ teaspoon garlic powder (or one clove garlic, minced)
- ⅛ teaspoon pepper
- 2 ripe tomatoes, thinly sliced
- ½ onion, thinly sliced
  salt and pepper
  sugar
- ½ cup grated Parmesan cheese
- 1 teaspoon dried basil (or 2 teaspoons fresh, chopped)

Steam eggplant until cubes are tender, about 10 minutes. Drain and mash. Sauté onion lightly in 1 tablespoon butter. Remove and set aside. Sauté 1 cup mushrooms in one more tablespoon butter. Add onions and mushrooms to eggplant. Add sugar, salt, garlic powder, and pepper. Mix well and adjust seasoning to taste.

Place eggplant mixture in a greased baking dish. Arrange thin slices of tomato and remaining mushrooms over the top. Top with thin slices of onion. Sprinkle generously with salt, pepper, and sugar. Garnish with basil and Parmesan cheese. Bake at 425 degrees for 30 minutes or until bubbly. Serves 4 to 6.

—Committee

❧ GARLIC GRITS

4½ cups boiling water
1 teaspoon salt
1 cup grits
½ cup (1 stick) margarine
2 eggs
  milk
1 5-ounce jar Old English cheese
1 clove garlic, minced
1 cup crushed cornflakes

To boiling water, add salt and grits. Cook until thick. Add margarine. In a cup, beat 2 eggs, then fill with milk. Add to grits along with cheese and garlic. Mix well and place in well-greased casserole. Sprinkle with cornflakes. Bake uncovered at 350 degrees for 40 minutes. Makes 8 servings.

—*Louise Lewis Grubb (Mrs. Ernest W.)*
—*Elizabeth Harper Collins (Mrs. Jackson R.)*

❧ FRIED GREEN TOMATOES

green tomatoes, good solid ones, cut in thick slices
flour
salt and pepper
butter
brown sugar

Dip tomato slices in flour, salt, and pepper on both sides. Fry in butter until good and brown. Place tomatoes in a shallow baking dish, darkest side down, and *be sure* the dish is well filled with tomatoes. Put pinch of brown sugar on each tomato. Cook in oven about 3 inches under top burner or under broiler until tomatoes are dark brown. One tomato serves one person.

—*Eleanor Williams Miles (Mrs. Clarence W.)*

❧ MUSHROOMS IN CREAM

1 pound mushrooms
1 clove garlic
3 tablespoons butter
  flour

½ pint heavy cream, or cream and milk
salt and pepper to taste

Fix mushrooms, removing stems. Rub heavy iron frying pan with garlic. Melt butter and gently sauté mushrooms, turning them every so often until they are cooked. Sprinkle lightly with flour and add cream, slowly stirring. Serve as soon as sauce is the desired consistency. Makes 6 servings.

—Lynette Morgan Nielsen (Mrs. Orsen)

MUSHROOMS À LA KING

3 tablespoons butter
1½ cups sliced mushrooms (about ⅓ pound)
1 tablespoon flour
3 hard-boiled eggs, diced
1 cup cooked, diced celery
¼ cup sliced stuffed olives
1 teaspoon salt
2 cups milk
1 tablespoon sherry
½ cup grated American cheese

Melt butter in skillet, add mushrooms and brown. Add flour and stir until blended. Slowly cook until thickened. Stir in other ingredients. Serve in patty shells, ramekins, or center of noodle ring. Serves 6 to 8.

—Isabel Atkinson Lieber (Mrs. Albert C.)

STEVENS POTATOES

This was told to us by the owner of The Lighthouse Restaurant in New London, Connecticut. However, cream is expensive and fattening, so we use evaporated milk instead of cream, and it is excellent.

Boil as many potatoes as you require. Cool them for at least 2 hours in the icebox so they will be easy to cut. Cut them into very tiny squares.

Grease a glass pie dish and spread the potato squares out in it. Pour in cream until it just shows through the top of the potatoes. Dot with butter, season with salt and pepper, sprinkle grated cheese over the top. Brown in the oven, or under the broiler.

—Claire Reynders Stevens (Mrs. Byam K.)

❧ *OIGNONS À LA GREQUE*

> 1 1-pound and 1 8½-ounce tin of white onions
> ¾ cup good strong stock
> ¼ cup vinegar
> ¼ cup seedless raisins
> 1 teaspoon tomato paste
> 1 tablespoon salad oil
> 2 tablespoons sugar
> ½ teaspoon salt
> ¼ teaspoon dried thyme
> 1 bay leaf
>   cayenne and black pepper

Bring the onions to a boil in the sauce made from combining the other ingredients. Place in casserole, cover and bake at 325 degrees for about an hour, or until tender. Chill and serve with cold meat. Serves 8 to 10.

—Marian Andrus (Mrs. Leon)

❧ *ONION CASSEROLE*

> 2 16-ounce jars canned onions (or equal amount green onions)
> ¼ pound butter
> 2½ tablespoons flour
> ½ cup half-and-half
> 1½ cups milk
> 2 tablespoons medium sharp cheese
> 1 teaspoon Worcestershire sauce
> 2 tablespoons chopped parsley
> 1 teaspoon salt (or to taste)
> ¼ teaspoon pepper (or to taste)
> 3 or 4 slices bread
> ¼ cup butter
>   Parmesan cheese
>   paprika

Cook onions in juice about 10 minutes. Drain. Brown butter, add flour, half-and-half, and milk. Cook until it thickens, stirring constantly. Add all seasonings and mix. Add onions, being careful not to break. Place in 1½-quart casserole. (Prepare up to this point the day before or early on the morning you plan to serve it.) Next day, break enough bread in fairly large pieces to make 1½ cups. Brown butter and pour over bread, mixing well. Spread this mixture over the casserole and sprinkle with Parmesan cheese and paprika. Bake at 375 degrees until brown. Makes 8 to 10 servings.

—*Sue Watson (Mrs. John G.)*

APPLE AND ONION CASSEROLE

Good with poultry or pork, and can be made a day ahead and reheated in microwave or oven.

6   tart apples (Granny Smith or Stayman Winesap),
        peeled and sliced
3   medium to large white onions (depending on your taste),
        peeled and sliced
    dark brown sugar (or light)
    ground cinnamon
    ground nutmeg
¼   pound butter

Butter 2-quart casserole that is at least 2 inches deep. Place layer of apples in casserole. Place layer of onions on top of apples. Sprinkle with brown sugar, cinnamon, small sprinkling of nutmeg, and square slices of butter. Repeat, ending with a layer of apples on top. Sprinkle top layer with cinnamon, brown sugar, nutmeg, and butter. Bake at least 1 hour at 350 degrees. If apples seem dry, I add apple juice or cider before I bake it. Serves 6.

—*Jean Blackman Todd (Mrs. Ben)*

GERMAN FRIED POTATOES

Peel and slice thin your raw potatoes. Drop in hot grease, season with salt and pepper to taste, let fry slowly until brown. Add about a gill of cream while frying and cover with lid. Turn off gas if gas stove is used, or if coal stove set on back part of stove until ready to serve.

—*John Charles Thomas, Baltimore.*
From Eat, Drink and Be Merry in Maryland

❧ YOUNGSTOWN CREAMED POTATOES

Very rich! These are wonderfully good; like no other potato dish I have ever tasted. My aunt, Mrs. Kenworthy, was famous for this dish.

5 medium potatoes, boiled with skins on the day before using
1 cup heavy cream
6 tablespoons butter
1 heaping tablespoon flour
   salt to taste

Skin and dice potatoes and put in casserole. Heat cream, add butter, salt, and flour. Stir. Pour sauce over potatoes and dot with butter. Cook at 325 degrees for about 45 minutes to an hour. Serves 4.

—*Virginia Ingles Freedland (Mrs. Samuel L.)*

❧ PATRICIAN POTATOES

4 cups mashed potatoes
3 cups cream style cottage cheese
¾ cup sour cream
1½ tablespoons grated onion
2 teaspoons salt
⅛ teaspoon pepper
   melted butter
½ cup toasted chopped almonds

Mash potatoes thoroughly, add no milk or butter. Press cottage cheese through sieve or run through blender. Mix together warm mashed potatoes and cheese. Add sour cream, onion, salt, and pepper, and mix well. Spoon into shallow buttered 2-quart casserole. Brush the surface with melted butter and top with almonds. Bake at 350 degrees for 30 minutes. Can be made the night before. Serves 8.

—*Janet Gadd Doehler (Mrs. William F.)*

❧ POTATOES ANNA

As good to eat as it is to look at.

6 cups potatoes, sliced as thinly as possible
½ teaspoon salt
   pepper to taste
½ cup butter or more

Soak thinly sliced potatoes in cold water. Drain and dry them well with towel. Season with salt and pepper. Butter a round mold or small baking dish. Arrange slices flat on the bottom of dish and up the sides. Then put in a layer of potato slices and spread them with 1 tablespoon butter over the top. Repeat the layers thus, with a final spreading of butter. Bake at 425 degrees for 40 to 50 minutes, or until potatoes are soft (test with small, sharp knife). To serve, invert on a serving dish so that potatoes slip out in a molded form, golden brown all over. Serves 12.

—*Mrs. Robert E. Atkinson*

SEED CATALOG LASAGNE

8 or 9 lasagne noodles depending on size to make 2 layers in large lasagne pan
3 large bunches (3 pounds) Swiss chard, spinach, broccoli rabe, or other substantial green
1 cup chopped onion
2 or 3 cloves garlic, minced
2 or 3 tablespoons oil
2 cups grated carrot
3 cups sliced fresh mushrooms
2 15-ounce cans tomato sauce (or, preferably, homemade)
1 cup chopped pitted olives
2 or 3 teaspoons dried oregano
3 cups ricotta or cream style cottage cheese
1 pound Monterey Jack or mozzarella, thinly sliced
1 cup grated Parmesan

Cook noodles according to package (8 to 10 minutes), drain, and set aside. Cook whatever green briefly in small amount of boiling, salted water. Drain well, chop, and set aside. Sauté onion and garlic in large skillet in oil until soft. Add carrots, mushrooms, tomato sauce, olives, and oregano, and heat thoroughly. Preheat oven to 375 degrees. Oil a large, deep casserole. Layer half each of the noodles, ricotta (or cottage cheese), drained greens, sauce mixture, and cheese slices. Repeat. Sprinkle with Parmesan. Bake 30 to 45 minutes until it bubbles. Makes 10 servings.

—*Joann W. Valliant (Mrs. James W.)*

🌿 *POTATO LATKES*

Serve with sauerbraten or pot roast, or with applesauce as a luncheon dish.

4 medium Idaho russet potatoes
¼ cup grated onion
½ teaspoon salt
¼ teaspoon freshly ground black pepper
1 egg, beaten
3 tablespoons flour
1 teaspoon baking powder
½ cup shortening

Peel potatoes, grate in blender, drain. Mix potatoes, onion, salt, pepper, egg, flour, and baking powder until very smooth. Heat the shortening in skillet. Drop the potato mixture into it by tablespoonsful. Fry until browned on both sides. Serves 4 to 6.

—*Janet Gadd Doehler (Mrs. William F.)*

🌿 *HOT POTATO LOAF*

This is an old Thompson family recipe.

8 medium potatoes (boiled, peeled, and diced)
4 green onions chopped fine (including tops)
1 small jar pimiento diced fine (drain oil off pimiento
    before using)

Add to the potato mixture a white sauce as follows: Melt ¼ cup margarine in large saucepan; slowly stir in ¼ cup flour, 1½ teaspoons salt, ¼ teaspoon pepper. When this has all blended, slowly add 1½ cups milk; stir constantly and cook until thick. Add to potatoes and mix well. Put in loaf pan and put in refrigerator at least 4 hours (better overnight). About 1 hour before serving remove from refrigerator and run a knife along sides. Invert on oven-proof platter. Bake 325 degrees for 45 minutes; sprinkle with an 8-ounce package of grated cheddar cheese and bake 15 minutes longer. Serve hot. Serves 6.

—*Stephanie Michalec Thompson (Mrs. Robert B.)*

🌿 *MARK'S POTATOES*

6 medium potatoes, cooked and grated
1½ teaspoons salt

> 1 cup sour cream
> 6 to 8 green onions, chopped
> 1 cup shredded cheddar cheese
> ½ cup butter or margarine, melted
> paprika

Combine all except butter and paprika. Spoon into 2-quart casserole. Pour butter over top and sprinkle with paprika. Bake at 400 degrees for about 25 minutes or until browned on top. Makes 6 to 8 servings.

—Diane Youngblood Freestate (Mrs. Mark M.)

❧ *TOMATO PIE*

> Pastry (recipe follows)
> 3 medium tomatoes, peeled and sliced
> ¾ cup mayonnaise
> 1 cup (4 ounces) shredded cheddar cheese
> 1 4-ounce can sliced mushrooms, drained
> 1 tablespoon chopped onion
> 1 tablespoon chopped green pepper

Arrange half of tomato slices in pastry shell. Combine remaining ingredients, stirring well. Spread half of mixture over tomato slices. Repeat with remaining tomatoes and mayonnaise mixture. Bake at 350 degrees for 30 to 35 minutes. Makes 1 9-inch pie.

Pastry

> 1¼ cups all-purpose flour
> 2 teaspoons baking powder
> ½ teaspoon salt
> ½ teaspoon dried whole basil
> ½ cup shortening
> ½ cup commercial sour cream

Combine first 4 ingredients; cut in shortening with pastry blender until mixture resembles coarse meal. Add sour cream; stir with a fork. Shape into a ball. Chill. Roll pastry to ⅛-inch thickness on a lightly floured surface. Place in a 9-inch pie plate; trim off excess pastry along edges. Fold edges under and flute. Makes 1 9-inch pastry shell. Serves 6 to 8.

—Katherine Maybeck Draper (Mrs. Frank W., III)

🍂 *BAKED PUMPKIN*

  ½ stick margarine (4 ounces)
  2 eggs, beaten
  1 cup sugar
  ½ teaspoon cinnamon
  ⅓ cup flour
  ¼ teaspoon soda
  ¼ teaspoon vanilla
  1 cup milk
  2 cups pumpkin, cooked and mashed
    pinch of salt

Melt margarine in baking dish. Mix ⅓ of the sugar and all the cinnamon and set aside. Mix other ingredients. Pour into baking dish. Sprinkle top with cinnamon and sugar mixture that was set aside. Bake at 425 degrees for 25 to 30 minutes. Can be used as a main dish or dessert. Serves 8.

—Jean Matthews LeCompte (Mrs. Neil R.)

🍂 *PINEAPPLE CASSEROLE*

  1 12-ounce can crushed pineapple
  ¼ pound soft butter
  3 eggs
  ½ cup sugar
  3 slices of bread, crusts removed and broken up
  1 teaspoon salt

Mix together and bake at 350 degrees for 30 minutes. Serves 6.

—Elizabeth Harper Collins (Mrs. Jackson R.)
—Anne Gadd Hennighausen (Mrs. Charles E.)

🍂 *GRATIN OF SCALLIONS*

  1 pound scallions
  1 cup water
  ½ cup half-and-half
  1 slice of bread
  2 tablespoons grated Parmesan cheese

¼ teaspoon salt

¼ teaspoon freshly ground black pepper

Remove the top 2 inches and any wilted leaves from the scallions. Rinse the scallions thoroughly. Place the scallions in a stainless steel saucepan with the water. Bring to a boil, cover, and cook over high heat for 5 minutes. Most of the liquid will have evaporated. Arrange the scallions in a gratin dish and pour the half-and-half over them. Break the bread slice into pieces, place the pieces in a food processor, and process them momentarily until crumbed (should yield nearly ¼ to ½ cup of crumbs). Put the bread crumbs in a small bowl and add the cheese, salt, and pepper, mixing the ingredients. Sprinkle this mixture over the scallions. Bake the dish at 450 degrees for about 10 minutes and serve.

The dish may be prepared up to final baking ahead of time and allowed to sit. If this is done, increase the baking time by an additional 5 minutes to ensure that the dish is hot. Makes 4 servings.

—*Lynda Eby Jordan (Mrs. Harold)*

SPINACH QUICHE

1 frozen deep-dish 9-inch piecrust

1 10-ounce package frozen chopped spinach (or broccoli)

8 ounces Swiss cheese, grated

2 tablespoons flour

3 beaten eggs

1 cup milk

½ teaspoon salt

⅛ teaspoon pepper

dash nutmeg

Thaw piecrust about a minute or two and prick bottom and sides with fork. Bake in a 425 degree oven for 6 to 8 minutes. Cook frozen spinach or broccoli as directed. Drain well and let cool. Combine Swiss cheese and flour. Toss and set aside.

Combine eggs, milk, salt and pepper, and nutmeg. Mix well. Stir in spinach and cheese mixture. Pour mixture into partially baked pie shell and bake at 350 degrees for 50 to 60 minutes. Cool slightly before serving. Serves 6 to 8.

—*Gail Pippin Calabrese (Mrs. Sam)*

❦ *SPINACH SOUFFLÉ I*

2 10-ounce packages frozen chopped spinach
9 eggs (or equivalent egg substitute)
1 24-ounce carton low-fat cottage cheese
3 cups shredded Monterey Jack
3 cups shredded cheddar cheese
½ cup flour
¾ teaspoon seasoned salt

Thaw and drain spinach. In large bowl, beat eggs. Stir in spinach and remaining ingredients until well blended. Pour into greased 9 × 13-inch pan and bake at 350 degrees for 1 hour or until set and top is light golden brown. Let stand 10 minutes before serving. Can be prepared ahead of time. Cover and refrigerate or freeze. Remove cover and bake as directed. Serves 12.

—Beth Strong (Mrs. Harlan)

❦ *SPINACH SOUFFLÉ II*

1 cup cooked spinach, drained and chopped
6 tablespoons butter
½ cup flour
1 teaspoon salt
¼ teaspoon pepper
2 cups light cream
3 eggs, separated
1 tablespoon lemon juice
1 teaspoon chopped onion

Melt butter over low heat; add flour, salt, and pepper; stir until well blended. Remove from heat. Gradually stir in cream and return to heat. Cook, stirring constantly, until thick and smooth. Add the egg yolks, lemon juice, and onion to the white sauce. Cool slightly. Stiffly beat the egg whites and fold into the sauce. Pour sauce over spinach. Mix well. Pour into greased baking dish or ring. Put ring in a larger pan filled with water that rises up 1 inch on side of baking dish. Bake at 325 degrees for 40 minutes in a pan of water. Serves 6 to 8.

—Isabel Atkinson Lieber (Mrs. Albert C.)

❧ *SQUASH CASSEROLE*

> *The above receipt was handed down from Aunt Pinkie, our old South Carolina Gullah nursemaid.*

6 to 12   summer squash (depending on size)
1   large onion
2 or 3   bouillon cubes (or chicken or beef broth)
    salt and pepper
    Worcestershire sauce
    sugar
    cracker crumbs
    Parmesan cheese
    butter (or margarine)
    crumbled cooked bacon (optional)
    toasted almonds (optional)

Boil squash with onion in a small amount of water with bouillon cubes. Add seasonings (enough of each to make it taste good). Mix well and pour into greased casserole. Cover heavily with cracker crumbs, sprinkle generously with Parmesan cheese, and dot with butter or margarine, and bake at 400 degrees until golden brown. Crumbled bacon and toasted almonds may be sprinkled on top before baking.

—*Elizabeth Parker Goldsborough (Mrs. John)*

❧ *PARMESAN TOMATOES*

3   medium or large tomatoes
¼   teaspoon salt
⅛   teaspoon pepper
4   teaspoons Parmesan cheese
2   tablespoons butter or margarine
    parsley sprigs

Cut tomatoes in half horizontally, place halves on small pan, cut side up. Sprinkle with salt, pepper, and Parmesan cheese. Dot with butter. Broil 3 or 4 inches from source of heat until hot through and tops are light golden brown. Garnish with parsley sprigs. Serve at once. Makes 6 servings.

—*Mary Davy Pippin (Mrs. James O., Jr.)*

The cupola was removed from the rectory and the rector says "the house is much easier to heat." (1925)

❧ ESCALLOPED TOMATOES

      1 large onion, chopped fine
     ¼ cup butter
    1¼ cups dry bread cubes
     ½ cup brown sugar (packed tight)
      1 1-pound, 3-ounce can tomatoes
      1 teaspoon salt
     ⅛ teaspoon pepper

Sauté onion in butter, using frying pan. Add bread cubes and sugar. Cook slowly. Stir in tomatoes and seasoning. Place mixture in buttered shallow pan and bake for 45 minutes or more at 375 degrees. Serves 8 to 10.

—*Frances Perry Horton*

❧ BAKED TOMATOES I

      1 pint tomatoes, cut up
     ½ stick margarine, melted
     ⅔ cup sugar
      4 regular slices bread, shredded
      1 rounded tablespoon flour
     ½ rounded teaspoon cinnamon
      1 teaspoon vanilla
         dash of nutmeg
     ½ teaspoon salt

Mix all ingredients well. Pour into greased casserole and bake at 350 degrees for about 45 minutes. Serves 6.

—*Jean Matthews LeCompte (Mrs. Neil R.)*

🌿 BAKED TOMATOES II

1 1-pound, 13-ounce can tomatoes
brown sugar
6 slices bread, buttered
salt and pepper

Drain most of the juice from can of tomatoes and place in a 9 × 13-inch baking dish. Season with salt, pepper, and brown sugar.

Place buttered bread slices on tomatoes; then spread with more brown sugar. Bake slowly for 2 hours at 225 degrees. Makes 8 to 10 servings.

—Katherine Wilson Barton (Mrs. W. Edward)

🌿 ZUCCHINI SCALLOP

½ stick butter or margarine
¼ cup chopped onion
4 medium zucchini (about 1 pound)
2 firm tomatoes
2 teaspoons sugar
¼ teaspoon oregano
1 teaspoon salt
⅛ teaspoon pepper
2 tablespoons grated Parmesan cheese

Melt 2 tablespoons butter or margarine in shallow 6-cup baking dish. Sprinkle onion over melted butter. Wash, trim ends and halve zucchini, then quarter each piece lengthwise to make 4 sticks. Wash, cut out stems, and slice each tomato into 8 wedges. Arrange zucchini and tomatoes over onion in baking dish.

Combine sugar, oregano, salt, and pepper in cup; sprinkle over vegetables; dot with remaining butter or margarine; cover.

Bake at 350 degrees for 1 hour, or until zucchini is tender. Sprinkle with Parmesan cheese before serving. Makes 4 servings.

—Margaret Gadd Ashley (Mrs. John M.)

🐝 *ZUCCHINI MADRONE*

        6 small unpeeled zucchini
        2 tablespoons butter
        1 tablespoon minced onion
        2 tablespoons lemon juice
        ½ cup heavy cream
1 to 1½ teaspoons salt
           pepper
        ¼ teaspoon oregano

Cut zucchini lengthwise in thin slices, about 2 inches long, then cut the sliced zucchini in julienne strips. Place squash in saucepan with very little water, butter, onion, lemon juice. Cook over low heat until tender but not soft. Drain thoroughly and add cream and seasoning. Heat, do not let boil. Serve very hot. Serves 6.

—*Janet Gadd Doehler (Mrs. William F.)*

The flag of the Episcopal church is red, white, and blue. A red cross on a white field (the St. George's cross) signifies its descent from the Church of England. The nine white crosses recall the nine original American dioceses. The crosses are arranged on a blue field in the form of a St. Andrew's cross signifying the fact that the first bishop in America was consecrated in Scotland.

🐝 *NO FEAR HOLLANDAISE*

1½ sticks cold, unsalted butter, cut into cubes
   3 large egg yolks, well beaten with 4 teaspoons fresh lemon juice
       dash of salt
       pinch of cayenne

Prepare a double boiler. Add just enough water so the top pan does not touch the water in the lower pan. Heat the water, but do *not* boil or simmer! Put ½ stick butter in the double boiler and melt. Stir in the egg yolks, beating constantly with a wire whisk. Add another ½ stick of butter and continue whisking (Be sure water does not boil!) and cooking until mixture begins to thicken. Add the last ½ stick of the butter, and whisk and cook until the emulsion has thickened. (Don't worry if the mixture isn't as thick as you would like. It will thicken as it cools.) Remove from the hot water and the heat. Stir in the salt and cayenne. Cover until ready to serve. *Caution:* Do not try to reheat! If the mixture should curdle, add 1½ tablespoons boiling water, whisking constantly to rebuild emulsion. Makes approximately 1 cup.

—Ann McQueeny North (Mrs. Gregory J.)

❧ WORLD'S EASIEST HOLLANDAISE

- 2 egg yolks
- 3 tablespoons fresh lemon juice
- 1 stick *frozen* butter

Beat yolks, add lemon juice, and frozen butter in small saucepan. Cook over the lowest heat while stirring with a wooden spoon. Low heat and slow cooking is the secret. Serve hot or at room temperature. If sauce separates, heat while slowly stirring in 1 teaspoon water. Makes 1 cup.

—Janie Eby Ashley (Mrs. Sydney G.)

❧ SAUCE MOUSSELINE

This is especially good with asparagus.

- 4 tablespoons vinegar
- pinch salt
- white pepper
- 4 egg yolks
- 2 pieces butter (size of walnut)
- 1¼ cups butter
- a little cold water
- juice of ½ lemon
- salt and pepper
- 6 tablespoons cream, beaten until stiff

Combine first 5 ingredients and cook slowly, stirring, until mixture thickens slightly. Remove from fire, place in double boiler and slowly add butter, cold water, and lemon juice. When thick, season with salt and pepper. Remove from fire and stir in whipped cream. Serve warm. Makes 2 cups.

—Isabel Atkinson Lieber (Mrs. Albert C.)

SALADS AND DRESSINGS

Blessed art thou, O Lord God, Ruler of the Universe.
From thy bounty thou providest for our needs.

❦ *AVOCADO SALAD RING*

    1 tablespoon unflavored gelatin
    ¼ cup cold water
    1 cup boiling water
    1 tablespoon mustard
    1 tablespoon lemon juice
    1 teaspoon sugar
    1 cup mashed avocado (generous portion)
    1 tablespoon mustard
    1 tablespoon lemon juice
    ½ cup heavy sour cream
    ½ cup mayonnaise
       salt and pepper (generous amount)
       few grains cayenne
       salad greens
   1½ cups peeled cut tomatoes
   1½ cups chopped watercress

Soak gelatin in cold water, add boiling water, mustard, lemon juice, and sugar. Stir until well blended. Chill mixture in refrigerator until slightly thickened. Sieve the mashed avocado, using a fine sieve. While sieving, add the mustard and lemon juice alternately with the sour cream and mayonnaise. Add the seasonings. Add the gelatin mixture and blend well. Pour into an oiled ring mold or individual molds. Chill until firm (2 to 3 hours). When ready to serve, turn out on well-chilled plate that has been covered with watercress or other salad greens. Fill center with tomatoes mixed with chopped watercress. Serves 4 to 6.

—*Eleanor Williams Miles (Mrs. Clarence W.)*

❦ *MOLDED AVOCADO SALAD*

    2 envelopes unflavored gelatin
  1¼ cups cold canned consommé or bouillon
       (nonfat, undiluted)
    ⅓ cup lime or lemon juice
    ½ teaspoon salt
    1 teaspoon minced onion
    3 cups sieved avocado
    ¾ cup mayonnaise

Sprinkle the gelatin on cold consommé to soften. Bring to a boil and dissolve. Add lemon juice and salt and other seasoning of your choice. Cool. When the consistency of egg white, add the avocado. *Comment:* 1 cup avocado may be diced. Makes 10 to 12 servings.

—*Ruth Branner Gadd (Mrs. A. Sydney, Jr.)*

🎋 BING CHERRY MOLDED SALAD

　1　4-ounce can black cherries, drained, reserving juice
　1　3-ounce package black cherry gelatin
　1　teaspoon lemon juice
　1　4-ounce can crushed pineapple
　　　salt
　　　small cream cheese balls rolled in ground nuts

Use the juice of the cherries to dissolve the gelatin. Add lemon juice and pineapple. Chill. Add pinch of salt and place in mold. Garnish with cream cheese balls. Serve on lettuce. Makes 6 servings.

—*Ruth Branner Gadd (Mrs. A. Sydney, Jr.)*

🎋 PEPPER CABBAGE (*Peffer Graut*)

This is a Pennsylvania Dutch recipe.

　1　head cabbage, grated
　1　small stalk celery, diced
　1　red pepper, sliced
　1　green pepper, sliced
　1　onion, sliced
　¼　teaspoon mustard seed
　¼　teaspoon celery seed
　3　tablespoons salt
　1　cup water
　¼　cup sugar
　2　tablespoons vinegar

Mix vegetables and seasonings thoroughly. Add water, sugar, and vinegar. Chill and serve.

—*G. Myron Latshaw*

🌿 *BROCCOLI SALAD*

  3 bunches fresh broccoli (use stalks: peel and chop)
  ½ cup dark raisins
  ½ pound bacon—crisp and crumble (optional)
  1 small red onion, chopped
  ¾ cup mayonnaise
  3 tablespoons vinegar
  ¼ cup sugar

Toss broccoli, raisins, and chopped onion in a large salad bowl. Mix remaining ingredients and pour over salad; mix well. Cover and refrigerate for several hours. This salad is better the next day. Add bacon just before serving or omit. Serves 8 to 10.

—*Roberta Barton Seger (Mrs. George)*

🌿 *WARM CHICORY SALAD WITH CROUTONS AND LARDONS*

  1 large head chicory or curly endive or young dandelion greens
  1 cup ½-inch cubes of slab bacon
  1 cup ½-inch cubes country bread, crusts removed
   salt and pepper
   mustard dressing (see below)

Wash and spin-dry head of chicory or curly endive or young dandelion greens. Break leaves into two or three pieces. Allow one good handful per person. Put the greens in the serving bowl and leave at room temperature. Render cubed slab bacon (rind removed) till crispy but not dry, reserving ¼ cup drippings. Toss a generous cup of country bread cubes in three or four tablespoons of the rendered bacon fat, season them with salt and pepper, and bake on a tray in the oven or toaster oven till lightly browned.

  Take a small, heavy-bottomed skillet and toss the lardons (rendered bacon) till pan is good and hot. Throw in the croutons and then the dressing, toss for exactly 2 seconds and pour the whole thing over the greens. Toss the salad thoroughly. If the pan and contents were hot enough, the salad will be warm. Don't overcook the dressing or the mustard will lose it's kick and make the whole thing oily.

One can add roast garlic cloves to this salad and it can be topped with Roquefort cheese or, more traditionally, a soft poached egg. Serves 4.

Mustard Dressing

1 shallot, finely diced not chopped
1 tablespoon real Dijon mustard (if possible, Bornier brand)
2 tablespoons red wine vinegar
5 tablespoons extra virgin olive oil
  salt and freshly ground pepper to taste (season very well)

Mix all ingredients except oil, then whisk in oil gradually.

—*Stephen Kirk Lyle*

Stephen Kirk Lyle is the eldest son of Cecily Lyle. He was born in France and did a standard apprenticeship there before coming to America to cook professionally. He is the executive chef of The Odeon, a restaurant on West Broadway, New York City.

CAESAR SALAD

4 anchovies (packed in oil)
2 or 3 cloves garlic
  ground black pepper to taste
  dash of Tabasco
  dash of Worcestershire sauce
1 teaspoon dry mustard
¼ cup red wine vinegar
½ to ⅔ cup olive oil
4 eggs, coddled (Immerse room temperature eggs in boiling water for 1 minute.)
2 heads romaine
  Parmesan cheese
1 cup croutons (prepared with garlic and butter)

Blend anchovies, garlic, seasonings, vinegar, and olive oil in blender. Add coddled eggs, one at a time, and continue blending until creamy. Cut romaine lettuce in 1½-inch lengths, put in salad bowl, add dressing, and toss greens in dressing. Add ½ cup Parmesan cheese and croutons. Makes 4 servings.

—*Elizabeth Lea Ferguson (Mrs. Spencer)*

🍃 COLE SLAW SOUFFLÉ

    1 3-ounce package lemon gelatin

    1 cup hot water

    ½ cup mayonnaise

    ½ cup cold water (or less)

    2 tablespoons vinegar

    ½ teaspoon salt (or less)

2 to 4 tablespoons chopped green peppers

    1 tablespoon diced onion

  1½ cups chopped cabbage

    ½ cup diced celery

    ½ cup chopped radishes (optional)

Dissolve gelatin in hot water. Blend in mayonnaise, cold water, vinegar, and salt. Chill until partly set. Place bowl with gelatin mixture in bowl of ice water and beat until fluffy. Add vegetables and put in ring mold or individual molds. Makes 8 servings.

—Anne Gadd Hennighausen (Mrs. Charles E.)

🍃 CRANBERRY SALAD

    1 envelope unflavored gelatin

    ¼ cup cold water

    ½ cup hot water

    1 1-pound can cranberry sauce (or 2 cups home-cooked, strained cranberries)

    ¼ teaspoon salt

    ½ cup celery, chopped

    ½ cup English walnuts, chopped

Soften gelatin in cold water; dissolve in hot water. Pour over cranberry sauce and beat with rotary beater. Chill until thickened; then add salt, celery, and nuts. Mold and chill. Serves 4 to 6.

—Nellie Brown Whiteley (Mrs. J. Harman)

❧ FROZEN FRUIT SALAD

1 cup shredded pineapple
2 tablespoons powdered sugar
1 cup maraschino cherries, cut in halves
8 marshmallows, cut in halves
2 3-ounce packages cream cheese
1 cup mayonnaise
1 cup heavy cream, whipped

Drain pineapple, add sugar, cherries, and marshmallows. Soften cream cheese, add mayonnaise, cream, and fruit. Freeze in refrigerator tray.

—*Ruth Newell (Mrs. Robert)*
—*Dorothy Keith Perkins (Mrs. Louis H.)*

❧ APRICOT CHICKEN SALAD

3 pounds skinless, boneless chicken breasts
1 cup cream
½ cup sour cream
½ cup mayonnaise
2 tablespoons dry vermouth
1 tablespoon dried tarragon
½ cup walnuts, lightly toasted
1 cup celery, sliced on a diagonal
1 cup dried apricots, slivered
1 small Vidalia onion, minced
   salt and pepper to taste

Bake chicken breasts in pyrex baking dish with cream at 350 degrees for approximately 25 minutes, or until done. Drain well. (You do not want the cooking cream in the salad.) Cool and cut into bite-sized pieces. Mix sour cream, mayonnaise, dry vermouth, and tarragon in a salad bowl. Add remaining ingredients. Stir gently until combined. Chill for at least three hours. Serves 6.

—*Miss Sydney Gadd Doehler*

✻ SLAW AND DRESSING

½ cup vinegar
½ cup water
1 egg
¾ cup sugar
1 tablespoon flour
1 teaspoon salt (scant)
1 teaspoon dry mustard
⅛ teaspoon red pepper
1 cabbage, cut up fine
    carrots, grated
    a little chopped onion
    celery, finely cut

Combine vinegar and water and heat. Beat egg and add it and sugar. Make a paste of flour, salt, pepper, and mustard, and, when smooth, add to sugar mixture. Pour the hot vinegar and water over egg mixture. Put back on stove and cook until thickened. Cool. Combine cut-up vegetables and add dressing just before serving. Serves 8.

—*Mary Foreman Brown (Mrs. W. Purnell)*

✻ MOLDED CHICKEN SALAD

1½ cups chicken broth
1 teaspoon minced fresh thyme (or ½ teaspoon dried)
1 teaspoon minced fresh rosemary (or ½ teaspoon dried)
2 envelopes unflavored gelatin
1 pound cottage cheese
1 pint sour cream (or 8 ounces cream cheese, softened)
2 tablespoons lemon juice
1 teaspoon lemon zest
½ teaspoon grated onion
2 tablespoons minced fresh parsley
3 cups cooked chicken, cut in large pieces
½ cup toasted almonds, slivered
2 cups seedless grapes, halved
½ cup ripe olives, sliced
    salad greens

In saucepan, sprinkle broth with thyme and rosemary. Simmer a few minutes to flavor with herbs. Add gelatin, stirring until dissolved. Do not boil. Process cottage cheese in food processor until smooth. Add sour cream, lemon juice, zest, and seasonings to broth mixture. Cool. Chill until consistency of unbeaten egg white. Gently fold in solids. Pour into 1½-quart mold. Chill until firm. Unmold onto a bed of bright greens. Serve with horseradish mayonnaise or curried chutney dressing.

—Committee

POTATO SALAD DRESSING

    2 eggs
    ½ cup sugar
    1 tablespoon flour
    1 teaspoon salt
    ½ teaspoon celery salt
    ½ cup water
    ½ cup vinegar
    1 tablespoon French's prepared mustard
    2 tablespoons butter
      dash cayenne

Beat eggs until light. Mix sugar, flour, salt, celery salt; add water and vinegar. Cook over low heat until it bubbles and thickens. Remove from fire. Add the mustard, butter, and cayenne. Makes 1 cup.

—Mabel Walls Valliant (Mrs. T. Rigby)

PEAR SALAD

    1 3-ounce package lime gelatin
    1 cup boiling water
    1 15½-ounce can pears, drained
    1 3-ounce package cream cheese, softened

Dissolve gelatin with boiling water and 1 cup pear juice. When cool, add softened cream cheese and blend, using blender or mixer. Add pears, diced or cut in pieces. Pour into a mold; if desired,maraschino cherries may be added. One can use any fruit, for example, pineapple or peaches.

—Dorothy Keith Perkins (Mrs. Louis H.)

❧ *QUEEN ELIZABETH CHICKEN SALAD*

This was served to Queen Elizabeth II of England at a bicentennial celebration in 1976 under the Rotunda at the University of Virginia.

- ¾ cup mayonnaise
- 1 teaspoon curry powder
- 2 teaspoons soy sauce
- 2 teaspoons lemon juice
- 2 cups cooked chicken, cut in large pieces
- ¼ cup water chestnuts, sliced
- ½ pound green grapes, halved
- ½ cup celery, chopped
- ½ cup slivered almonds, toasted
- 1 8-ounce can pineapple chunks, drained
  mixed greens

Combine mayonnaise, curry powder, soy sauce, and lemon juice. Mix dressing with salad ingredients. Chill well and serve on crisp, mixed greens. Serves 4 to 6.

—Committee

❧ *CUCUMBER-LIME MOUSSE*

Nice accompaniment to chicken, seafood, or ham.

- 1 3-ounce package lime gelatin
- 1 cup hot water
- 2 large cucumbers
- 1 tablespoon lime juice
- 1 teaspoon Worcestershire sauce
- 1 teaspoon salt
- ¾ teaspoon pepper
- ¼ teaspoon liquid hot pepper sauce
- 1½ tablespoons horseradish
- ½ cup mayonnaise
- 2 cups sour cream

Dissolve gelatin in hot water and chill until consistency of unbeaten egg white. Meanwhile, peel cucumbers, discard seeds, chop fine (to make about 1½ cups). Sprinkle with lime juice. Let stand 5 minutes. Drain thoroughly, add remaining ingredients and blend well. Fold into chilled gelatin. Turn into 5-cup mold. Chill until set. Serves 6 to 8.

—*Janet Gadd Doehler (Mrs. William F.)*

In Epiphany, green is the symbol of growth and development.

❧ CUCUMBERS IN SOUR CREAM

      2 large cucumbers, peeled and very thinly sliced
   1½ teaspoons salt
      1 cup sour cream
      2 tablespoons lemon juice (fresh or frozen)
      1 tablespoon finely chopped onion
      2 tablespoons chopped dill pickle
     ¼ teaspoon sugar
          dash pepper
      3 radishes, thinly sliced
          lettuce
   1½ teaspoons finely chopped parsley

Lightly toss cucumbers with 1 teaspoon salt; refrigerate until well chilled. Meanwhile, combine sour cream, lemon juice, ½ teaspoon salt, onion, dill pickle, sugar, pepper, and radishes. Reserve ½ cup sour cream mixture for garnish. Toss cucumbers with remaining sour cream mixture. Refrigerate. To serve: Arrange well-chilled cucumbers in sour cream on a bed of lettuce; garnish with reserved sour cream mixture. Sprinkle with chopped parsley. Makes 4 to 6 servings.

—*Isa Louise Blaney (Mrs. Arthur J.)*

❦ SUMMER SALAD

2 packages unflavored gelatin
1 cup tomato juice
1 10-ounce can tomato soup
3 3-ounce packages cream cheese
1 cup mayonnaise (not salad dressing)
dash of Tabasco sauce
1 cup mixed grated carrot, cabbage, radishes,
    onion, diced celery

Soften the gelatin in the tomato juice. Heat tomato soup to a boil and dissolve gelatin in it. Beat cream cheese with egg beater; add other ingredients. Put in oiled 4-cup mold and chill. Makes 8 servings.

—Barbara Porter (Mrs. John)

❦ EASTERN SHORE SALAD

celery
shrimp
crabmeat
olives, green and ripe
capers
cress
hard-boiled eggs
mayonnaise

Mix crab with mayonnaise and place in mound on center of large plate covered with lettuce, circle shrimp around it. Mix a few chopped capers and chopped ripe olives with a little mayonnaise and place dab in center of each shrimp.

Garnish with quartered hard-boiled eggs which have been dusted with paprika, celery, cress, and olives.

Committe note: Allow ½ cup of shrimp (or seafood) and crab per person.

—From Eat, Drink and Be Merry in Maryland

❧ *HORSERADISH MOUSSE*

Delicious with roast beef. This can be halved easily.

6 ounces lemon gelatin
1 cup water
¼ teaspoon salt
2 tablespoons vinegar
1 cup horseradish, drained
¼ teaspoon Tabasco
2 cups heavy cream

Dissolve lemon gelatin in hot water. Add salt and vinegar. Stir in horseradish and Tabasco. Whip cream and fold into mixture. Pour into a 4-cup mold and refrigerate until served. Serves 4 to 6.

—Anne Gadd Hennighausen (Mrs. Charles E.)

❧ *HERBED TOMATOES*

Serve with potato salad and cold cuts.

6 ripe tomatoes
¼ teaspoon coarse black pepper
¼ cup finely snipped parsley
¼ cup snipped chives or onion
1 teaspoon salt
few leaves fresh thyme or marjoram (½ teaspoon of
dried herbs)
⅔ cup salad oil
¼ cup tarragon vinegar

Peel tomatoes. Place in bowl; sprinkle with seasonings and herbs. Combine oil and vinegar and pour over tomatoes. Cover and chill an hour or so, occasionally spooning the dressing over tomatoes. At serving time, drain off dressing to pass in bowl; arrange tomatoes in serving dish. Snip additional parsley or chives and sprinkle over tomatoes. Makes 6 servings.

—Margaret Gadd Ashley (Mrs. John M.)

❧ HORSERADISH RING MOLD

Serve on lettuce leaves filled with chicken salad.

1 package lemon gelatin and 1 package lime gelatin
    or 2 packages lemon-lime gelatin
1 cup chopped pecans
¾ 12-ounce carton small-curd cottage cheese
4 heaping teaspoons horseradish
1 cup mayonnaise
  salt to taste

Mix gelatin as directed on package and let set slightly; then fold in rest of ingredients and chill in a mold until firm. Serves 10.

—*Julia Browne Sause (Mrs. John W., Jr.)*

❧ LIME SALAD

1 3-ounce package lime gelatin
1 cup hot water
1 small can crushed pineapple
1 cup marshmallows, cut in small pieces
1 cup medium-sharp grated cheese
  pinch of salt
½ cup whipped cream
⅓ cup mayonnaise
  lettuce

Dissolve gelatin in hot water. Cool and add other ingredients, folding in the whipped cream and mayonnaise last. Pour into mold and chill. Serve on lettuce cups. Makes 8 servings.

—*Mildred Lee Thompson Murray (Mrs. Gerald)*

❧ MOLDED BEET SALAD

2 envelopes unflavored gelatin
½ cup cold water
2 cups boiling liquid (use drained beet juice and water)
3 tablespoons vinegar
⅓ cup sugar
1 teaspoon salt

1⅔ cups (1 16-ounce can) chopped beets, drained, juice reserved
⅓ cup diced celery
2 teaspoons prepared horseradish

Soften gelatin in cold water, letting it stand 5 minutes. Then stir into boiling water. When dissolved, add vinegar, sugar, and salt. Chill until it begins to thicken. Then add beets, celery, and horseradish. Makes 8 servings.

—*Julia G. Bishop Long (Mrs. H. Lawrence)*

MOLDED TUNA SALAD

1 tablespoon (1 envelope) unflavored gelatin
¼ cup cold water
¾ cup hot water
2 tablespoons lemon juice
1 teaspoon prepared mustard
¼ teaspoon salt (if tuna is salted be careful)
¼ teaspoon paprika
2 7-ounce cans flaked tuna fish
1 cup finely chopped celery
½ cup heavy cream, whipped
chopped olives or pimiento strips

Soften gelatin in cold water, dissolve in hot water. Add lemon juice and seasonings. Chill until partially set. Add tuna and celery. Fold in cream. Add a few chopped olives or strips of pimiento in bottom of molds. Chill in individual molds. May be served with cucumber dressing. Serves 6.

Cucumber Dressing

1 cup of mayonnaise or ½ cup mayonnaise and ½ cup sour cream
3 tablespoons lemon juice
¼ teaspoon Tabasco sauce
½ teaspoon dillweed (optional)
1 cucumber, finely chopped

Blend all ingredients except cucumber. Drain the cucumber and combine with mayonnaise mixture. Chill for several hours before serving. Makes 1½ cups.

—*Susie Harris Jones (Mrs. Oliver C.)*

MOLDED VEGETABLE SALAD

        1   3-ounce package lemon gelatin
        1   cup hot water
       ½   cup mayonnaise
       ½   cup cold water
        2   tablespoons vinegar
       ¼   teaspoon salt
     1½   cups shredded cabbage
       ½   cup diced radishes
       ½   cup diced celery
  2 to 4   tablespoons diced green pepper
        1   tablespoon grated onion

Dissolve gelatin in hot water. Blend in mayonnaise, cold water, vinegar, and salt. Chill until partially set; then beat until fluffy. Add vegetables and put in oiled mold. Serves 8 to 10.

—*Julia G. Bishop Long (Mrs. H. Lawrence)*

CORNED BEEF MOLD

        1   tablespoon unflavored gelatin
       ½   cup water
     1½   cups tomato juice or V-8
        1   12-ounce can corned beef, shredded
        3   chopped hard-cooked eggs
        2   tablespoons chopped onion
       ½   cup chopped celery
       ½   cup chopped cucumber
        1   cup mayonnaise or light mayonnaise
        1   tablespoon horseradish (generous)

Dissolve gelatin in water. Heat tomato juice, then add gelatin. Add rest of ingredients. Makes 10 servings. *Comment:* I prefer V-8 and double horseradish.

—*Bette Blackwood (Mrs. Terence)*

WILD RICE SALAD

       ½   cup oil
       ¼   cup lemon juice

  1 teaspoon sugar

  1 teaspoon salt

 ¼ teaspoon pepper

 ⅛ teaspoon tarragon

  1 6-ounce box Uncle Ben's Original Long Grain and Wild Rice

 ¼ cup diced green pepper

 ¼ cup diced green onion

     pineapple cubes, fresh or canned

 ½ cup whole or slivered almonds

Combine for dressing the oil, lemon juice, and seasonings. Prepare rice according to package directions. Add vegetables and toss with dressing. May be prepared ahead except adding pineapple and almonds. Serves 6.

—*Gail Pippin Calabrese (Mrs. Sam)*

✺ RELISH SALAD

Excellent with most any kind of meal and very nice for a Christmas salad.

  1 3-ounce package lemon gelatin

  2 cups water, less 2 tablespoons

  2 teaspoons vinegar

  2 cups chopped celery

  1 cup chopped pimiento

  1 cup black walnut meats (no substitutes)

  2 teaspoons relish (plain or India)

     pinch of salt

     lettuce

     mayonnaise

     olives or paprika

Dissolve gelatin in 1 cup hot water; add the cold water and chill for a while. Add rest of ingredients, mixing well. Pour into individual molds or a ring mold. Serve on lettuce with mayonnaise. Garnish with olives or paprika. Serves 12.

—*Ruth Branner Gadd (Mrs. A. Sydney, Jr.)*

SEVEN LAYER SALAD

½ head of lettuce, torn
½ bag spinach, stemmed and torn
1 head cauliflower, broken into florets
1 pepper, chopped
1 10-ounce box frozen peas, defrosted and patted dry
5 stalks celery, chopped
1 red onion, sliced
1 pound bacon, cooked crisp and broken
2 cups mayonnaise
⅔ cup Parmesan cheese
¼ cup sugar

Layer vegetables and bacon in order given. Mix mayonnaise, Parmesan, and sugar, and spread over top of salad, sealing to edge of bowl. Refrigerate 24 hours. Serves 8 to 10.

—*Betty Gannon Woodford (Mrs. Walter E., Jr.)*

SUMMER WHITE BEAN SALAD

1 pound dried beans (cannellini or Navy beans)
½ cup fresh sage leaves (or use less dried)
½ cup good grade extra virgin olive oil
   juice of 1 lemon
1 onion, finely chopped
   ground pepper to taste
1 nice fresh bunch parsley, chopped fine

Soak beans overnight and drain. Cover with fresh water, add sage and 1 tablespoon olive oil. Simmer until tender but not mushy. (They should be beans still, not mush). Drain; add olive oil, lemon juice, onion, pepper, and parsley. Refrigerate. Best done a day ahead. Makes 8 to 10 servings.

—*Nina DuPont Curran (Mrs. Edward A.)*

CURRY SHRIMP SALAD

1¾ pounds cooked, cleaned shrimp
⅓ cup mayonnaise
2 teaspoons lemon juice

⅛ teaspoon salt

⅛ teaspoon pepper

¼ teaspoon curry powder

¼ cup chopped celery

   lettuce

Cut shrimp into halves or thirds. In a bowl, combine the mayonnaise, lemon juice, salt, pepper, and curry powder. Blend well and add the celery and shrimp. Cover and refrigerate until served. Arrange on lettuce leaves. Serves 6.

—Henrietta Holton Dallam (Mrs. John)

❧ TOMATO ASPIC

2 envelopes unflavored gelatin

3 cups tomato juice

2 teaspoons lemon juice

1 teaspoon brown sugar

2 tablespoons celery, chopped

2 tablespoons onion, chopped

½ teaspoon salt

2 whole cloves

1 bay leaf

Sprinkle gelatin on ½ cup tomato juice. Simmer remaining juice and other ingredients 5 minutes. Strain. Stir in softened gelatin until dissolved; chill until as thick as unbeaten egg white. Fold in any chopped vegetable additions you desire. Pour into 4- to 6-cup mold. Chill until firm. Unmold. Makes 5 cups (3 cups liquids, 2 cups solids).

Committee Note: We recommend using Friel's tomato juice, which is canned locally in Queenstown, Maryland.

—Committee

The first American Episcopal bishop, Dr. Samuel Seabury (1729-1796), had to be ordained in Scotland because he would not pledge allegiance to the king of England.

🌿 STRING AND KIDNEY BEAN SALAD OR PICKLE

⅓ cup sugar
⅓ cup salad oil
⅓ cup vinegar
1 1-pound can green string beans
1 1-pound can yellow string beans
1 1-pound can kidney beans
1 small grated onion
small amount grated green pepper

Combine sugar, oil, and vinegar until dissolved. Marinate the beans, onion, and green pepper overnight in refrigerator in covered container. Serves 12 to 14.

—*Ruth Willis Draper (Mrs. Frank W., Jr.)*

🌿 HONEY SALAD DRESSING

This dressing gets its name from the honeylike consistency.

1 teaspoon celery seed
1 teaspoon paprika
½ teaspoon salt
1 teaspoon dry mustard
½ cup sugar
¼ teaspoon onion juice
¼ cup vinegar
1 cup salad oil

Place all ingredients in jar together and shake, or mix in a bowl with an eggbeater.

—*Mrs. John Morrison*

🌿 TACO SALAD

Sounds awful, looks strange, tastes great! Men love it with beer as a summer meal. It can be made in large quantities and tossed in plastic bags. The ideal tailgate lunch at football games, horse shows, etc.

1 pound ground round, browned and seasoned
1 15-ounce can kidney beans, drained

1 Bermuda onion, diced
4 tomatoes, diced
1 avocado, diced at serving time
1 head iceberg lettuce, torn
1 5¼-ounce bag taco flavor tortilla chips, crushed
8 ounces sharp cheddar cheese, grated
1 7-ounce package Italian salad dressing mix, prepared
   according to directions, or your own
 salt and pepper

Combine meat and beans; refrigerate (in plastic bag). Combine onion, tomatoes, lettuce; refrigerate (in plastic bag). To assemble, put all ingredients in bowl and toss with salad dressing. Season with salt and pepper. Can be transported in plastic bags in cooler and then cooler can be used as salad bowl for mixing at last moment. Serves 10 to 12.

—*Katherine Grove Sailer (Mrs. John R.)*

❧ ZITI SALAD

2 tomatoes, cored and chopped into ¼-inch cubes
2 small green peppers, chopped into ¼-inch cubes
3 tablespoons chopped fresh dill (or 1 tablespoon dried)
1 red onion, chopped into ¼-inch cubes
6 sweet pickles, chopped
1 large shallot or small green onion, minced
1 pound cut ziti, cooked (or any pasta)
¼ cup milk
1½ cups mayonnaise
½ cup sour cream
1 packet beef bouillon (MGT or Knorr's only)
 salt and pepper
 dash wine vinegar
1 tablespoon pickle juice

Reserve 1 tablespoon of each vegetable for garnish. Mix ziti with milk. Mix mayonnaise and sour cream together with powdered bouillon, salt, pepper, wine vinegar, and pickle juice. Add vegetables and ziti. Garnish with reserved vegetables. Makes 8 servings.

—*Jane Corey (Mrs. R. Reece)*

🍃 SPICY ASPIC

 1 3-ounce package lemon gelatin
1¼ cups hot water
 1 8-ounce can tomato sauce
1½ tablespoons vinegar
 ½ teaspoon salt
    dash of pepper
    dash of onion juice
    dash of celery salt
 1 teaspoon to 1 tablespoon horseradish powder to taste

Dissolve lemon gelatin in hot water. Add tomato sauce, vinegar, and seasonings, then horseradish. Blend well. Chill until firm in 4 to 6 individual molds. Makes 4 to 6 servings.

—Anne Stoney Cantler (Mrs. James E.)

The Rev. James Cantler was rector at St. Paul's Parish 1965-1972.

🍃 SEAFOOD PASTA SALAD

This salad tastes best when eaten in view of the water, either from a deck, porch, or beach. Some crusty French bread and a good bottle of wine are all you need for a happy summer menu.

 1 pound medium shrimp, shelled and deveined
 1 pound bay scallops, rinsed
 ½ pound pasta shells or twists (spinach, tomato,
      or mixed flavors)
 2 tablespoons chicken broth
 2 tablespoons red wine vinegar
 1 cup fresh peas (or frozen, defrosted)
 ½ cup diced sweet pepper (green, red, yellow, or mixed)
 ½ cup red onion, diced
 1 cup cherry tomatoes
 ¾ cup black olives
 ½ cup celery, cut on diagonal
    artichokes, quartered (optional)
 4 tablespoons pesto sauce (see below)
 4 tablespoons lite sour cream

1 cup lite mayonnaise
2 tablespoons fresh parsley
  salt and pepper

Bring a large saucepan of salted water to a boil. Drop in the shrimp and scallops for one minute. Remove and drain. In another pot of boiling salted water, drop in the pasta. Return water to boil and cook pasta until just tender. Do not overcook or pasta will break up in salad. Place in large bowl. Mix chicken broth and red wine vinegar. Add to pasta and mix well. Add peas. Add sweet pepper, onion, tomatoes, black olives, celery, and artichokes. Toss again gently. Mix pesto sauce, sour cream, mayonnaise, chopped parsley, and salt and pepper to taste. When blended, mix into salad and refrigerate. Fresh tomato wedges may be used to garnish this salad rather than adding cherry tomatoes into the mixture. Makes 12 to 14 servings.

Pesto Sauce

3 cups sweet basil leaves, packed (Italian large leaf)
2 large cloves garlic, minced
½ cup English walnuts
¾ cup fresh parsley, packed
¾ cup Parmesan cheese
½ cup olive oil
¼ cup melted butter
  salt and pepper to taste

Process first 5 ingredients in processor or blender. Add olive oil and butter slowly in thin stream to sauce until smooth. Pack unused pesto in small jars, film top with olive oil and refrigerate or freeze.

—Committee

FRUIT SALAD DRESSING

Delicious over greens or fruit salad.

2 tablespoons undiluted frozen limeade concentrate
1 cup sour cream

Stir concentrate into sour cream. Makes just over 1 cup.

—Miriam P. Chambers

CLUB DRESSING

¾ cup sugar
¾ cup vinegar
1 small onion, grated
1 teaspoon celery seed
1 teaspoon Colman's mustard
1 teaspoon paprika
1 teaspoon salt
½ cup catsup
1 teaspoon Worcestershire sauce
1 cup salad oil

Boil sugar and vinegar together for 4 minutes. Add other ingredients, except oil, and beat with rotary beater. Add oil very slowly. Keeps well in the refrigerator. Makes 2 cups.

—*Elizabeth Harper Collins (Mrs. Jackson R.)*

SALAD DRESSING

½ tablespoon Dijon style mustard
3 tablespoons balsamic vinegar
salt and black pepper
1 clove garlic, crushed
1 cup olive oil, best quality

Whisk mustard and vinegar together in bowl; season with salt and pepper to taste. Add garlic. Dribble olive oil into the bowl, whisking all the time. Cover and let stand at room temperature until used. Whisk again well before using. Refrigerate covered if not used at time of preparation. Makes 1¼ cups.

—*Murray Bradley Peck (Mrs. Charles R.)*

The balance in the St. Paul's Parish operating budget at one point during the period of the Great Depression was $1.20. Donations of coal were greatly welcomed.

MAYONNAISE

Mrs. Valliant made this dressing for chicken salad served at Queen Anne's County Garden Club May Marts and St. Paul's Bazaars.

1 teaspoon salt
¼ teaspoon paprika
½ teaspoon dry mustard
  dash of cayenne
2 egg yolks
2 tablespoons vinegar
2 cups salad oil
2 tablespoons lemon juice
1 tablespoon hot water

Mix dry ingredients, add egg yolks, and blend. Add vinegar and mix well. Add salad oil, 1 tablespoon at a time, beating with rotary beater until ½ cup has been added; add remaining oil in increasing amounts, alternating last half-cup with lemon juice. Add hot water; this takes away oily appearance. Makes 2 cups.

—*Genevieve Hall Valliant (Mrs. Edwin S., Sr.)*

CHICKEN SALAD DRESSING

½ cup sugar
2 teaspoons salt
¼ teaspoon red pepper
3 tablespoons flour
1½ teaspoons dry mustard
4 eggs, beaten
½ cup vinegar
1 pint chicken stock (some fat)

Mix all dry ingredients. Add well-beaten eggs. Add to this the vinegar and chicken stock. Bring to a slow boil, stirring constantly, until it thickens. Let cool. Makes 2½ cups.

—*Sara Catherine Valliant (Mrs. Edwin S., Jr.)*

✤ SLAW DRESSING

    2 eggs
    2 teaspoons dry mustard
    1 heaping teaspoon salt
    3 tablespoons sugar
  ½ cup vinegar
  ½ cup cream
    1 teaspoon celery seed
    1 lump butter

Beat eggs until well mixed. Add mustard, salt, sugar, and vinegar, and mix well. Cook in double boiler until thick. When cool, add cream, celery seed, and butter (mixture must be warm enough to melt butter). Makes about 1½ cups.

—Clara Bayless (Mrs. C. B.)

✤ COOKED SLAW DRESSING

    2 round (scant) tablespoons flour
    3 heaping tablespoons sugar
    1 heaping teaspoon salt
 1½ level teaspoons dry mustard
    1 egg
       tip end of ¼ teaspoon measure of cayenne
  ¾ cup cold water
  ½ cup vinegar
 1½ ounces butter
 1½ teaspoons celery seed

Mix flour, sugar, salt, and dry mustard. Drop in whole egg and mix well. Add cayenne, cold water, vinegar, and butter. Put over high heat, stirring constantly. When mixture commences to boil, reduce heat and boil 5 minutes; continue stirring or it will lump and burn. Remove from fire and add celery seed. Let get cold before stirring in cabbage (about a 3-pound head). A little mayonnaise may be added before the cabbage. A bit of chopped celery will provide a new taste.

—Louise Perry (Mrs. John W.)

❧ HOT BACON SALAD DRESSING

    3   slices bacon
    1   egg, well beaten
    1½ tablespoons flour
    1   cup milk
    ¼   cup vinegar
    ¼   cup sugar
    ½   teaspoon salt

Chop bacon and fry until crisp; remove bacon and add to salad greens. Add all other ingredients to beaten egg and pour into hot bacon fat. Cook until thickened. Pour at once over 1 quart crisp, dry salad greens. A combination such as lettuce, endive, dandelion, and spinach may be used (whatever you happen to have). A little chopped onion may be added to the greens if desired. Makes about 2 cups (4 to 6 salad servings).

—Sara Warren Kidd (Mrs. A. L.)

❧ MUSTARD SALAD DRESSING

Add ½ cup mayonnaise to this for a dressing that's good for fresh garden lettuce, slaw, or chicken salad.

    2   eggs
    1   tablespoon sugar
    1   teaspoon salt
    1   teaspoon dry mustard
    1   shake flour
    1   dessert spoon butter, melted
    1   cup milk
    ¼   cup vinegar, heated

Beat eggs; add sugar, salt, and mustard. Shake in flour. Stir in melted butter, then milk and hot vinegar. Cook until it thickens. Makes about 1½ cups.

—Fanny Earle Wright (Mrs. Henry)

❧ *QUICK MAYONNAISE*

            1 tablespoon dry mustard
            1 whole egg
            1 teaspoon salt
    1½ to 2 cups oil
            ¼ teaspoon Tabasco sauce
            ½ teaspoon Worcestershire sauce
               juice of 1 lemon

Blend mustard, egg, and salt in blender. With motor running, add slowly the remaining ingredients. Makes 2 cups.

—Lillian Hardy (Mrs. William)

DESSERTS AND SAUCES

Thank you for the world so sweet,
Thank you for the food we eat,
Thank you for the birds that sing,
Thank you, God, for everything.

❧ APPLE BROWN BETTY

This comforting dessert was served at the Centreville Tea Room and always found its way to the bazaar luncheons in Donaldson Hall where it was a popular favorite.

Fill a well-buttered baking dish with alternate layers of thinly sliced tart apples or canned unsweetened apples and buttered bread crumbs. Sprinkle each layer generously with sugar and cinnamon. Dot with butter, add a little water. Bake at 375 degrees for 30 minutes.

Serve warm with fresh lemon sauce, not too thick, or a little bourbon in place of the lemon. Four cups of apples makes approximately 6 to 8 servings.

—*Bessie Dadds Bedford (Mrs. Morte)*

❧ BAKED APPLE DUMPLINGS

      2 cups flour
     ¾ cup shortening
     ¼ cup water
      1 teaspoon salt
         sugar
         cinnamon
      6 apples
         butter
      2 cups water
      4 tablespoons butter
     ½ teaspoon cinnamon
    1½ cups granulated sugar
    1½ cups brown sugar (or 1½ cups granulated)

Make a pastry of the flour, shortening, water, and salt. Cut up apples and mix with butter, sugar, and cinnamon to taste. Place apples in squares of pastry and fold over pastry to form dumplings. Put in deep baking pan. Combine water, butter, cinnamon, and sugars. Boil for 3 minutes. Pour syrup over dumplings in pan and cook at 500 degrees until tan. Reduce heat to 325 or 350 degrees and continue baking until apples are soft, basting occasionally. Makes 6 servings.

—*Mrs. R. Allen Day*

APPLE STREUSEL

¼ pound butter or margarine
¾ cup light brown sugar
1 teaspoon cinnamon
½ teaspoon nutmeg
1 cup flour
5 apples, pared and thinly sliced

Blend butter, sugar, cinnamon, nutmeg, and flour. Put apples in a buttered 6 × 10-inch baking dish. Place butter mixture over apples, packing it down. Bake at 350 degrees for 30 to 45 minutes, or until apples are done. Serve while warm with cream or ice cream. Makes 8 servings.

—*Nellie Brown Whiteley (Mrs. J. Harman)*

APRICOT SOUFFLÉ

A delightful "comfort" dessert.

⅔ cup water
⅓ cup sugar
1 cup dried apricots
  butter
  confectioner's sugar
5 eggs at room temperature
¼ teaspoon cream of tartar

Bring water and sugar to boil in a small saucepan. Add apricots and simmer for 12 minutes. Puree in processor and set aside to cool. Butter a 9-inch soufflé dish and dust with confectioner's sugar. Preheat oven to 400 degrees. Separate eggs. Reserve yolks for another use (perhaps hollandaise for the main course). Whip the whites until stiff, but not dry. Gently fold in cream of tartar. Fold in the apricot puree and pour into prepared baking dish. Set dish in a pan of hot water. Bake for 10 minutes and reduce heat to 350 degrees. Bake for 50 minutes more; serve immediately with fresh whipped cream. Makes 6 to 8 servings.

—*Hallie Rogers Rugg (Mrs. Daniel)*

❧ *APRICOT MOUSSE*

From the collection of Lolly and Jim Mitchell.

1 16-ounce can apricot halves
1 6-ounce can apricot nectar
1 envelope unflavored gelatin
4 eggs, separated
½ cup sugar
¼ teaspoon salt
⅓ cup apricot brandy or rum
1 cup whipping cream

Drain apricot halves and blend to a puree. Pour nectar into top of double boiler and sprinkle with gelatin. Let stand 5 minutes to soften. Beat egg yolks lightly and add to nectar along with ¼ cup of sugar and the salt. Set over boiling water and cook 5 to 10 minutes, stirring constantly, until mixture thickens. Remove from heat and stir in apricot brandy. Cool until mixture begins to set up. Beat egg whites to a fine foam. Gradually beat in remaining ¼ cup of sugar and beat to stiff meringue. With same beater, beat cream stiff. Fold both into gelatin mixture and turn into a 5-cup dish. Chill 'til firm, at least three hours. Serves 8.

—*Joan Vest Withington (Mrs. Charles F.)*

❧ *TROPICAL BAVARIAN CREAM*

1½ cups apricot nectar, or juice and pulp from a can of whole
        fruit
⅓ cup sugar
    salt to taste
1 envelope unflavored gelatin
2 tablespoons lemon juice
¼ cup undrained crushed pineapple
½ cup whipping cream

Heat the nectar with sugar and salt. Soften gelatin in lemon juice. Dissolve in hot nectar. Add crushed pineapple and allow to cool. Fold in stiffly beaten cream. Mold and chill. Serves 5 or 6.

—*Ruth Branner Gadd (Mrs. A. Sydney, Jr.)*

❧ BREAD PUDDING WITH BROWN SUGAR SAUCE

> 1 pint milk
> 2 slices bread, crumbled
> 2 eggs
> ¼ cup sugar
> pinch of salt
> 1 teaspoon vanilla
> 2 cups brown sugar
> sherry

Soak bread in milk. Beat eggs, sugar, and salt. Add vanilla. Mix all together and place in a casserole which has been put in a pan of water. Bake for 1 hour at 350 degrees. Mix brown sugar with enough sherry to dissolve sugar. Pour over pudding. Makes 4 servings.

—*Nannie Wright (Mrs. Clayton)*

❧ BISCUIT TORTONI

> 1 envelope unflavored gelatin
> ¼ cup cold water
> 1 cup scalded milk
> 2 eggs
> ½ cup sugar
> ⅛ teaspoon salt
> ½ teaspoon vanilla or 2 tablespoons sherry
> 1 cup heavy cream
> ¼ cup vanilla cookie crumbs
> maraschino cherries (optional)

Sprinkle gelatin on water in small bowl to soften. Add hot milk and stir until dissolved. Beat eggs until thick, adding sugar gradually. Stir in milk mixture, salt, and vanilla or sherry. Chill until thick and syrupy.

Whip cream until just thick enough to hold soft peaks, and fold into chilled mixture. Pour into 8 or 10 paper cups, or into freezing tray. Sprinkle cookie crumbs over the top. Freeze in freezing compartment until firm—2 to 3 hours. Serve topped with maraschino cherries, if desired. Serves 8 to 10.

—*Henrietta Holton Dallum (Mrs. John)*

BABA AU RHUM

3 eggs, separated
¾ cup sugar
1 cup bread flour, sifted
pinch salt
1 teaspoon baking powder
3 tablespoons milk

Beat yolks well, add sugar and mix well. Sift flour, salt, and baking powder together and add to mixture in three parts, starting with milk and stirring well with each addition. Beat egg whites until stiff but moist and fold in. Put cake in 8-inch tube pan, filling so cake will not fill container to top when done. Bake at 350 degrees until cake is up, then raise heat to 375 degrees, and bake for 20 minutes more. When done, leave cake in pan and, while still hot, pour syrup slowly over cake, allowing it to soak in. Leave in pan until ready to serve. When ready to serve, pour more of the syrup over cake. Makes 12 babas.

Syrup Suggestions for Baba au Rhum

½ cup orange juice
1 cup sugar
Cointreau or Grand Marnier

Combine orange juice and sugar in pan and heat. Allow to cool; then add Cointreau or Grand Marnier to taste. Be generous.

1 cup sugar
½ cup water
rum

Combine sugar and water and heat. Remove from heat, allow to cool, and flavor with rum.

Juice from fruit compote in this book makes an excellent syrup and can also be flavored with rum if desired.

—Lynette Morgan Nielsen (Mrs. Orsen)

COFFEE-NUT TORTONI

1 cup whipping cream
¼ cup sugar
1 tablespoon instant coffee granules

few drops almond extract
1 egg white
2 tablespoons sugar
¼ cup finely chopped toasted almonds
¼ cup flaked coconut, toasted and crumbled

Whip cream, fold in sugar, instant coffee, and flavoring. Beat egg white until soft peaks form, gradually add sugar, and beat to stiff peaks. Mix almonds and coconut. Fold egg white and ½ nut mixture into whipped cream. Spoon into 8 paper bake cups set in muffin tins. Sprinkle remaining nut mixture over top. Freeze firm. Serves 8.

—*Anne Stoney Cantler (Mrs. James E.)*

🐚 *FORT POINT TARTE CHOCOLATE*

This is a tricky dessert—it doesn't always look pretty, but the taste never disappoints.

4 ounces bittersweet chocolate, chopped
1½ ounces unsweetened chocolate, chopped
10 tablespoons (1¼ sticks) unsalted butter, room temperature
½ cup plus 2 tablespoons sugar
3 large eggs, room temperature
½ cup plus 2 teaspoons all-purpose flour
1½ tablespoons unsweetened cocoa powder
¾ teaspoon baking powder
   vanilla ice cream or whipped cream (optional)

Lightly butter 6 1-cup ramekins. Melt both chocolates in double boiler over water until smooth. Add butter and sugar and stir until butter and sugar melt. Transfer to large bowl. Add eggs, then flour, cocoa powder, and baking powder. Using electric mixer, beat until mixture thickens to mousse consistency, about 8 minutes. Divide mixture among prepared ramekins, cover with plastic wrap, and freeze at least 3 hours or up to 3 days ahead. Near serving time, position rack in center of oven and preheat to 375 degrees. Remove plastic. Bake until edges are set and centers are still moist and shiny, about 11 minutes. Do not overbake. Cool 10 minutes, invert each dessert onto plate, and serve warm with ice cream or whipped cream, if desired. Makes 6 servings.

—*Nina DuPont Curran (Mrs. Edward A.)*

❦ *CHOCOLATE AND ALMOND BAVAROIS RING*

    2½ cups milk
     ⅔ cup sugar
         pinch salt
     ½ cup blanched almonds, toasted and finely ground
     4 teaspoons unflavored gelatin
     1 teaspoon almond extract
     1 cup heavy cream

Heat over boiling water 2 cups milk mixed with sugar and salt. When hot, add almonds. Cover and remove from heat. Let stand for 15 minutes to blend flavors. Soak gelatin in ½ cup cold milk. Add to above and heat until dissolved. Cool and add almond extract.

When mixture begins to thicken, beat hard with rotary beater until fluffy. Beat cream until stiff. Fold into milk mixture and spoon into a 5-cup ring mold. When firm, turn out on a deep platter and coat with Chocolate Sauce. Ring may be sprinkled with additional ground or grated almonds if desired. Makes 8 servings.

Chocolate Sauce

    1⅓ cups milk
     3 squares unsweetened chocolate
     ¼ teaspoon salt
     ⅓ cup sugar
     2 teaspoons cornstarch
     1 teaspoon vanilla

Heat milk and chocolate in top of double boiler. When chocolate is melted, blend well and add salt and sugar and heat until sugar is dissolved. Mix cornstarch with a little cold water and stir into chocolate; cook, stirring constantly, until smooth and thick and no starch taste remains. Cool slightly, add vanilla, and beat to the consistency of very thick cream. Coat ring with some sauce and serve balance in center of ring.

—Isa Louise Blaney (Mrs. Arthur)

❦ *HOT CHOCOLATE PUDDING*

    4 ounces unsweetened baking chocolate
    1 pint grated bread crumbs
    1 quart milk

    3 eggs
    1 cup sugar

Melt chocolate and add bread crumbs. Heat milk to boiling and add to chocolate mixture. Let mixture cool then add eggs which have been well beaten with sugar. Pour into buttered 2-quart casserole and bake at 350 degrees for 1 hour or until cake tester inserted in center comes out clean. Serve with hard sauce. (Make up early and bake in time to serve hot.) Serves 6 to 8.

—Louise Perry (Mrs. John W.)

❧ CHOCOLATE ROLL

    1 cup granulated sugar
    5 eggs, separated
    6 ounces Baker's German's Brand Sweet Chocolate
    2 cups heavy whipping cream
       maraschino cherries and grated chocolate for decorations
       vanilla or rum (optional)

Beat ¾ cup sugar into egg yolks. Melt chocolate in water. When partly cooled, mix with yolks, then add stiffly beaten egg whites. Butter cookie sheet or jelly roll pan lined with wax paper. Spread mixture evenly in pan. Bake 10 minutes at 350 degrees and 5 minutes more at 325 degrees. When baking is finished, place damp towel over pan and cool 1 hour in refrigerator. Remove from refrigerator and spread with seasoned whipped cream, reserving some cream for top of cake. Roll and cover with remaining cream, sprinkle with grated chocolate, and stud with quartered cherries. Cream may be seasoned with a little sugar and vanilla, or rum, or any other seasoning desired. Makes 8 to 10 servings.

—Mrs. Henry Merlier

❧ LEMON SHERBET

    2 quarts milk or half-and-half
  3½ cups sugar
  1½ cups lemon juice
       grated rind of 3 lemons

Mix all ingredients together and freeze. Makes 12 servings.

—Ann Dudley Brower Turner (Mrs. J. B., Jr.)

❧ *COEUR À LA CRÈME*

   2 8-ounce packages cream cheese
½ cup sugar
   1 cup heavy cream, whipped
      strawberries and raspberries

Line a heart-shaped mold (about 6 inches across and 2 inches deep) with dampened cheesecloth, completely covering bottom and sides of mold. In medium bowl, let cream cheese stand at room temperature about 1 hour to soften. With wooden spoon, beat sugar and cheese until smooth. Beat in whipped cream, a small amount at a time, until mixture is light and smooth. Turn into prepared mold, filling evenly. Smooth with spatula. Refrigerate, covered, overnight or until well chilled. To serve, turn onto a serving dish with a rim. Surround with strawberries and raspberries. Serves 8 or more. This is very rich—dessert servings should be small.

Strawberries and Raspberries

   1 10-ounce package frozen strawberries, thawed
   1 10-ounce package frozen raspberries, thawed
   1 tablespoon cornstarch
¼ cup kirsch

Drain fruits, reserving juice. Add water to juice to measure 1¾ cups. In small saucepan, combine cornstarch and juice, mixing until smooth. Bring to a boil over medium heat, stirring constantly. Reduce heat and cook 5 minutes or until thickened and translucent. Let cool. Add strawberries, raspberries, and kirsch. Refrigerate, covered, overnight. Makes 2½ cups.

—*Barbara Colthurst Bryan (Mrs. David C.)*

❧ *CREAM CHEESE PANCAKES*

These are very easy, wonderfully delicious, and quick.

   2 3-ounce packages cream cheese, at room temperature
   1 egg
   1 tablespoon flour
      confectioner's sugar
      currant jelly (optional)
      brandy (optional)

Blend all together into smooth batter. Drop onto griddle from spoon, making cakes about 3 inches in diameter and ⅛-inch thick. Serve warm, three cakes per person, with jam between. Dust with confectioners' sugar; or make a sauce of currant jelly and brandy. Serves 3.

—*Clare Reynders Stevens (Mrs. Byam K.)*

CRÈME BRULÉE

4 egg yolks
⅛ teaspoon salt
⅓ cup brown sugar
1½ cups table cream, scalded in double boiler

Beat egg yolks well. Add salt and half the sugar. Slowly add cream, stirring vigorously. Cook in double boiler over simmering water until mixture thickens slightly and coats spoon. Pour immediately into individual baking dishes. Cool. Chill several hours. To serve, sieve remaining sugar over top. Brown sugar slowly under broiler. (Watch carefully so sugar does not scorch.) Cool for short time. Makes 4 servings.

—*Maria McKenney*

DATE-NUT SURPRISE

Best made a day or two ahead.

1 8-ounce package chopped dates
1 cup chopped walnuts
2 teaspoons baking powder
2 cups broken pieces graham crackers (not crumbs)
2 eggs, beaten
1 cup white sugar
½ cup cooking oil
1 cup milk
   pinch of salt

Mix dates, walnuts, baking powder, and graham cracker pieces, and put into well-buttered 8-inch-square baking dish. Combine remaining ingredients and pour over nut mixture. Bake for 30 minutes at 350 degrees. Cool and cut in squares. Serve cold with whipped cream. Makes 6 to 8 servings.

—*Anne Gadd Hennighausen (Mrs. Charles E.)*

❦ DEVIL'S FOOD WAFFLES

         1 cup sugar
      1½ cups flour
         2 teaspoons baking powder
        ⅛ teaspoon salt
         2 egg yolks
        ½ cup milk
         1 teaspoon vanilla
         2 squares unsweetened chocolate
        ½ cup fat
         2 egg whites

Sift together sugar, flour, baking powder, and salt. Add egg yolks, milk, and vanilla. Melt chocolate and fat and add to the mixture. Fold in beaten egg whites last. Makes 6 medium waffles.

—*Mrs. C. Norwood Shockley*

❦ ENGLISH TRIFLE

> *My grandmother's recipe.*

        ¼ pound macaroons
         1 sponge cake
         1 cup apricot or peach jam
      1½ pints sherry
            brandy
         1 cup thin custard
         1 pint whipped cream
         1 teaspoon vanilla
         2 teaspoons sugar
         2 ounces shredded almonds
            maraschino cherries

Put cookies in a deep glass serving dish. Cut sponge cake into slices, spread with jam, and place on top of cookies in even layers. Soak well with wine and 2 tablespoons brandy. Pour on custard. Flavor whipped cream with vanilla, sugar, and 1 teaspoon brandy. Force through pastry bag with decorative tip over mold and garnish with almonds and cherries. Chill. Serves 8 to 10.

—*Trixie Price (Mrs. Ellsworth)*

❧ *FRUIT COMPOTE*

    1 10-ounce can black cherries
    1 10-ounce can peaches
    1 10-ounce can apricots
    1 orange
    1 lemon
    ½ cup brown sugar
    2 tablespoons Grand Marnier

Drain fruit. Pit cherries, if necessary. Grate rind off orange and lemon and squeeze juice. (Too much orange spoils it, so use less rind if peel is thick and full of oil.) Mix fruit, lemon and orange juice, and a good part of rind and brown sugar in baking dish. Sprinkle rest of rind on top. Bake in moderate oven until flavors are blended. Chill. Add Grand Marnier. Serve cold. Freezes well. Makes 8 to 10 servings.

—Lynette Morgan Nielsen (Mrs. Orsen)

❧ *LEMON SUPREME*

    6 eggs, separated
    1½ cups sugar
    ½ cup lemon juice
    1½ teaspoons grated lemon rind
    1 envelope unflavored gelatin soaked in ¼ cup water
    1 small angel food cake
       whipped cream

Beat egg yolks well, add ¾ cup sugar, and beat well. Add lemon juice and rind. Cook in double boiler until thick. Add gelatin and stir until dissolved. Let mixture cool. Make a meringue of egg whites by beating ¾ cup sugar into beaten egg whites. Add to the cooled lemon mixture. Break angel food cake into chunks. Put a layer of cake in a deep dish and then add a layer of lemon custard on top, repeating until all is used. Let the cake set in the refrigerator overnight. An hour before serving, take it out of the refrigerator and turn upside down onto serving plate. Cover with whipped cream. Can be stored in deep freeze. Serves 12.

—Genevieve Hall Valliant (Mrs. Edwin S., Sr.)

✤ FUNNY COBBLER

    1 cup flour
    1 cup sugar
    1½ teaspoons baking powder
    1 cup milk
       pinch of salt
    2 tablespoons butter
    4 cups fruit (peaches, cherries, or such)

Mix together first 5 ingredients. Grease a 1-quart baking dish with butter; then pour in cake mixture. Spread fruit on top. Season to taste with nutmeg, cinnamon, or lemon juice. Bake at 375 degrees for 45 minutes. Batter rises to top and browns. Serves 4 to 6.

—*Harriet Willcox Gearhart (Mrs. David)*

✤ FRUMMERY

> *This recipe came from the Truitt family preceding the Civil War but originally was from France through the Paradee-Pardu-Purdue family. Use it as breakfast cereal or dessert.*

    4 cups new wheat
    4 cups hot milk
    1 cup seeded raisins and 1 cup currants (or 1½ cups raisins in all)
    1 teaspoon salt (scant)
    4 teaspoons honey or syrup
    ⅙ teaspoon powdered nutmeg

Crack wheat by moistening and pounding in a cloth or bag. Remove chaff. Soak overnight in cold water. Cook in water until very soft, adding boiling water if necessary. Add milk, raisins, currants, salt, honey, and nutmeg, and stir. Cook 10 minutes lightly. Makes 8 to 10 servings.

—*Dr. Reginald V. Truitt*

✤ HOT FUDGE PUDDING

    1 cup sifted all-purpose flour
    3 teaspoons baking powder
    ¼ teaspoon salt
    ¾ cup sugar
    2 tablespoons cocoa

½ cup milk
2 tablespoons melted shortening
1 cup chopped black walnuts
1 cup brown sugar
4 tablespoons cocoa
1¾ cups hot water

Sift dry ingredients together; stir in the milk; add shortening and mix until smooth. Add nuts and spread in an 8-inch-square pan. Mix brown sugar and cocoa for topping and sprinkle over batter. Pour hot water over entire batter. Bake at 350 degrees for 40 to 45 minutes. Remove from oven and cool. (During baking the cake comes to the top and sauce goes to the bottom.) Cut cake into squares; invert pan onto a plate and allow sauce to drip over all. Makes 4 to 6 servings.

—*Ruth Newell (Mrs. Robert)*
—*Julia Goldsborough Long (Mrs. H. Lawrence)*

LADYFINGER DESSERT

This looks elegant and makes a wonderful dinner dessert. It also freezes very well.

½ cup orange juice
1 orange, grated
1 tablespoon lemon juice
1 egg, beaten
2½ tablespoons flour
½ cup sugar
   pinch of salt
½ pint whipped cream
3 tablespoons brandy
1½ dozen ladyfingers

Cook orange juice and grated rind of half the orange, lemon juice, beaten egg, flour, sugar, and salt until thick as heavy cream. Cool and fold in whipped cream and brandy. Line a 9 × 5-inch loaf pan with ladyfingers, cover with portion of filling and add another layer of ladyfingers, then rest of filling. Cover with ladyfingers and put in refrigerator to set and chill. When ready to serve, turn out and cover with more whipped cream that has 1 tablespoon brandy added, if desired. Makes 8 servings.

—*Lynette Morgan Nielsen (Mrs. Orsen)*

🍂 SEEDLESS GRAPES AND WHIPPED CREAM

A light, refreshing summer dessert, festive enough for any party but quick and easy to do.

4 to 5 cups seedless grapes
 ½ pint whipping cream
 1 tablespoon of sugar
 1 tablespoon of white rum

Wash and stem the grapes. Whip cream and add sugar and rum. Mix well with grapes. Serves 6.

—*Virginia Ingles Freeland (Mrs. Samuel L.)*

🍂 JELLIED GRAPEFRUIT DESSERT

 1 envelope unflavored gelatin
 ¼ cup cold water
 ½ cup hot water
 ⅔ cup sugar
 2 grapefruit

Soften gelatin in cold water and dissolve in hot water. Put sugar in bowl and cut and section grapefruit over it to get all juice. Then add dissolved gelatin. Stir to mix and chill. Makes 4 servings.

—*Katherine Wilson Barton (Mrs. W. Edward)*

🍂 ICEBOX CAKE

 2 8-ounce bars Baker's German's Brand Sweet Chocolate
 4 tablespoons water
 4 tablespoons sugar
 4 eggs, separated
 ½ pound ladyfingers

In a double boiler, put chocolate, water, and sugar, and melt. Beat egg yolks well and pour chocolate mixture over them. Beat again and fold in well-beaten egg whites. Line a 2-quart mold with waxed paper. Line mold bottom and sides with ladyfingers. Pour in chocolate mixture to cover and then another layer of ladyfingers. Cover with chocolate, and continue until all has been used. End with ladyfingers. Put in refrigerator and chill. To serve, turn out on plate, remove waxed paper, and decorate with whipped cream. Serves 4. This can be made a day ahead.

—*Elizabeth Bland Nesbit (Mrs. Thorpe)*

LORRAINE'S COFFEE SPANISH CREAM

This is a very elegant looking and deliciously light dessert for dinner.

1½ cups coffee infusion (see below)
½ cup milk
⅔ cup sugar
1 package unflavored gelatin, soaked in 2 tablespoons water
¼ teaspoon salt
3 eggs, separated
½ teaspoon vanilla
grated bittersweet chocolate
whipped cream

Mix coffee infusion, milk, and half of the sugar and heat in double boiler. Add gelatin and dissolve. Add remaining sugar, salt, and beaten egg yolks and cook, stirring constantly, until mixture coats the spoon. Remove from stove and allow to cool somewhat. Beat egg whites until stiff but not dry. Fold into cooling mixture. Add vanilla. Pour into 4-cup mold in the bottom of which grated chocolate has been generously sprinkled. Put into refrigerator and allow to set. When ready to serve, turn out on plate and decorate with whipped cream and sprinkle over top grated bitter chocolate. Serves 5 or 6.

Coffee Infusion

The better the infusion the better the dessert. Instant coffee can be used. Don't pour hot infusion into milk that is right out of the refrigerator—it can curdle it. Put a little of the hot infusion-milk mixture into beaten egg yolks and mix before adding egg yolks back into the infusion; this prevents lumping.

—*Lynette Morgan Nielsen (Mrs. Orsen)*

❦ INDIAN PUDDING

This is an old Truitt family recipe. Colonists used imported spices, but Indians used local, wild condiments and juices for flavoring.

½ cup cornmeal
4 cups milk
1 cup brown sugar
1 teaspoon ground ginger
½ teaspoon ground nutmeg
½ teaspoon ground cinnamon
1 teaspoon salt
½ cup dark molasses
2 cups light cream
2 cups heavy cream

Preheat oven to 275 degrees. Combine cornmeal with 1 cup of milk and scald remaining 3 cups of milk in saucepan over medium heat. Stir in cornmeal mixture a little at a time and cook, stirring constantly, for 15 minutes, until thick as cooked cereal. Keep stirring to avoid lumps. Remove from heat. Stir combined sugar, spices, and salt into cornmeal mixture. Add molasses and light cream. Pour into greased 2-quart baking dish. Bake 2 hours. Set aside at least an hour to cool. Serve warm with heavy cream in pitcher to pour over each portion at the table. Serves 8.

—*Dr. Reginald V. Truitt*

❦ SUMMER PUDDING

1 pint blueberries
1 pint strawberries
1 pint raspberries (or any berries will do in any combination)
½ loaf of good bread (Arnold or Pepperidge Farm) crust removed
⅓ cup water
⅓ cup sugar (optional)
   heavy cream or crème fraiche (optional)

Wash fruit. Cut strawberries into bite size pieces. In a heavy saucepan, combine fruit, water, and sugar (optional). Cook gently over low heat until fruit gets mushy and runny.

Line bottom and sides of a 2-quart mixing bowl with slices of bread. Overlap the bread around the sides of the bowl so that the fruit won't spill out when unmolded. *Do not* butter bowl! Ladle warm fruit into the bread-lined bowl. Cover the top with another layer or two of bread. Cover loosely with plastic wrap. On top of plastic wrap, place a small, sturdy plate that will fit inside the bowl. Place a brick on top of the plate and refrigerate pudding overnight. Unmolding pudding is easy: the weight of the pudding usually pulls it away from the bowl. If it needs help, run a thin knife around the edge of the bowl. Cut like a cake and serve in bowls. Pass the heavy cream or crème fraiche. Makes 8 servings.

—*Melissa Clarke (Mrs. Garry E.)*

ORANGE CAKE

- 1 cup butter at room temperature
- 1½ cups sugar
- 3 eggs, separated
- 2 cups flour
- 1 teaspoon baking powder
- 1 teaspoon soda
- 1 cup sour cream
  grated rind of 1 orange
- ½ cup chopped walnuts or pecans
- ¼ cup orange juice
- ⅓ cup Grand Marnier or Cointreau
- 2 tablespoons slivered almonds (optional)

Preheat oven to 350 degrees. Cream together butter and 1 cup sugar until light. Beat in egg yolks. Sift together the dry ingredients and add them alternately with the sour cream, stirring well. Stir in orange rind and nuts. Beat egg whites stiff and fold into batter. Grease tube cake pans, one 10-inch or two 8-inch, and bake 50 minutes or until cake tests done.

Combine remaining ½ cup sugar, orange juice, and liqueur, and spoon the mixture over the cake as soon as it is taken from oven. Let it soak in. Decorate cake with almonds if you wish. Let cake cool in the pan. Serve with more of the above sauce slightly thickened. Serve slightly warm. This cake freezes well. Serves 12.

—*Lynette Morgan Nielsen (Mrs. Orsen)*

❧ *A DELICIOUS, QUICK, EASY, AND VERY PRETTY DESSERT*

   6 oranges
   ½ gallon orange ice or orange sherbet
      candied orange peel (see below)

Slice oranges and arrange on platter around ice or sherbet. Sprinkle with candied peel. Strawberries with their caps on, cherries, or sprigs of mint can be used for a touch of color.

Candied Peel

      orange peel from 2 oranges
   ½ cup water
   1 cup sugar

Boil orange peel and remove pith. Boil water and sugar until syrup spins a thread. Cook peel in syrup 5 minutes and drain.

—Mary Wood (Mrs. Howard, III)

❧ *SWEET POTATO PUDDING OR PIE*

1 pint boiled and mashed sweet potatoes. To this add butter the size of an egg, 1½ cups of sugar, the grated rind of a lemon and juice of same, the yolks of three eggs and beat well. Then add 1½ cups of milk and lastly the well beaten whites of the eggs. This can be baked either in pastry shells or a greased dish as a pudding.

—Readbourne Receipts, Queen Anne's County (courtesy of Swepson Earle).
From Eat, Drink and Be Merry in Maryland

❧ *LEMON CREME*

   2 eggs
   1 cup sugar
   ⅓ cup fresh lemon juice
   1 tablespoon cornstarch

½ cup water

1 teaspoon vanilla extract

1 cup (½ pint) whipping cream, whipped

In bowl, beat together eggs, ½ cup sugar, and lemon juice. In saucepan, combine remaining sugar and cornstarch; stir in water. Cook and stir until thickened; remove from heat. Gradually beat in egg mixture. Over low heat, cook and stir until thickened. Add vanilla. Cool and fold in whipped cream. Serve with cut fruit.

—Carol Carter (Mrs. Clayton C.)

QUEEN OF PUDDINGS

1 quart of milk

1 quart diced bread (stale) light measure

1 cup sugar

4 egg yolks

rind of 1 lemon grated

butter the size of an egg

Scald the milk and soak the bread in it for an hour or more. Stir butter in while hot, also sugar. When cooked add yolks of eggs and lemon rind. Put in greased baking dish and bake about 30 minutes.

When done spread with preserves, any kind desired, raspberry was usually used at "Readbourne," then add meringue of egg whites and place in oven until brown. Serve cold with cream.

—Readbourne Receipts, Queen Anne's County (Courtesy of Misses Clara and Bessie Hollyday). From Eat, Drink and Be Merry in Maryland

---

With tobacco as the currency of the Eastern Shore economy in the eighteenth century, the Vestry would tax the parish to help support the church: In 1698, "each white male over 16 years . . . assessed forty pounds of tobacco" and all persons were taxed 10 pounds of tobacco for church repairs and buying of books.

❧ MAPLE SPONGE PUDDING

    2 envelopes plus 1 teaspoon unflavored gelatin
    2 cups good, full-bodied maple syrup
    6 egg whites
    1 well-packed cup macaroon crumbs
      whipped cream
      grated maple sugar (use fairly coarse grater and be sure
        sugar is cold)

Soak gelatin in ½ cup cold water. Boil maple syrup 3 minutes. Add gelatin and stir until dissolved. Set syrup mixture in cold water to cool and thicken. Beat egg whites until stiff. Oil 10-inch ring mold. When syrup cools and is slightly thickened, beat until frothy (about 3 minutes). Add beaten egg whites and macaroon crumbs. Fold until even consistency is reached. Put into mold. After filling, give mold a couple of whacks on table. This is best made the day before. Requires 6 hours in the refrigerator. To serve, unmold on platter, fill center with whipped cream and grate maple sugar all over it. Around outside of ring, alternate little mounds of grated maple sugar and whipped cream. Serves 8.

—*Isa Louise Blaney (Mrs. Arthur J.)*

❧ BRIDGE MERINGUE TORTE

    6 egg whites
    2 teaspoons vanilla
    ½ teaspoon cream of tartar
      dash salt
    2 cups sugar
    12 Heath bars, crushed
    2 cups whipping cream

Have egg whites at room temperature. Add vanilla, cream of tartar, and salt. Beat to soft peaks, then gradually add sugar, beating to stiff peaks. Cover 2 cookie sheets with plain, unglazed shelf paper or parchment paper and draw 9-inch circles on each. Spread meringue evenly on paper within circles. Bake at 275 degrees for 1 hour. Turn off heat and let dry in oven, keeping door closed for at least 2 hours. Fold crushed candy (reserve some for garnish) and dash of salt into whipped cream. Spread one third of cream between meringue layers, one third on top, and last third on sides. Garnish with Heath bar pieces and chill 8 hours or overnight. Serves 8.

—Julia Browne Sause (Mrs. John W., Jr.)

❧ *NORWEGIAN PANNE-KAKA*

    2   tablespoons butter
    ½   cup plus 1 tablespoon flour
    ½   cup milk
    ½   cup water
    ¼   teaspoon salt
    2   tablespoons sugar
    3   eggs, separated
        butter
        jam (strawberry is very good)
        confectioners' sugar

Melt butter in double boiler, stir in flour, milk, water, and salt to make a thick white sauce. Do not allow to cook very long, and stir occasionally, so it does not become lumpy. When cool, add egg yolks beaten with sugar. Beat egg whites stiff but moist, and fold into egg mixture. Melt enough butter in two heavy frying pans, No. 6 or 7, to cover bottom well. Divide egg mixture between pans and cook over medium flame (as for fluffy omelette, covered) about 20 minutes. Pancake should be puffed and nicely browned on bottom; it begins to pull away from pan. To serve, turn upside down on warm plate, quickly and generously spread with jam. Turn second cake on top of jam to form a sandwich and dust with powdered sugar. Serve as soon as possible. Makes 4 or 6 servings.

Note: The original recipe called for making one cake at a time, keeping the first hot in a warm oven while second is cooking, which can be done, but I find it tricky and am more successful with cooking both at once. A lot depends on right heat to cook pancakes—not too fast to toughen, but fast enough to make them rise. You may have to experiment. This is a perfectly delicious and different dessert worth the struggle, if any.

—Lynette Morgan Nielsen (Mrs. Orsen)

❧ ORANGE ALASKA

       2 large oranges
          brown sugar or marmalade
          brandy (optional)
          vanilla ice cream
       2 egg whites
          pinch salt
       ¼ cup white sugar

Halve, core, and loosen quarters of oranges by cutting around sections. Sprinkle oranges with brown sugar or melted marmalade according to taste; ¼ teaspoon brandy per half orange may be added. Place in refrigerator to chill. Make meringue: Add pinch of salt to 2 egg whites, beat until stiff but not dry. Gradually add sugar, beating until very stiff. Place in refrigerator until ready to use but not for more than a couple of hours. To serve, place oranges on baking sheet. Put a round of vanilla ice cream on top and cover well with meringue. Bake a minute or two in a very hot oven, long enough to brown top. Serve immediately. Serves 4.

—Lynette Morgan Nielsen (Mrs. Orsen)

❧ OZARK PUDDING

       1 egg
       1 cup sugar
       1 cup chopped pecans or walnuts
       3 apples, pared and chopped
       ½ cup flour
       1 teaspoon baking powder
          pinch of salt

Beat egg, add sugar, nuts, apples, and mix well. Then sift in flour, baking powder, and salt. Put in a greased 9-inch pie plate and bake for 45 minutes at 375 degrees. Serve with whipped cream or ice cream. Makes 8 servings.

—Matilda Sause (Mrs. William)

❧ PEARS IN MAPLE BRANDY SAUCE

This is not quick or easy, but well worth the trouble.

       8 large pears (russets are best), peeled
       2 cups sugar

   1 pint maple syrup
  ½ pound butter, soft
  ½ cup French brandy
  1 teaspoon Jamaica rum

Cover pears with water, add sugar, and cook gently. When pears are cooked, drain off pear syrup and boil until syrup is one fourth its volume. (This should make about a half pint of pear syrup.) Boil maple syrup to half its volume. Whip maple syrup to cool, and when it is lukewarm add butter while whipping. Add pear syrup, brandy, and rum. Whip and let stand to cool.

Before serving, whip sauce again and pour over chilled pears. Or put half a pear on a slice of ice cream and pour sauce over. Serves 8 to 10 people.

—Lynette Morgan Nielsen (Mrs. Orsen)

✺ PEACH COBBLER

      2 cups flour
      3 teaspoons yeast powder [baking powder]
      1 teaspoon salt
      ½ cup shortening
      ½ cup milk
 5 or 6 peaches, peeled and sliced
      ½ cup brown sugar
      ½ teaspoon cinnamon
      2 tablespoons butter, melted
      1 cup hot water
      ½ cup sugar
      1 tablespoon lemon juice
         piece of butter

Sift flour, yeast, and salt into a bowl. Cut in shortening. Add milk and stir just to mix. On a floured surface, roll out into a rectangle. Combine peaches with sugar, cinnamon, and butter. Put this on rolled dough. Roll up as jelly roll and seal ends. Slice in 6 pieces. Put these slices in a small pan to which has been added water, sugar, lemon juice, and butter. Cook at 425 degrees for 35 minutes. Makes 6 servings.

—Margaret Fesmyer Wolcott (Mrs. Milton)

🎣 STUFFED FRESH PEACHES

 6 large, ripe, good-flavored peaches
⅓ cup blanched almonds
¼ cup blanched toasted almonds
 3 tablespoons confectioners' sugar
 8 small macaroons, crushed to fine crumbs
 1 tablespoon candied fruit peel, finely chopped
    cognac
    whipped cream

Scald the peaches for a minute or two in boiling water, then peel off skin. Halve lengthwise, remove stones, and scoop out a little of the pulp from each. Grind the almonds and pound them until mealy. Mix with sugar, macaroons, peel, and scooped-out peach pulp. Moisten with cognac; when mixture is well blended, put some into each of the peach halves. Rejoin the peach halves and fasten together with toothpicks. Brush with cognac and dust lightly with sifted confectioners' sugar. Bake at 350 degrees for about 20 minutes. Remove toothpicks. Serve ice cold with whipped cream.

—*Lynette Morgan Nielsen (Mrs. Orsen)*

🎣 PEACH ICE CREAM

Strawberries may be substituted for peaches.

 4 cups milk
1½ cups sugar
 ½ teaspoon salt
 4 eggs, separated
 2 teaspoons vanilla
 1 pint whipping cream
 2 cups crushed, ripe peaches
 1 tablespoon lemon juice

Scald milk, sugar, and salt in top of double boiler. Pour a little of this mixture over beaten egg yolks. Return to the double boiler and cook until slightly thickened. Chill, add vanilla, and fold in stiffly beaten egg whites. Add whipped cream. Freeze mixture in ice cream freezer until slightly thick. Fold in crushed peaches and lemon juice. Continue to turn freezer until very stiff. Makes 1 gallon.

Chocolate Ice Cream

Use 5 squares of semisweet chocolate and 2 cups sugar, melted in scalded milk. Beat to blend. Add 1 teaspoon almond extract, if desired.

—*Lou Snyder Eby (Mrs. J. Walter)*

PINEAPPLE UPSIDE-DOWN CAKE I

butter
1   cup brown sugar
1   1-pound 4½-ounce can sliced pineapple, drained,
        reserving juice
    maraschino cherries (optional)
2   eggs, separated
1   cup granulated sugar
1   cup flour
1½ teaspoons baking powder
¼   teaspoon salt

In an iron frying pan (one No. 10 or two No. 6 if smaller cakes are desired) melt 3 tablespoons butter (1½ to 2 tablespoons in smaller pans) and brown sugar, firmly packed (slightly more than half this amount in two smaller pans). Take off stove and arrange pineapple slices flat in brown sugar (maraschino cherries can be placed in pineapple holes for decoration). In a bowl, beat together egg yolks, sugar, and 3 tablespoons of pineapple juice. Sift flour, baking powder, and salt and beat into egg yolk mixture with 4 more tablespoons of pineapple juice. Beat egg whites stiff but not dry and fold into dough. Pour over pineapple and bake at 375 degrees for 30 to 45 minutes. Turn upside down on plate and serve slightly warm with whipped cream.

A large cake makes 8 generous portions, a small one a generous 4 servings. These freeze well, so I freeze one for another day. Cover a plate with a piece of foil large enough to wrap cake, turn cake upside down onto foil-covered plate, and wrap to freeze.

❧ PINEAPPLE UPSIDE-DOWN CAKE II

This is an excellent, quick dessert.

4 tablespoons butter
½ cup brown sugar
1 1-pound 4½-ounce can sliced pineapple, drained,
    reserving juice
    maraschino cherries (optional)
24 ladyfingers

Melt 4 tablespoons butter in a heavy iron frying pan (No. 6 or 7) or an 8-inch square cake pan. Add brown sugar and stir until melted. Place pineapple slices in sugar and put cherries in holes of pineapple, if desired. Place ladyfingers on top of pineapple in such a way as to make a covering layer. Moisten ladyfingers with pineapple juice (be careful not to make them soggy). Make another layer of ladyfingers and moisten with juice. Bake at 350 degrees for 20 minutes.

Turn upside down onto dish and serve with whipped cream. Makes 8 servings.

—*Lynette Morgan Nielsen (Mrs. Orsen)*

❧ PRUNES WITH PORT

34 large prunes
4 cups good red port
1 cup sugar
½ vanilla bean
1 cup whipping cream
    macaroons, powdered

Soak prunes for 24 hours in 2 cups of port. Add the sugar, 2 cups port, and ½ vanilla bean. Cook in covered enamel or steel saucepan over low heat for a half-hour. When cool, put in refrigerator for 3 days. Serve covered with whipped cream and sprinkled thickly with powdered macaroons. This can be frozen, but thaw well before serving. Serves 8 to 10.

—*Lynette Morgan Nielsen (Mrs. Orsen)*

🌺 *TYLER PUDDING*

This is a very old recipe.

1 cup butter
½ cup brown sugar
1½ cups white sugar
1 cup cream and 1 cup milk (or 1 large can evaporated milk
    with enough water to make 2 cups)
5 eggs
2 teaspoons vanilla
2 unbaked pastry shells

Heat first 4 ingredients together and beat in eggs and 2 teaspoons vanilla. Pour into pastry shells and bake as for custard pies (slowly) at approximately 350 degrees for thirty minutes. Dust with nutmeg and sprinkle with pecans, if desired. Makes 2 pies.

—*Katherine Nichols Grove (Mrs. J. Robert)*

🌺 *VANILLA ICE CREAM*

5 cups milk
5 eggs
2 cups sugar
2 tablespoons flour
¾ teaspoon salt
5 cups cream
4 teaspoons vanilla flavoring

Scald the milk. Combine the eggs, sugar, flour, and salt. Add to scalded milk and cook slowly, stirring constantly, until slightly thickened. Chill thoroughly. (This can be chilled overnight). Add cream and vanilla. Mix well. Pour into 1-gallon size ice cream maker can (will be about three-fourths full), place can in ice cream maker, pack with ice and salt. Freeze until mixture is thick. Remove from ice cream maker and remove paddle. Put the can back in with more ice and salt. Wrap the ice cream maker with an old piece of burlap, etc., and let stand until ready to serve.

—*Marguerite Marshall Thomas (Mrs. William T.)*

🐝 *IRISH PLUM PUDDING*

 ½ pound beef suet, chopped fine
 1 pound and 2 ounces bread crumbs
 ¼ teaspoon nutmeg
 6 ounces (¾ cup sugar)
 2 teaspoons ginger
    grated rind of 1 lemon
 1 wine glass (½ cup) whiskey
 1 tablespoon lemon juice
 ½ pound currants
 ½ pound raisins
 6 eggs, well beaten
 1 cup milk

Mix well all ingredients. Boil 3 hours in cloth (floured), securely tied with string. This is best when mixed at least a week before using and kept in a cool place. Pudding may be boiled 2 hours at this time and then for 1 hour before serving. Serve hot with Brandy Sauce. Serves 12.

Brandy Sauce

 ¼ pound butter
 1 cup sugar
 4 ounces (½ cup) brandy

Cook butter and sugar in double boiler, add brandy, and serve hot. Makes about 1 cup.

—*Sarah Robinson Blackwood (Mrs. Temple)*

🐝 *ENGLISH PLUM PUDDING*

 ½ pound beef suet
 ½ pound bread crumbs
 ¼ pound flour
 1 pound seedless raisins
 ½ pound ground almonds

½ pound brown sugar
¼ pound diced lemon peel
¼ pound diced citron
1 pound currants
1 large carrot, grated
½ teaspoon salt
½ teaspoon nutmeg
½ teaspoon cinnamon
½ teaspoon allspice
½ teaspoon cloves
5 eggs, slightly beaten
6 ounces rum
  juice of 1 lemon

Mix all thoroughly. Divide into desired size puddings. (Remember, this is very rich). Place each in a square of muslin. Secure with string or twist ties. Steam for 5 hours. Hang on porch or other cool place until ready to use. May be frozen. Serve with hard sauce. For Christmas, place a sprig of holly in middle. Pour warm brandy over pudding and ignite. Makes 12 servings.

—Sarah E. Cantler (Mrs. William D.)

❧ PERSIMMON PUDDING

This makes quite a lot but is a favorite with so many I freeze it and so can have it all year.

¾ pound pitted, strained persimmons
1 pound sugar
¾ pound butter
1 quart milk
6 eggs
1 nutmeg, grated

Combine all ingredients in kettle and cook slowly, constantly stirring until as thick as boiled custard. Pour into baking dishes and bake at 225 degrees for 1 hour or until knife inserted in center comes out clean.

—Isabel Atkinson Lieber (Mrs. Albert C.)

❧ *RASPBERRIES MARSALA*

>   2 10-ounce packages frozen raspberries, thawed
>   Marsala
>   1 cup heavy cream
>   ⅓ cup confectioners' sugar
>   2 tablespoons toasted, slivered almonds

Place undrained berries in serving bowl. Pour over 3 or 4 tablespoons Marsala and mix gently. Refrigerate, covered, 2 hours, or until well chilled. Beat cream with sugar until stiff. Fold in 1 tablespoon Marsala. Mound cream over berries in center of bowl; sprinkle with almonds. Serve at once. Serves 6 to 8.

—*Janet Gadd Doehler (Mrs. William F.)*

❧ *RICE PUDDING*

> *Another Centreville Tea Room favorite. Also popular at bake sales on the Courthouse Green and at the Bazaar Luncheons.*

> 4 or 5 eggs
>   ¾ cup sugar
>   dash salt
>   1 teaspoon vanilla
>   1 quart milk
>   ¾ cup cooked rice
>   ¾ cup raisins (optional)
>   nutmeg

Beat eggs, sugar, salt, and vanilla together. Add the milk, then the rice and raisins. Stir well and place in a 1½-quart baking dish. Sprinkle with nutmeg. Place dish in pan of water and put in preheated 350-degree oven. Cook for about a half hour or less. When pudding begins to thicken, place a spoon in the side of the dish and move gently to distribute rice and raisins through mixture. When finished, sprinkle a little nutmeg where you put the spoon (makes the top look better).

—*Bessie Dadds Bedford (Mrs. Morte)*

❧ RICE PUDDING ADOLFINE

  1 quart milk
  1 vanilla bean, split
  1 cup white rice
  ¾ cup sugar
  2½ pints whipping cream
  1 package frozen strawberries or raspberries, defrosted

Put milk in top of double boiler, add split vanilla bean, and let come to a boil. Add rice and sugar and cook until all milk is absorbed and rice is soft. Remove vanilla bean and set rice aside to cool. When cool, mix in cream, which has been whipped. (At this time, add 1 teaspoon vanilla if you did not have the vanilla bean). Grease 2-quart mold, pour in mixture, and let stand in refrigerator 4 hours or more. Remove from mold and serve with defrosted fruit. Serves 10 to 12.

—Louise Forstmann Wilson (Mrs. Kenneth)

❧ STRAWBERRY MOUSSE

  2½ envelopes unflavored gelatin
  2 cups milk
  2 10-ounce packages frozen strawberries, thawed
    juice of 1 lemon
  1 teaspoon orange extract
  ¼ cup sugar
  1½ cups whipping cream

Soften gelatin in ¼ cup cold milk and dissolve in rest of milk which has been heated. Puree strawberries when sufficiently thawed, and strain to remove seeds. Flavor strawberries with lemon juice and orange extract. When milk mixture is cool, add the strawberry mixture slowly. Chill until thick and syrupy, then beat until fluffy. Whip cream with sugar. Fold into strawberry mixture and chill until it begins to thicken, stirring occasionally. Pour into a 2-quart mold and refrigerate until very firm. Serve on platter with more strawberries and whipped cream. Raspberries may be used in place of strawberries. Makes 8 to 10 servings.

—Ruth Branner Gadd (Mrs. A. Sydney, Jr.)

🐚 *SPONGE PUDDING*

    1 pint milk
    4 tablespoons flour
    6 eggs, separated
       butter, the size of an egg

Bring milk to a boil, then add flour that has been mixed to a soft paste with a little cold milk. Cook slowly, stirring until thickened. Remove from fire and let cool. Add yolks of eggs, well beaten, then fold in stiffly beaten egg whites. Butter a 2-quart pudding dish. Pour in mixture, place in pan of hot water. Bake at 350 degrees for about 35 minutes or until firm. Serve at once with Wine Sauce.

Wine Sauce

This is also wonderful on English Plum Pudding.

    2 eggs
 1½ cups sugar
    ¼ pound butter
       a little nutmeg
       wine or brandy

Mix eggs and sugar in top of double boiler. Add butter and nutmeg. Cook, without boiling, until thick, remove from heat, and add a wine glass of wine or brandy.

—*Mary Emory Atkinson*

🐚 *VIENNESE PALATSCHINKEN*

    1 cup cottage cheese
    ¾ cup sugar
    2 tablespoons cream
       grated rind of 1 lemon
    2 eggs, plus 1 egg yolk, well beaten
    1 recipe Shrove Tuesday pancake batter

Mix cottage cheese, sugar, cream, and lemon rind with eggs. Put some of the mixture in the middle of each pancake, and roll. Serve hot. Makes 2 cups filling.

Shrove Tuesday Pancake Batter

2 tablespoons flour
dash salt
2 eggs plus 3 egg yolks
milk
dash of brandy

Mix dry ingredients, add eggs and yolks (beaten but not whipped), then add enough milk and a dash of brandy to make thin batter. Makes 12 pancakes.

—*Isabel Atkinson Lieber (Mrs. Albert C.)*

WINE JELLY I

1 cup sherry
1 package unflavored gelatin
1 cup orange juice (frozen)
1 teaspoon lemon juice
¾ cup sugar

Soak gelatin in sherry. Heat fruit juices to just under a boil; add to gelatin with sugar. Stir until fully dissolved. Pour into glasses. Refrigerate. Serves 4.

—*Margaret Hoey Fox (Mrs. Albert C.)*

WINE JELLY II

2 envelopes unflavored gelatin soaked in 1 cup cold water
2 cups boiling water
1¼ cups wine (sherry, port, or Madeira)
¾ cup sugar
¼ cup lemon juice
red food coloring

Make this a day ahead. Add gelatin soaked in cold water to the boiling water. Combine with remaining ingredients. Stir until dissolved and well blended. Chill. Serve with whipped cream. Serves 8.

—*Katherine Nicols Grove (Mrs. J. Robert)*

∾ *CHOCOLATE SAUCE*

2 squares unsweetened chocolate
1 tablespoon butter
⅓ cup boiling water
1 cup sugar
2 tablespoons light corn syrup
1 teaspoon vanilla
  salt

Melt chocolate in saucepan over hot water, and then add butter. Add to this very slowly the boiling water. Bring to boiling point, add sugar and corn syrup. Just bring to a boil. Cool slightly. Then add vanilla and a few grains of salt. Serve either hot or cold over ice cream. Makes 1 cup.

—*Marjorie McKenney (Mrs. William, Jr.)*

∾ *ULTIMATE CHOCOLATE SAUCE*

¼ cup semisweet chocolate chips
¼ cup butter
¼ cup cocoa (imported—Droste is the best)
½ cup sugar
½ cup heavy cream
⅛ teaspoon salt
1 teaspoon vanilla

Melt chocolate chips and butter. Stir until smooth. Add cocoa, sugar, cream, and salt. Bring to boiling point, stirring continuously. Remove from heat, add vanilla. Can be refrigerated indefinitely. This recipe can be doubled. Makes 1½ cups.

—*Amanda Bryan Marx (Mrs. Peter J.)*

∾ *SNOW PUDDING*

2 tablespoons unflavored gelatin
½ cup cold water
¾ cup boiling water
¼ teaspoon salt
1 cup granulated sugar

1½ cups strained fresh orange juice

¾ cup strained fresh lemon juice

4 egg whites

Soak gelatin in cold water, add salt, let set a few minutes, then pour boiling water over gelatin, stirring well over heat. Add sugar, cook until dissolved, then remove from heat, add cold water, and orange and lemon juice. Put in refrigerator to jell slightly. Beat egg whites 10 minutes and fold in jelled mixture, which has been beaten until light and fluffy. Return to refrigerator and let stand several hours until firm. To serve, pour cold boiled custard or whipped cream over each serving of snow.

—*Louise Perry (Mrs. John W.)*

BRANDY SAUCE

¼ pound butter

½ cup sugar

2 egg whites

½ cup boiling water

½ cup brandy

Cream butter and sugar for 5 minutes. Add egg whites, beaten, but not too stiff. Fold in ½ cup boiling water. Put above ingredients in double boiler. Add brandy. Stir until light. Do not boil.

—*Clara Bayless (Mrs. C. B.)*

MISS ALICE TURPIN'S PLUM PUDDING SAUCE

2 ounces (¼ cup or ½ stick) butter

6 ounces (¾ cup) sugar

2 eggs, well beaten

grated rind and juice of 1 lemon

4 ounces (½ cup) brandy

Cream butter and sugar; add eggs and lemon juice and rind. Place in double boiler and stir until blended, using moderate heat. Add brandy before serving. Makes 1 cup.

—*Miss Caroline Wilson*

❧ *BUTTERSCOTCH SAUCE*

    1¼ cups brown sugar
    ⅔ cup light corn syrup
    4 tablespoons butter
        salt
    ⅔ cup evaporated milk

Combine brown sugar, corn syrup, and butter in saucepan. Boil until thick. Cool, then add evaporated milk and a pinch of salt. Maple syrup may be substituted for corn syrup. Makes 2 cups.

—Katherine Nicols Grove (Mrs. J. Robert)

$\mathcal{P}$ASTRIES

Bless me, O Lord, and let my food
Strengthen me to serve thee,
For Jesus Christ's sake.
—A New England Primer

🍂 ANGEL PIE

    2 egg whites
    ½ cup sugar
    ⅛ teaspoon cream of tartar
    ⅛ teaspoon salt
    1 6-ounce package chocolate chips
    3 tablespoons water
    1 teaspoon vanilla
    1 cup heavy cream, whipped

Beat egg whites until stiff. Add sugar gradually, then cream of tartar and salt. Beat until they stand in peaks. Line buttered pie plate with this and bake at 300 degrees for 55 minutes. Cool. Melt chocolate chips with 3 tablespoons water over hot water. Cool. Add 1 teaspoon vanilla and fold in whipped cream. Pour into meringue shell. Chill several hours, or overnight. Makes 1 9-inch pie.

—Dorothy Keith Perkins (Mrs. Louis H.)

🍂 CHEESE PIE

    1 unbaked 8-inch graham cracker crust
    3 eggs
    1 cup sugar
    ⅛ teaspoon salt
    1 teaspoon lemon juice
    ½ teaspoon vanilla
    1 8-ounce package cream cheese
    1 cup sour cream
    1 tablespoon sugar
    ½ teaspoon vanilla

Beat eggs with the sugar and salt until creamy. Add lemon juice, vanilla, and cream cheese, and beat all together until smooth. Pour into unbaked crust. Bake at 325 degrees for 45 to 60 minutes. Remove from oven and top with sour cream to which sugar and vanilla have been added. Turn off heat, put back in oven, and let cool in oven. Makes 1 8-inch pie.

—Mary Morris Young (Mrs. George, Sr.)

❧ *CHOCOLATE ANGEL PIE*

> 2 egg whites
>   pinch salt
> ⅛ teaspoon cream of tartar
> ½ cup sugar
> ½ teaspoon vanilla
> ½ cup finely chopped walnuts or pecans
> 1 4-ounce bar Baker's German's Brand Sweet Chocolate
> 3 tablespoons water
> 1 teaspoon vanilla
> 1 cup whipping cream

Beat egg whites with salt and cream of tartar until foamy. Add sugar (2 tablespoons at a time), beating well after each addition. Continue beating until very stiff peaks form. Fold in vanilla and nuts. Spoon into lightly greased 8-inch pie pan to form nestlike shell. Build sides up ½ inch above edge of pan. Bake at 300 degrees for 50 to 55 minutes. Cool. Stir chocolate in water over low heat until melted. Cool, then add vanilla. Whip cream and fold into chocolate mixture. Pile into shell. Chill 2 hours or more. Serves 6 to 8.

—*Matilda Sause (Mrs. William)*

❧ *CHOCOLATE BROWNIE PIE*

> 3 egg whites
>   pinch of salt
> ¾ cup sugar
> ¾ cup fine chocolate wafer crumbs
> ½ cup chopped nuts
> ½ teaspoon vanilla

Beat egg whites and salt until peaks form. Slowly add sugar and beat until stiff. Fold in crumbs and nuts. Add vanilla. Spread in pie plate. Bake at 325 degrees about 45 minutes. Let cool and put in refrigerator. Serve cold with whipped cream. Makes 1 9-inch pie.

—*Lois S. Duffey (Mrs. Harry J., Jr.)*

❦ *RICH CHOCOLATE PIE*

        1 baked 9-inch pie shell
        1 pint hot milk
        3 heaping tablespoons cocoa
    1½ ounces butter
        3 eggs, separated
        1 cup sugar
        2 heaping tablespoons cornstarch
      ¼ teaspoon salt
        1 tablespoon vanilla
        6 tablespoons sugar
      ¼ teaspoon salt
      ½ teaspoon baking powder (scant)

Pour hot milk slowly over cocoa, add butter, and heat until butter melts. Beat egg yolks until light, add sugar, beat until light, add cornstarch and salt. Combine milk and egg mixtures. Cook in double boiler to thicken. Let cool, add vanilla, and pour into baked pie shell. Beat egg whites 10 minutes, add sugar and beat until glossy. Add salt and baking powder. Spread meringue over filling to edges of crust to prevent shrinkage. Bake at 350 degrees for 15 to 20 minutes. Burns easily. Set on rack to cool. Makes 1 9-inch pie.

—*Louise McFeely Perry (Mrs. John W.)*

❦ *QUICK APPLE PIE*

This is the best apple pie I've ever eaten. It's the lemon juice that makes the difference.

        unbaked pastry for 9-inch 2-crust pie
    4 cups peeled, cored, thinly sliced apples
    ¾ cup sugar, or more if apples are tart
    ¼ cup water
    1 teaspoon cinnamon
    ¼ teaspoon nutmeg
        juice and grated rind of 1 lemon

Simmer all these ingredients 20 minutes while you make crust. Pour apple mixture into unbaked crust; dot with butter. Place top crust, crimp edges, smear top with softened butter, flour, then milk. Cut a slash or two in middle of crust. Bake for 20 minutes at 450 degrees. Sprinkle liberally with powdered sugar while hot.

—Virginia Ingles Freeland (Mrs. Samuel L.)

BLACK BOTTOM PIE

- 1 baked 9-inch piecrust (graham cracker or chocolate chip cookie; I prefer chocolate chip)
- 1 envelope unflavored gelatin
- 1¾ cups milk
- 4 eggs, separated
- 1 cup granulated sugar
- ½ teaspoon salt
- ½ teaspoon cornstarch
- 1½ squares unsweetened or bittersweet chocolate, melted
- 1 teaspoon vanilla
- 3 tablespoons rum, or to taste (not extract)
- 1 cup heavy cream
- 2 tablespoons confectioners' sugar
- ½ square bittersweet chocolate, shaved

Soak gelatin in ¼ cup milk. Scald remaining 1½ cups milk in double boiler. Beat egg yolks; beat in ½ cup sugar, salt, and cornstarch. Add hot milk slowly, stirring constantly. Return to double boiler and cook slowly about 4 minutes, stirring constantly until custard coats the spoon. Remove from heat. Remove ½ cup custard and add gelatin to remaining custard. Stir until dissolved. Melt chocolate in small bowl over boiling water, stir in ½ cup custard and vanilla. Beat until blended and cool to room temperature. Pour chocolate into chilled baked crust. Chill until firm. Chill remaining custard until it begins to set, and add rum. Beat egg whites until stiff but not dry and gradually beat in ½ cup sugar and fold into custard. Pour custard over chocolate mixture in pie shell. Chill until firm. Whip cream until stiff, fold in confectioners' sugar. Put cream on top of pie with pastry tube. Finely shave ½ square chocolate and sprinkle over cream. Chill before serving. Serves 8 to 10.

—Janet Gadd Doehler (Mrs. William F.)

❦ *COCONUT CREAM PIE*

    1 baked 9-inch pie shell
    2 cups milk
    3 eggs
    ½ cup sugar
  2½ tablespoons cornstarch
    2 tablespoons butter
    1 cup shredded coconut
    1 teaspoon vanilla
    6 tablespoons sugar

Scald milk in double boiler. Add beaten egg yolks, sugar, and corn-starch. Cook until very thick. Add butter, coconut, and vanilla. Pour into baked pie shell. Beat egg whites until frothy, then begin adding sugar, a little at a time, until whites are stiff but not dry. Spread meringue on top of filling. Bake at 350 degrees until brown.

—Margaret Fesmyer Wolcott (Mrs. Milton)

❦ *COCONUT CUSTARD PIE*

    1 cup granulated sugar
    3 egg yolks
    2 cups milk
    1 tablespoon (heaping) cornstarch
    ¼ teaspoon salt
    ¾ cup shredded coconut
    1 teaspoon vanilla

Cream together sugar and egg yolks. Add milk, cornstarch, and salt. Cook until mixture thickens. Add the coconut and cook a few seconds longer. Add vanilla. Cool slightly, stir, and pour into baked piecrust. Cover with meringue, if desired (see Rich Chocolate Pie above). Makes 1 9-inch pie.

Piecrust

  1½ cups sifted bread flour
    ½ teaspoon salt
    1 teaspoon baking powder
    ⅓ heaping cup lard
    3 tablespoons cold water

Mix dry ingredients. Cut lard into dry ingredients, then add water and blend together. Flour board and roll out. Bake 8 or 10 minutes at 450 degrees on bottom shelf before adding custard. Makes 2 9-inch crusts. (Save one for another pie or double the filling recipe).

—*Louise McFeely Perry (Mrs. John W.)*

❧ LEMON PIE

  1½ cups cold water
  ¾ cup sugar
  ¼ teaspoon salt
  1 tablespoon grated lemon rind
  4 tablespoons flour
  2 tablespoons cornstarch
  3 egg yolks
  1 tablespoon melted butter
  4 tablespoons lemon juice

Mix all ingredients together thoroughly; cook in double boiler until thick. Cool; pour into baked crust.

Pastry

  1½ cups sifted pastry flour
  ½ teaspoon salt
  ½ cup shortening
4 to 5 tablespoons cold water

Sift together flour and salt. Cut in shortening with a fork, half at a time. Add the water. Form into ball. Let stand, roll out. Bake at 450 degrees.

Meringue

  3 egg whites
  ¼ teaspoon salt
  6 tablespoons sugar
  1 teaspoon vanilla

Beat egg whites and salt until frothy. (Whites will whip better at room temperature.) Add sugar, one tablespoon at a time. Beat until stiff and glossy. Add vanilla. Spread over pie, being careful to seal edges. Bake until meringue is brown.

—*Miss Caroline W. Owings*

❦ *GRAHAM CRACKER PIE*

1 baked 9-inch pastry shell
1 pint cream
4 eggs, separated
¼ cup sugar
1 tablespoon cornstarch
1 teaspoon vanilla
  sugar
14 graham crackers (crumbled)

Make a custard of cream, egg yolks, sugar, and cornstarch and cook in double boiler until it thickens. Remove double boiler from heat and put cold water in the bottom of the boiler. Continue beating until the custard is cool. Add vanilla. Sprinkle the bottom of the pastry shell with a little sugar and some cracker crumbs, and spread a layer of custard. Then spread another layer of cracker crumbs and another layer of custard until pie is filled. Reserve some crumbs for garnish. Beat the whites of the eggs stiff, add a little sugar, and spread on top of pie. Sprinkle on top a few more cracker crumbs and brown in the oven. Chill and serve. Makes 1 9-inch pie.

—Eleanor Williams Miles (Mrs. Clarence W.)

❦ *FROZEN LEMON PIE*

½ cup sugar
3 eggs, separated
¼ teaspoon salt
  grated rind and juice of 1 lemon (use extra rind if desired)
1 cup heavy cream, whipped
3 cups graham cracker crumbs
½ cup chopped pecans

Combine sugar and egg yolks, lemon juice and rind, and salt in double boiler. Cook over hot but not boiling water until thickened, stirring constantly. Cool, then fold in whipped cream and stiffly beaten egg whites (beat eggs 10 minutes). Mix ⅔ cup graham cracker crumbs with chopped pecans. Sprinkle half of crumb mixture in bottom of ice tray, add lemon mixture and top with rest of crumbs. Better made day before serving. Serves 6 to 8.

—Frances Perry Horton

❧ *LEMON CHIFFON PIE*

 1 9-inch baked pastry shell
 3 eggs, separated
 1 cup sugar
 3 tablespoons water
  grated rind and juice of 1 lemon
  pinch of salt

Beat egg yolks with ½ cup sugar and water. Add lemon juice and rind. Add salt. Cook over hot water until slightly thickened. Beat whites with ½ cup sugar until stiff. Fold into the custard. Pour into baked pie shell. Brown at 400 degrees for about 10 minutes. Makes 1 pie.

—Dorothy Keith Perkins (Mrs. Louis H.)

❧ *OSLO PASTRY (Easy Method for Puff Pastry)*

 1¼ cups butter
 2 cups plus 2 tablespoons unsifted flour
 8 tablespoons water

Take ⅓ of butter, cold, and mix with all the flour. Work in with fingers. Pour in water and knead gently until smooth. Roll in a ball and place in refrigerator for at least 15 minutes. Roll out to knife thinness and spread with part of butter which has softened while standing out. Fold by lifting edges over each other, then both ends over each other. Let rest in refrigerator 15 minutes and repeat until all butter is used. When ready for tart, cut in rounds; place cooked, well-drained fruit or meat or fish hash in center and fold over; seal edges. Bake at 375 degrees for about 20 minutes. Watch, as they burn easily. When used as a dessert, sprinkle powdered sugar on top or decorate with a sugar icing.

  The original recipe called for 250 grams flour and 250 grams butter—always use equal *weights* of flour and butter. The more often this dough is rolled out and buttered the lighter it will be. Butter can be put on thickly, but it is better when thinly spread. This dough freezes well and can be used for patty shells, as well as turnovers or Napoleons—layers of pastry with fruit filling between. Filling should be quite dry. Makes about 1 pound of pastry.

—Lynette Morgan Nielsen (Mrs. Orsen)

🌸 *MERINGUE SHELL BERRY PIE*

    10 soda crackers, rolled very fine
    ½ cup finely chopped nuts
    1 teaspoon baking powder
    3 egg whites
        pinch of salt
    1 cup granulated sugar
    1 teaspoon vanilla
        whipped cream
        berries or fruit

Mix thoroughly first three ingredients. Add pinch of salt to egg whites and beat until stiff. Fold in 1 cup of sugar and vanilla. Add cracker mixture. Spread in well-buttered 9-inch pie tin. Bake 30 minutes at 325 degrees or less. Serve with a dash of whipped cream and sprinkle with berries or fruit. Makes 1 pie.

—Elizabeth Harper Collins (Mrs. Jackson R.)

🌸 *PUMPKIN PIE I*

    1 unbaked 10-inch pastry shell
    2 eggs
    ¾ cup sugar
    1 teaspoon cinnamon
    1 teaspoon ginger
    ½ teaspoon salt
    1 tablespoon molasses
  1½ cups pumpkin
    1 tablespoon flour
    1 tablespoon melted butter
  1½ cups milk

Beat eggs; add sugar, spices, salt, molasses, and pumpkin. Then add flour and butter. Add milk last. Put in unbaked piecrust and bake at 425 degrees for 35 to 45 minutes. Makes 1 10-inch pie.

—Frances Wright Hilleary (Mrs. Robert)

🍂 *PUMPKIN PIE II*

    2 unbaked 9-inch pastry shells (see below)
    1 quart canned pumpkin
  ¼ pound butter
    3 eggs, separated, plus 1 egg white
 1½ cups sugar
  ½ rounded teaspoon ginger
  ¼ level teaspoon powdered cloves
 1½ heaping teaspoons cinnamon
    1 cup rich milk or cream
  ½ cup whiskey or brandy
  ¼ teaspoon salt
    2 level tablespoons cornstarch
    1 heaping teaspoon baking powder

Melt butter with pumpkin in pan over low heat, stirring often. Beat yolks until light, add sugar and beat well. Add ginger, cloves, and cinnamon. Stir in milk, whiskey or brandy, salt, cornstarch, and baking powder. Fold in stiffly beaten egg whites. Bake on bottom shelf at 450 degrees for 15 minutes, then on middle shelf at 350 degrees for 45 to 55 minutes or until custard is set but not dry. Makes 2 pies.

Crust for Pumpkin Pie

 1½ cups sifted flour (level cups)
    1 teaspoon cinnamon
  ¼ teaspoon salt
      scant ½ teaspoon Calumet baking powder
  ⅓ heaping cup lard
    3 tablespoons cold water

Make crust before making filling. Sift all dry ingredients together and then work in lard, then cold water. Form into 2 balls and roll them out. Makes 2 9-inch crusts.

—Louise McFeely Perry (Mrs. John W.)

❧ RITZ PIE

    3 egg whites
    1 cup sugar
    ½ teaspoon baking powder
   14 Ritz crackers, crushed
    ⅔ cup chopped pecans
    1 teaspoon vanilla
       whipped cream

Beat egg whites until stiff. Beat in sugar and baking powder. Fold in cracker crumbs, nuts, and vanilla. Spread in well-greased 9-inch pie pan. Bake at 325 degrees for 1 hour. Cool. Spread top with thin layer of whipped cream. Put in refrigerator until ready to serve. Makes 1 9-inch pie.

Committee note: Cream may be flavored with a liqueur such as Cointreau.

—*Mrs. George Kennedy*

❧ RUM PIE

    1 baked 8- or 9-inch graham cracker crust
    2 cups milk
    ¾ cup sugar
       pinch of salt
    5 egg yolks
    ¼ cup flour
    2 tablespoons cornstarch
    ½ cup butter
    2 teaspoons dark rum
       whipped cream
       chopped pecans
       grated chocolate

Heat 1½ cups milk in a double boiler with ¾ cup sugar and a pinch of salt. Beat egg yolks lightly with ½ cup milk, and beat in the flour and cornstarch. Stir the egg yolk mixture into the hot milk mixture and cook the sauce, stirring until it is thick and smooth without boiling. Cool slightly and beat in ½ cup softened (room temperature) butter. Flavor with rum. Pour the cream mixture into pie plate lined with a graham cracker crust and chill. Just before serving, decorate the pie with whipped cream, chopped pecans, and grated chocolate. Makes 1 8- or 9-inch pie.

—*Jean Weller*

❧ *SHOO-FLY PIE*

In the Dutch country this is not a dessert. It is a breakfast treat.

- 1 unbaked 9-inch pastry shell
- 1½ cups flour
- 1 cup brown sugar
- ½ cup butter (or margarine)
- ¾ teaspoon soda
- ⅛ teaspoon nutmeg
- ⅛ teaspoon ginger
- ⅛ teaspoon cinnamon
- ¼ teaspoon salt
- ¾ cup dark molasses
- ¾ cup hot water

Work the flour, sugar, and butter together. In a separate bowl, mix remaining ingredients. Put some of crumb mixture into unbaked pie shell, then alternate liquid and crumbs, ending with crumbs on top. Bake 15 minutes at 450 degrees, then 20 minutes at 350 degrees. Makes 1 9-inch pie.

—*Katharine Nicols Grove (Mrs. J. Robert)*

❧ *FRESH PEACH PIE*

- 1 unbaked 9-inch pastry shell
- 5 cups sliced fresh peaches
- ⅓ cup butter, melted
- 1 cup sugar
- ⅓ cup all-purpose flour
- 1 egg
  dash of nutmeg

Place peaches in pastry shell. Combine remaining ingredients and pour over peaches. Bake at 350 degrees for 1 hour and 10 minutes.

—*Mary Davy Pippin (Mrs. James O., Jr.)*

🌿 WHITE POTATO CUSTARD PIE

 1 unbaked 10-inch pastry shell
 1 pound white potatoes, peeled and cut up
 ¼ pound butter
 5 eggs, separated
 1½ cups granulated sugar
  grated rind and juice of 1½ lemons
 ¼ teaspoon salt
 ¼ teaspoon nutmeg
 1 teaspoon baking powder (rounded)

Cook potatoes in slightly salted water until tender, then put through ricer. Add butter to hot potatoes and mix well. Beat egg yolks until thick and lemon colored, adding sugar slowly. Pour over potatoes and mix together. Beat egg whites 10 minutes and fold in. Add the rind and juice of lemons. Add salt, nutmeg, and baking powder. Put into unbaked pastry shell. Sprinkle extra nutmeg over top before putting in oven. Bake at 450 degrees on bottom shelf for 15 minutes; then on middle shelf at 350 degrees for 30 minutes more. Makes 1 10-inch pie.

—*Louise McFeely Perry (Mrs. John W.)*

🌿 HELEN MILLER'S WHITE POTATO PIE

 1 unbaked 9-inch pastry shell (see below)
 1 cup peeled, cooked, and mashed russet potatoes
 ½ stick butter (¼ cup)
 1 cup milk
 ½ cup sugar
 ½ teaspoon salt
 2 eggs, separated
  grated rind and juice of ½ lemon
 1 teaspoon vanilla
 ½ teaspoon nutmeg

Put hot potatoes in mixer along with butter. Slowly add milk. Add sugar, salt, and beaten egg yolks. Add grated lemon rind. Strain lemon juice and add to mixture with vanilla. Beat egg whites until they form a peak. Fold into mixture. Pour into pastry shell. Sprinkle with nutmeg. Preheat oven to 350 degrees and bake for 45 to 60 minutes, or until toothpick inserted in center is clean.

Pastry

⅓ cup water
1 egg, lightly beaten
1 tablespoon vinegar
3 cups unbleached, all-purpose flour
1 cup shortening
1 teaspoon salt

Blend water, egg, and vinegar together. Blend flour, shortening, and salt until consistency of coarse meal. Toss two mixtures together lightly, and form loose ball. Let stand for half an hour and then divide into 4 equal parts. Wrap and freeze in plastic until ready to use. Makes 4 9-inch pastry shells.

❦ *FRUIT TORTE*

½ cup butter
1 cup sugar
1 cup flour, sifted
1 teaspoon baking powder
2 eggs
    salt (about ¼ teaspoon, depending on salt in butter)
    fresh fruit

Cream butter and sugar. Sift flour, baking powder and salt together and work into butter mixture. Beat eggs slightly and beat into mixture. Cover bottom of 9-inch springform with batter.

Cover entire surface of batter with fruit, such as 1 pint blueberries or 24 halves pitted Italian plums (skin side up); sliced apples or peaches or sliced Raffetto brand Harlequin stuffed oranges. If you have no fresh fruit, use frozen or canned fruits but drain well. Sprinkle top of fruit and torte with sugar, lemon juice, flour (if fruit is very juicy), and cinnamon.

Bake at 350 degrees for 1 hour. Delicious when served with vanilla ice cream or whipped cream. Best served slightly warm. Serves 8.

—*Nancy Jane Reed (Mrs. Adrian)*

🌿 *PECAN PIE*

  1 uncooked, chilled 9-inch pie shell
¾ cup sugar
  1 cup dark Karo syrup
  3 eggs, beaten
  4 tablespoons butter or margarine
  1 teaspoon vanilla
  1 cup coarsely broken pecans
     pecan halves

Boil sugar and syrup together about 2 minutes. Pour slowly over beaten eggs, stirring constantly. Add butter, vanilla, and pecans. Stir until butter is melted. Pour into shell. Decorate with pecan halves. Bake at 350 degrees for 50 to 60 minutes. Makes 6 to 8 servings.

—Anne Stoney Cantler (Mrs. James E.)

🌿 *MOCHA WALNUT TORTE*

  1 16-ounce package brownie mix (Duncan Hines is best)
  2 eggs
¼ cup water
½ cup walnuts
  2 cups whipping cream
½ cup brown sugar
  1 scant tablespoon instant coffee granules

Mix together brownie mix, eggs, water, and nuts as directed on brownie mix box and bake in two 8-inch round cake pans as directed on package. Whip cream, gradually adding brown sugar and coffee granules. Ice brownie cake. Chill overnight. Serve garnished with chocolate shavings.

—Janet Gadd Doehler (Mrs. William F.)

𝒞AKES

The gifts of God for the people of God;
Therefore let us keep the feast.

—Book of Common Prayer

APPLESAUCE CAKE

  2½ cups unsweetened applesauce, heated
  ¾ cup shortening
   4 teaspoons baking soda
   1 cup lukewarm water
  1¾ cups sugar
     pinch salt
   1 teaspoon cinnamon
   1 teaspoon nutmeg
   1 teaspoon ground allspice
   1 teaspoon ground cloves
   1 pound seedless raisins dipped in flour to keep separated
  ¼ pound chopped nuts
  3½ cups flour

Add shortening to pan of hot applesauce and continue heating until it dissolves. Remove from stove and add soda dissolved in the water. Add remaining ingredients. Stir slowly by hand. When ingredients are well mixed, pour into a 10-inch tube pan that has been greased and floured. Bake at 350 degrees for about 1 hour, 15 minutes. Makes large cake, 18 to 20 average slices.

—Nellie Brown Whiteley (Mrs. J. Harman)

APRICOT BRANDY CAKE

   1 cup butter or ½ cup butter and ½ cup margarine
   3 cups sugar
   6 eggs
   3 cups flour
  ½ teaspoon salt
  ¼ teaspoon baking soda
   1 cup sour cream
  ½ cup apricot brandy
   1 teaspoon vanilla
  ½ teaspoon rum extract
  ½ teaspoon lemon extract
  ½ teaspoon almond extract
     powdered sugar

melted butter
brandy

Cream together butter and sugar. Add eggs, one at a time. Sift flour, salt, and baking soda together. Mix sour cream, apricot brandy, and all extracts together. Alternately add sour cream mixture and flour mixture to creamed butter and sugar. Pour into a greased and floured 10-inch angel food cake pan. Bake at 325 degrees for 70 minutes or until done. Mix powdered sugar with small amount of melted butter. Add brandy to make necessary consistency for a glaze. Prick cake and brush with glaze. Makes a large cake.

—*Ruby Young (Mrs. Herbert)*

BLACKBERRY JAM CAKE

This very old recipe by an Ozark mountain woman travelled with the pioneers westward and over the mountains. It was a very special treat at Christmas.

2 cups sugar
1 cup shortening (originally I used butter)
4 eggs, separated
1 teaspoon vanilla
3 cups flour
1 teaspoon soda
2 teaspoons cinnamon
1 teaspoon nutmeg
1 teaspoon ground cloves
1 teaspoon allspice
1 cup buttermilk
1 cup seedless blackberry jam
1 cup chopped black walnuts

Cream sugar and shortening. Beat in the egg yolks and vanilla. Add combined dry ingredients alternately with buttermilk. Stir in jam and nuts and then fold in beaten egg whites that are stiff but not dry. Pour into a greased 10-inch tube pan or 2 9-inch greased cake pans. Bake at 325 degrees for 30 minutes then increase to 350 degrees and bake for 40 more minutes.

—*Jane Corey (Mrs. R. Reece)*

🐝 BLACK WALNUT CAKE

> 1 cup butter
> 2 cups sugar
> 4 eggs
> 1 cup milk
> 4 cups all-purpose flour
> 3 teaspoons baking powder
> 1½ cups black walnuts
> ½ pound seedless raisins

Cream butter and sugar. Add eggs, one at a time, beating thoroughly after each. Add dry ingredients alternately with milk. Add nuts and raisins which have been well floured with some of the flour called for in the recipe. Bake at 325 degrees for about 1 hour, 20 minutes in large loaf pan which has been buttered and floured well, or a 9-inch tube pan.

—Ruth Newell (Mrs. Robert)

🐝 HALLIE'S FRENCH COUNTRY STYLE CHEESECAKE

> 3 to 4 tablespoons unsalted butter
> ½ cup (more or less) graham cracker crumbs
> 2 pounds cream cheese at room temperature
> ¾ cup heavy cream
> 1½ cups sugar (superfine if you have it)
> 6 eggs
> grated rind and juice of 1½ lemons
> 1 to 2 teaspoons vanilla
> 1 teaspoon grated fresh ginger (if you have it)

Grease 9- or 10-inch soufflé dish with butter, sprinkle with crumbs. Reserve excess for top. Place cream cheese in bowl of electric mixer. Start beating at low speed. Add cream and then sugar and lemon rind. Continue beating, adding eggs one at a time, then lemon juice, vanilla, and ginger. Increase speed until ingredients are blended, smooth, and fluffy. Pour batter into prepared dish; sprinkle crumbs on top. Put dish in larger pan of hot water, 1½ inches deep. Bake in preheated oven at 325 degrees for 1½ hours. Turn off and let sit for another ½ hour. Place pan on rack until cool. Flip onto serving plate. Serves 10 to 12.

—Hallie Rogers Rugg (Mrs. Daniel M.)

🍂 HAZELNUT CHEESECAKE

     4 tablespoons butter
     2 tablespoons honey
     2 cups finely crumbled graham crackers
     1 cup hazelnuts
     2 pounds cream cheese at room temperature
 1¾ cups sugar
     4 eggs
     ½ teaspoon lemon zest
     ⅓ cup graham cracker crumbs
        hazelnuts for decoration

Melt butter and honey together. Add to graham cracker crumbs and mix well. Press firmly into buttered 8-inch springform pan 3 inches high. Bake 10 minutes in 350 degree oven. Cool thoroughly.

Spread hazelnuts in a shallow pan and bake in preheated oven at 325 degrees , stirring occasionally, for about 15 minutes, or until the skins begin to flake off and nuts are lightly browned. Now, a few at a time, place in a terrycloth towel and rub vigorously. Most of the skin will come off. If a few bits of skin remain, just leave them. Pick out the nuts and discard the skins. Grind nuts and save some ground nuts for garnish. Beat cream cheese in a bowl until very smooth. Scrape sides of bowl frequently. When cheese is smooth, beat in sugar very well, then add the eggs, one at a time. After adding the eggs, beat only to blend the ingredients. Stir in the lemon zest and hazelnuts with spatula. Turn batter into previously prepared crust in springform pan. Level batter and place pan in a larger pan with hot water to a depth of 1½ inches. Bake in a preheated oven at 350 degrees for 1¼ hours or until top is golden brown and dry to touch. Cool cheese cake in the pan on a rack for a few hours or until completely cool. Sprinkle graham cracker crumbs and hazelnuts on top for garnish if desired. Serves 10 to 12.

—*Barbara Colthurst Bryan (Mrs. David C.)*

During the fuel shortages of World War II, Gunston School students rode horses to St. Paul's and tethered them at the church house hitching post while they attended services.

🍃 CHEESE CAKE

1½ pounds ricotta
  1 pound cream cheese
  1 pint sour cream
  6 eggs
1½ cups sugar
  1 tablespoon vanilla
  1 teaspoon lemon juice
  6 heaping tablespoons flour

First cream ricotta, cream cheese, and sour cream; then add 6 eggs, one at a time, beating well; then add sugar and flavoring; last add flour. Pour into a greased and floured 10-inch springform pan. Bake at 350 degrees for 1 hour; shut off oven and let stand in oven overnight.

You can use light cheeses, light sour cream, and egg substitute, and it will turn out so well no one would know.

—*Margaret Gadd Kelly (Mrs. B. J.)*

🍃 CHOCOLATE CAKE

Here is a disastrously good, rich, moist sheet cake to serve a crowd.

     2 sticks margarine
     1 cup water
4 to 6 heaping tablespoons of good cocoa (not instant)
     2 cups sugar
     2 eggs
     2 cups flour
    ½ teaspoon baking soda
    ½ cup sour cream

Bring margarine, water, and cocoa to a boil. Remove from heat and add sugar. Beat eggs until light. Pour into the cocoa mixture. Beat in flour mixed with soda. Beat in sour cream. Pour into a greased and floured pan (11½ × 15½ inches). Bake at 350 degrees for 25 minutes or until done. Spread icing (see below) on cake while still hot. After icing and cooling, cut in brownie-sized squares. Really heavenly. Makes 24 servings.

Icing

1 stick margarine
4 tablespoons cocoa
6 tablespoons milk
1 cup chopped pecans
1 1-pound box confectioners' sugar
1 teaspoon vanilla

Bring margarine, cocoa, and milk to a boil. Remove from heat and stir in nuts, confectioners' sugar, and vanilla. Beat until smooth.

—Janie Eby Ashley (Mrs. Sydney G.)

DOUBLE DELIGHT CHOCOLATE CAKE

2 3-ounce packages cream cheese
½ cup soft margarine
1 teaspoon vanilla
6½ cups (1½ pounds) powdered sugar
⅓ cup milk
5 squares unsweetened chocolate, melted and cooled
4 tablespoons margarine, soft
3 eggs
2¼ cups all-purpose flour
1 teaspoon baking powder
1 teaspoon baking soda
1 teaspoon salt
1¼ cups milk

Cream cheese, margarine, and vanilla. Alternately beat in sugar and milk. Blend in chocolate. Reserve 2 cups for frosting. Cover and refrigerate. Cream together remaining chocolate mix and margarine. Add eggs, one at a time; beat well. Stir together dry ingredients. Beat into creamed mix alternately with milk. Turn into 2 greased and floured 9 × 1½-inch cake pans. Bake at 350 degrees for 30 minutes. Cool in pans 10 minutes. Remove and cool on cake racks. Remove frosting from refrigerator 15 minutes before frosting cake.

—Beverly Leager Carter (Mrs. James H.)

🐾 GINGER CHEESECAKE

¾ pound pecans, ground
2 tablespoons brown sugar
1 egg white, beaten until frothy
1 teaspoon finely grated lemon rind
2 pounds cream cheese, softened
¾ cup sugar
4 eggs, lightly beaten
½ cup heavy cream
1 teaspoon vanilla extract
1 cup minced ginger preserves
2 teaspoons ground ginger
1 tablespoon finely grated fresh ginger
1 ounce candied ginger, minced

Preheat oven to 300 degrees. Butter a 9-inch springform pan. To make the crust, in a large bowl mix the first 4 ingredients. Press the mixture onto the bottom and sides of the pan.

In a bowl, beat the cream cheese and sugar until the mixture is smooth and light. Add the remaining ingredients, except the candied ginger, and mix well. Pour the filling into the crust in the springform pan. Bake at 300 degrees for 1 hour, 40 minutes. Turn off the heat and leave the cheesecake in the oven to cool for 1 hour. Remove from oven and chill.

To serve, remove the outside of the pan. Sprinkle the cheesecake with the candied ginger. Makes 12 servings. This can be frozen; defrost before serving.

—Barbara Colthurst Bryan (Mrs. David C.)

🐾 BRAZIL NUT FRUITCAKE

Nuts and fruit are left whole and when slices are cut with a sharp knife they are boldly mosaic in appearance.

3 cups shelled Brazil nuts
1 pound pitted dates

    1 cup drained maraschino cherries
    ¾ cup sifted all-purpose flour
    ¾ cup sugar
    ½ teaspoon baking powder
    ½ teaspoon salt
    3 eggs
    1 teaspoon vanilla

Put nuts, dates, and cherries in large bowl. Sift flour, sugar, baking powder, and salt over nuts and fruits. Mix with hands until nuts and fruits are coated. Beat eggs until foamy; add vanilla. Stir into nut-fruit mixture until well mixed. Turn into greased and waxed paper-lined pan, 9½ × 5½ × 2¾ inches. Bake at 300 degrees for 1 hour and 45 minutes. Cool before removing from pan. Makes a 3-pound cake.

—Jane Hollingsworth Voshell (Mrs. Edward)

❧ MANGO CHEESECAKE

    1 9-inch graham cracker pie shell
    1 large finely chopped mango (1¼ cups)
    ½ cup sugar
    2 teaspoons lime juice
    1 envelope unflavored gelatin
    12 ounces cream cheese
    ¾ cup sour cream
    1 teaspoon vanilla

Combine finely chopped mango, sugar, and lime juice. Cover and refrigerate 20 minutes, then drain liquid from mango (½ cup). Soften gelatin in mango liquid; dissolve over hot water, then return gelatin mixture to mango. Beat cream cheese until light. Stir in sour cream and vanilla. Fold mango into cheese mixture. Turn into pie shell and refrigerate. Garnish with sliced mangoes. Serves 8 to 10.

—Nancy Jane Austin Reed (Mrs. Adrian P.)

🍂 *DARK FRUITCAKE*

I make these at Thanksgiving for Christmas. Pour whiskey, brandy, or other liquor over cake several times during the month.

1½ cups butter
 2 cups sugar
 6 eggs
 ½ cup black molasses
 ¼ cup brandy (or grape juice)
 1 teaspoon soda
 ½ cup black coffee
 4 cups flour (sift before measuring)
 1 teaspoon cinnamon
 1 teaspoon nutmeg
 1 teaspoon cloves
 ½ pound blanched almonds
 ½ pound broken English walnuts
 ½ pound stoned and chopped dates
 1 pound currants
 1 pound raisins
 1 pound candied cherries
 1 pound candied pineapple

Cream butter, sugar; add eggs, molasses, brandy, soda dissolved in coffee; then flour and spices. Last, add nuts and fruit which have been floured with part of the measured flour. Line tube of angel food cake pans with greased, heavy tinfoil. Bake at 275 degrees for 2 to 4 hours. Serves 18 or more. Store in a large tin can with 1 apple to keep it moist. This makes 2 large cakes, about 9 pounds.

—*Margaret Gadd Ashley (Mrs. John M.)*

🍂 *BLACK FRUITCAKE*

¼ pound candied cherries
¼ pound candied pineapple
¼ pound candied orange peel
¼ pound candied lemon peel
½ pound candied citron

1 pound raisins

1 package dates

½ pound figs

1 cup English walnut pieces

1 cup black walnut pieces

½ pound butter

½ pound sugar

6 eggs

¼ cup brandy

¼ cup wine

½ pound flour

1 teaspoon nutmeg

2 teaspoons cinnamon

¼ teaspoon cloves

½ teaspoon salt

½ teaspoon soda

1 teaspoon baking powder

3 tablespoons molasses

Chop fruit and nuts in large bowl. Set aside. Cream butter and sugar. Add eggs, one at a time, beating well. Blend in brandy, wine, and molasses. Sift flour with spices, soda, and baking powder, and dredge prepared fruit and nuts with some of it. Mix thoroughly and add to batter. Bake 2½ hours at 250 degrees. This will make 2 large cakes or 3 2-pound loaves.

—*Reba Wright Turpin (Mrs. J. R. E.)*

BOILED ICING

5 tablespoons cold water

2 unbeaten egg whites

1½ cups sugar

1 teaspoon vanilla

Place cold water, egg whites, and sugar over boiling water. Beat constantly for about 7 minutes. Remove from water and add vanilla. Continue beating until icing is the right consistency.

—*Committee*

❧ *LIGHT FRUITCAKE*

  1 pound butter
  1 pound sugar (2 cups)
10 eggs
  4 cups flour
  1 tablespoon cinnamon
  1 tablespoon nutmeg
  1 teaspoon salt
     grated rind of 1 orange
  2 pounds white raisins
1½ pounds sliced citron
  1 pound figs
  6 slices conserved pineapple
  1 pound candied cherries
  1 pound nuts
 ¾ cup whiskey or rum

Cream butter and sugar; beat eggs and add alternately with flour which has been sifted with cinnamon, nutmeg, and salt. Add orange rind, floured fruits and nuts, then whiskey. Line pans with greased brown paper. Bake 4 hours if in one extra-large pan (a 4-pound tube pan) or 2 hours (if you're using 2 2-pound loaf pans) at 250 degrees to 300 degrees. Keep a pan of water in bottom of oven. A 2-pound loaf pan serves 18 to 24; a 4-pound tube pan serves 3 or 4 dozen.

—Katherine Nicols Grove (Mrs. J. Robert) from original cookbook

❧ *FUNNY CAKE*

A Pennsylvania Dutch recipe.

  1 unbaked 9-inch pastry shell
 ¾ cup sugar
 ¼ cup cocoa powder
 ¾ cup hot water
  1 teaspoon vanilla
1¼ cups sugar

½ cup shortening

2 eggs

1 cup milk

2 cups flour

2 teaspoons baking powder

Mix together sugar, cocoa, water, and vanilla, and set aside to cool. Cream sugar and shortening together, then add eggs. Add milk alternately with flour which has been sifted with baking powder. Put cake batter in large unbaked pie crust. Pour over this the chocolate mixture. Bake at 350 degrees for 30 minutes or more. Chocolate goes to bottom. Serves 8 to 10.

—*Harriet Willcox Gearhart (Mrs. David)*

COUSIN ELSIE SUDLER'S GINGERBREAD

1 cup lard or vegetable shortening

1 cup sugar

2 eggs

1 cup black molasses

1 cup water

1 teaspoon soda in a little hot water

2 teaspoons cinnamon

pinch of salt

2 teaspoons ginger

3 cups flour

1 cup raisins (optional)

½ cup chopped nuts (optional)

Cream shortening and sugar together. Add eggs and molasses, beating well. Then add water, soda, and sifted dry ingredients. Raisins and nuts may be added. Bake in greased and floured muffin tins or a sheet pan, 9 × 13 inches, for 35 minutes at 350 degrees. Makes 12 muffins.

—*Margaret Gadd Ashley (Mrs. John M.)*

❧ CHOCOLATE ICING

- ½ stick butter (or margarine)
- 2 ounces unsweetened chocolate
- ¼ teaspoon salt
- ¼ cup light corn syrup
- ½ cup milk
- 2 cups sugar
- 1 teaspoon vanilla

Mix all together, stir over low heat. Boil rapidly for 1 minute. Remove and beat until lukewarm. Add vanilla and beat until thick enough to spread. Makes about 1½ cups.

—Pearle E. Bishop

❧ DEVIL'S FOOD CAKE

- 1 cup (½ pound) butter
- 2 cups sugar
- 4 eggs, separated
- 1 cup sour milk
- 2½ cups sifted flour
- ¼ teaspoon salt
- 4 ounces unsweetened baking chocolate, melted
- 1 teaspoon vanilla
- 1 level teaspoon soda dissolved in 1 tablespoon hot water

Cream butter and sugar, add beaten egg yolks. Mix in sour milk and flour with salt, alternately, then chocolate, vanilla, and soda. Beat egg whites stiff but moist and fold in (don't put soda in until you are ready to fold in whites). Grease and flour 9-inch cake pans, fill, and bake at 350 degrees for 20 to 30 minutes, or until cake tests done (a longer time for a sheet cake).

Committee note: Sour cream may be substituted for sour milk, in which case use 2 fewer tablespoons butter; ¼ cup milk may be added to thin sour cream, more if very stiff.

—Louise Perry (Mrs. John W.)

✖ *CINNAMON CAKE*

    ¼ pound (1 stick) butter
 1½ cups sugar
   2 eggs
   2 cups flour
   2 teaspoons baking powder
   1 cup milk
   1 teaspoon vanilla
      brown sugar
      cinnamon

Cream butter and sugar. Add beaten eggs and mix well. Add dry ingredients alternately with the milk and vanilla. Put in shallow 9-inch-square baking dish and cover with a thin layer of brown sugar. Sprinkle generously with cinnamon. Bake at 375 degrees for 25 to 30 minutes. Check so as not to burn. Remove from oven and dot liberally with butter while hot.

—Isabel Atkinson Lieber (Mrs. Albert C.)

✖ *GINGERBREAD*

   1 cup butter
   2 cups sugar
   4 eggs, beaten
   1 cup sour cream
   2 cups blackstrap molasses
   4 cups flour
   1 teaspoon soda
   1 tablespoon ginger
   1 tablespoon cinnamon
   1 pound raisins

Cream butter with sugar. Add beaten eggs, then add sour cream and molasses. Sift and add dry ingredients, then add raisins dusted with flour. Pour into 9 × 13-inch pan lined with waxed paper greased and floured. Bake at 350 degrees for 45 to 50 minutes.

—Mabel Walls Valliant (Mrs. T. Rigby)

🌿 MINNEHAHA CAKE

    1 cup butter
  1½ cups sugar
    1 cup milk
    4 cups flour
    2 teaspoons baking powder
    1 teaspoon almond flavoring
    5 egg whites
       English walnuts, almonds, and raisins

Grease and flour 2 9-inch round cake pans. Cream butter and sugar. Add dry ingredients and milk alternately. Beat until light. Add almond flavoring. Beat egg whites until stiff but not dry. Fold into the batter. Bake at 350 to 375 degrees for 25 minutes. Use Boiled Icing and decorate between layers and on top with English walnut halves, almonds, and raisins.

—Isabel Atkinson Lieber (Mrs. Albert C.)

🌿 LORD BALTIMORE CAKE

  3½ cups cake flour
    4 teaspoons double-acting baking powder
   ½ teaspoon salt
    2 cups sugar
    1 cup butter
    1 cup milk
    1 teaspoon vanilla extract
   ¼ teaspoon almond extract (if desired)
7 or 8 egg whites

All ingredients should be at about 75 degrees. Sift flour before measuring. Resift it twice with baking powder and salt. Sift sugar. Cream the butter well. Add the sifted sugar gradually and continue creaming until very light. Add the flour mixture to the butter mixture in 3 parts, alternately with thirds of the milk. Stir the batter until smooth after each addition. Beat in vanilla extract and almond extract if desired. Whip until stiff, but not dry, the egg whites. Fold them lightly into the cake batter. Bake in 3 greased pans (8 or 9 inches) at 350 degrees for about 25 minutes. While the cake is cooling, make the filling.

Filling

- 6 figs or dates
- ½ cup seeded raisins
- 1 cup chopped nutmeats
- 2 cups sugar
- 1 cup water
- 2 egg whites
- ⅛ teaspoon salt
- ⅛ teaspoon cream of tartar or a few drops of lemon juice
- 1 teaspoon vanilla

Chop figs or dates. Add raisins and nutmeats. Set aside. In saucepan, combine sugar and water, stirring until sugar is dissolved. Bring to a boil. Cover and cook for about 3 minutes, until the steam has washed down any crystals which may have formed on the sides of the pan. Uncover and cook to 238 degrees. At that temperature, the syrup will spin a very thin thread on the end of a coarser thread. This final thread will almost disappear, like a self-consuming spider web. Whip the egg whites until frothy. Add the syrup in a thin stream, whipping egg whites constantly. When these ingredients are all combined, add cream of tartar or lemon juice and vanilla. Add fruits and nuts at the last minute, then spread on top of and between the layers of the cake.

—Barbara Seaman Efland (Mrs. Herman)

✺ QUICK BROWN SUGAR FROSTING

- 1½ cups brown sugar
- ¼ cup milk
- 1 tablespoon butter
- dash salt
- 1½ cups confectioners' sugar
- 1 teaspoon vanilla

Boil brown sugar, milk, butter, and salt for 2 minutes; then add confectioners' sugar. Beat until smooth, and add vanilla. Frosts a 3-layer cake.

—Mary Stewart Gadd (Mrs. John D.)

❧ OATMEAL CAKE

    1⅓ cups boiling water
    1 cup quick oats
    2 eggs
    ½ cup shortening
    1 cup brown sugar
    1 cup white sugar
    1⅓ cups flour
    ½ teaspoon cinnamon
    1 teaspoon soda
    ½ teaspoon salt
    1 teaspoon vanilla

Pour boiling water over quick oats, mix well, and set aside to cool. When cool, add to eggs which have been creamed with the shortening. Add sugars and other ingredients and mix well. Pour into 9 ×12-inch pan and bake at 350 degrees for 35 minutes. When cool, spread with Topping.

Topping

    ¼ cup butter
    1 teaspoon vanilla
    ½ cup brown sugar
    1 cup nuts
    ¼ cup evaporated milk
    1 cup coconut

Combine ingredients and spread on cake. Put in oven under broiler until topping bubbles.

—*Kathy Maybeck Draper (Mrs. Frank)*

❧ ORANGE CAKE AND ICING

    2 cups sugar
    2⅔ ounces butter
    2 whole eggs plus 3 egg yolks, beaten
    2½ cups sifted flour (then sift again into cake)
    ¼ teaspoon salt
    2 round teaspoons baking powder
       juice of 1 large orange and enough water to make 1 cup

Cream sugar and butter, add eggs and egg yolks beaten light, sift flour with salt and baking powder and add to cake alternately with orange juice and water. Pour into 13 × 9-inch pan and bake at 350 degrees for 30 minutes, or until cake tester comes out clean.

Icing

2½ cups sugar
½ cup water
    grated rind of 1 orange
3 egg whites, beaten

Cook sugar, water, and rind without stirring until it forms a thin thread when dropped from spoon, without bubbles on it (240 degrees on candy thermometer). Pour slowly over stiffly beaten whites and beat until creamy. Spread.

—*Louise Perry (Mrs. John W.)*

❦ MYSTERY CAKE

½ cup granulated sugar
1 cup sifted flour
2 teaspoons baking powder
⅛ teaspoon salt
1 ounce unsweetened baking chocolate
2 tablespoons butter
½ cup milk
1 teaspoon vanilla
½ cup brown sugar
¼ cup white sugar
4 tablespoons cocoa
1 cup cold double-strength coffee

Mix and sift first 4 ingredients. Melt chocolate and butter together over warm water. Add to first mixture and blend well. Combine milk and vanilla. Add. Mix well and pour into greased 8-inch-square pan. Combine the brown and white sugar and cocoa. Sprinkle evenly over batter and pour coffee on top. Bake at 350 degrees for 40 minutes. Serve hot or cold with whipped cream.

—*Barbara Porter (Mrs. John)*

🍃 *LEMON POUND CAKE*

½ cup vegetable shortening
½ pound butter
3 cups sugar
5 eggs
1 teaspoon baking powder
3 cups sifted cake flour
1 cup milk
1 teaspoon vanilla
1 teaspoon lemon extract

Cream shortening with butter and sugar. Add eggs, one at a time, beating thoroughly after each. Add baking powder to sifted cake flour. Add flour alternating with milk (room temperature). Fold in vanilla and lemon extract. Grease pan and flour lightly. Put in large stem pan (10-inch tube pan) in cold oven. Do not open oven door while baking. Bake at 350 degrees for 1 hour and 15 minutes.

—*Katherine Barton Johnson (Mrs. Marshall P.)*

🍃 *SIS'S LEMON-FILLED CAKE*

¼ pound butter
1½ cups sugar
3 eggs
2 cups plus 2 tablespoons flour
1 teaspoon baking powder
1 scant cup milk
¾ teaspoon vanilla

Cream butter and sugar together, then add eggs and beat well. Sift flour and baking powder together. Add first part of flour then part of milk to creamed mixture, until all is added. Add vanilla. Bake in 2 9-inch-square or round greased and floured pans at 375 degrees for 25 to 30 minutes.

Lemon Filling

1 cup sugar
1 tablespoon flour (blend with sugar)
½ cup boiling water
1 egg, beaten lightly

juice and grated rind of 1 lemon

⅛ pound butter

Use a double boiler. Mix dry ingredients and slowly add water. When it begins to thicken, fold in egg then lemon juice and grated rind. Cook until thick and clear, then add butter. Makes 10 servings.

—*From the collection of Sarah Wright, given from kitchen of Miss Nannie Wright*

❧ YELLOW LILY CAKE

  2 cups sugar

  1 cup butter

  1 cup milk

  3 cups flour

  3 teaspoons dry yeast [baking powder]

  5 egg yolks plus 1 whole egg

  1 teaspoon vanilla

Cream sugar and butter. Add milk, flour, yeast [baking powder], and eggs. Flavor with vanilla. Pour into 3 8-inch round cake pans. Bake at 375 degrees for 25 to 35 minutes. Frost with icing of your choice.

—*Genevieve Hall Valliant (Mrs. Edwin S., Sr.)*

❧ POUND CAKE

  ¾ pound margarine

  3 cups sugar

  5 eggs

  3 cups flour, rounded

  ½ teaspoon baking powder

  1 cup milk

  1 teaspoon flavoring, almond or lemon as desired

  ½ teaspoon vanilla

Cream soft margarine with sugar. Add eggs, one at a time, beating on medium speed. Add flour mixed with baking powder and milk, alternately. Add flavorings and blend well. Bake in a greased and floured tube pan or 2 loaf pans. Put into a cold oven. Turn to 325 degrees and bake for 1 hour and 40 minutes. Test with a toothpick to see if it is done. This cake keeps well and the flavor improves after a day or two. Freezes well when wrapped in foil and sealed.

—*Lou Snyder Eby (Mrs. J. Walter)*

❧ MY MOTHER'S SPICE CAKE WITH CARAMEL ICING

      6 ounces butter
      2 cups sugar
      4 eggs, separated
    2½ cups sifted flour
      2 scant teaspoons cloves
      2 level teaspoons allspice
     ¼ teaspoon salt
      2 round teaspoons baking powder
      1 cup half cream, half milk
      1 teaspoon vanilla
      2 heaping teaspoons cinnamon

Cream butter and sugar until mushy, add egg yolks, beat lightly. Sift flour, spices, salt, and baking powder and add to butter, sugar, and egg mixture. Add milk gradually, fold in egg whites that have been beaten 10 minutes. Bake in 4 9-inch pans, greased and floured, about 15 to 17 minutes at 350 degrees until cake leaves sides of pan and does not sizzle.

Caramel Icing

      3 cups dark brown sugar, packed
     ¼ pound butter
     ¾ cup half milk and half cream (use 6 ounces butter if all
          milk is used)

Cook as you would caramels (to soft ball stage—takes about 20 minutes to form a soft ball in water as a test). Beat until creamy.

—*Louise Perry (Mrs. John W.)*

❧ SPONGE-ANGEL FOOD CAKE

      4 eggs, separated
      7 tablespoons water (little over ⅓ cup)
      1 cup sugar
      1 cup all-purpose flour, sifted
     ½ teaspoon cream of tartar
      1 teaspoon baking powder
          pinch of salt
      1 teaspoon vanilla

Beat egg yolks and water in large mixing bowl, using high speed of electric mixer. Beat in sugar, beat 5 minutes at high speed. Sift dry ingredients, add to yolk mixture and beat 5 minutes at medium speed. In a separate bowl, beat egg whites until stiff; add salt. Fold the vanilla and egg whites into yolk mixture. Bake in angel food cake pan for 45 to 55 minutes at 350 degrees from a cold start (do not preheat oven).

—*Frances Wright Hilleary (Mrs. Robert)*

LEMON FILLING FOR CAKE

Very good! Recipe belonged to Molly Wright Earle.

    2 eggs
 1½ cups sugar
    ½ cup water
        rind of 2 lemons grated (do not grate in white of rind)
    ¼ pound butter

Beat eggs, add sugar, water, and lemon rind. Put on low flame, or over hot water. Add butter and let simmer until proper consistency to spread when cool. Cool. Use as inner filling for layer cake, using powdered sugar to top. Makes about 1½ cups.

—*Fanny Earle Wright (Mrs. Henry)*

SUGAR CAKES

Pennsylvania Dutch. A breakfast cake for dunkers.

    2 cups granulated sugar
    4 cups flour
 2½ teaspoons baking powder
    1 teaspoon salt
    ½ cup shortening
    1 teaspoon vanilla
    2 eggs
    1 cup milk (or a bit more so batter will pour)
        cinnamon sugar

Sift together sugar, flour, baking powder, and salt. Add shortening and vanilla. Add eggs and milk. Pour into 4 8-inch pie tins. Sprinkle top of batter with cinnamon sugar. Bake at 350 degrees for 20 to 25 minutes.

—*G. Myron Latshaw*

🍃 *TANDY CAKE*

> 4 eggs
> 1 teaspoon vanilla
> 2 cups sugar
> 2 cups flour
> 1 cup milk
> 2 tablespoons oil
> 2 teaspoons baking powder
> pinch of salt
> 1 cup peanut butter
> 10 ounces semisweet chocolate bits

In a large mixing bowl beat eggs until fluffy (2 to 3 minutes). Add remainder of ingredients. Mix all together for 2 minutes (batter will be thin). Bake in a greased and floured 12 × 17-inch pan at approximately 350 degrees until golden. Spread a thin layer of peanut butter on the cake while it is hot. Then refrigerate ½ to 1 hour until the peanut butter is no longer gooey or shiny. Melt chocolate and spread over the cooled cake. Cool; cut in bars. Makes 24 servings.

—Suzanne Cartier James (Mrs. Oliver)

🍃 *PECAN CAKE*

> ¾ cup butter
> 2 cups sugar
> 3 eggs, separated
> ½ cup molasses
> 1 teaspoon soda
> 2 nutmegs, grated
> 1 cup bourbon
> 3 cups sifted flour
> 1 teaspoon baking powder
> 1 pound shelled pecans
> 2 pounds seedless raisins

Cream butter and sugar. Add beaten egg yolks, then molasses to which soda has been added. Add nutmeg and bourbon. Use part of flour to flour nuts and raisins. Sift rest with baking powder. Add flour, then nuts and raisins. Last, fold in stiffly beaten egg whites. Pour in greased, floured tube pan, 9 to 10 inches in diameter and 3½ to 4 inches deep. Bake at 300 degrees for 3 hours or until done.

—Sara Warren Kidd (Mrs. A. L.)

SPONGE CAKE

    6 eggs, separated
2¼ cups sugar, less 1 tablespoon
    ½ teaspoon salt
    ½ teaspoon lemon extract
        grated rind of 1 orange
    6 teaspoons cold water
    ¾ cup hot water
2¼ cups flour, less 1 tablespoon
    ½ teaspoon cream of tartar

Beat egg yolks. Add sugar gradually, beating all the time. Add salt, lemon extract, and orange rind. Add cold water, then hot water, beating all the while. Fold in flour, cream of tartar, and beaten whites. Do not beat whites dry, just in peaks. Bake 1 hour in ungreased angel food pan at 350 degrees.

—Jennie Mae Hauser Fisher (Mrs. W. Henry)

COOKIES AND CANDY

Bless, O Lord, these thy gifts to our use,
And us to thy loving service,
And make us ever mindful of the needs of others.

❦ *ALBANY COOKIES*

> *Old receipt.*

3½ cups flour
1 pound dark brown sugar
½ pound butter
1 tablespoon lard
2 eggs
1 teaspoon soda dissolved in 1 cup sour cream
2 ounces cinnamon

Mix all together. Chill overnight and use small quantities at a time. Roll out on white sugar. Cut out with cookie cutters. Bake at 400 degrees for 8 to 10 minutes. Makes 80 cookies.

—*Eliza Brown (Mrs. Hampton)*

❦ *ALEXANDRITES*

1 egg, beaten
2 tablespoons flour
1 cup light brown sugar
½ cup butter, melted
¼ teaspoon salt
½ teaspoon baking powder
1 cup quick-cooking oatmeal
½ teaspoon vanilla

Combine all ingredients. Drop ½ teaspoon at a time onto buttered and floured waxed paper on cookie sheet. Bake at 350 degrees for 5½ to 7 minutes.

Note: Cool, and paper will come off easily. To store, leave on waxed paper and layer in box. Makes 80 cookies.

—*Elizabeth Barton (Mrs. Marvin)*

❦ *ALMOND COOKIES*

2 cups all-purpose flour
1 teaspoon baking powder

1 teaspoon baking soda

1 cup shortening

1 cup sugar

1 teaspoon vanilla extract

½ teaspoon almond extract

1 egg

1 egg yolk

1 tablespoon water

4 dozen whole almonds (about ½ cup) skinned

Combine first three ingredients; set aside. Cream shortening; gradually add sugar, beating until light and fluffy. Stir in vanilla and almond extracts. Add egg, beating well. Add dry ingredients and mix well. Combine egg yolk and water; mix well. Shape dough into ¾-inch balls. Press an almond into center of each cookie; brush with egg yolk mixture. Bake on ungreased cookie sheets at 350 degrees for 10 to12 minutes. Cool on wire racks. Enjoy! Makes 4 dozen cookies.

—*Sally Clark (Mrs. John T., III)*

AUDREY'S SUGAR COOKIES

This makes a very crisp cookie that can be decorated with colored sugar or nuts. The quantity is large, but it keeps perfectly in refrigerator, so cookies can be done at odd times for several days.

¾ pound butter

1 pound sugar

4 eggs

2 teaspoons baking powder

1 teaspoon vanilla

pinch of salt

½ teaspoon mace

5 to 6 cups flour

Cream butter and sugar. Add beaten eggs and flavoring. Add flour until able to handle. Chill overnight. Remove enough for rolling and cutting quickly. Should be rolled thin, then decorated as desired before baking. Bake at 325 degrees for 8 to 10 minutes. Makes 12 dozen.

—*Ruth Branner Gadd (Mrs. A. Sydney, Jr.)*

❧ BASIC ICEBOX DROP COOKIES

   ½ cup butter
   ½ cup margarine
 1½ cups sugar
   2 eggs, beaten
2¾ cups sifted flour
   2 teaspoons cream of tartar
   1 teaspoon soda
   ½ teaspoon salt
   1 teaspoon vanilla
   ½ teaspoon lemon extract
     dash of nutmeg
   3 tablespoons sugar
   2 teaspoons cinnamon
     currants (optional)
     maraschino cherries (optional)

Mix together butter, margarine, sugar, and eggs. Sift together and stir in flour, cream of tartar, soda, and salt. Add flavorings. Leave in refrigerator all night. Make balls about 1 inch in diameter. Roll in mixture of sugar and cinnamon. Currants for eyes and a slice of maraschino cherry for mouth make a cute cookie for a children's party. A half cherry or a pecan half, or a bit of jam in an indentation in the ball make a varied cookie.

    Other variations: Add chopped nuts or grated lemon rind and extra lemon flavoring to part of dough; sprinkle with colored sugar. Makes 72 cookies.

—*Elizabeth Barton (Mrs. Marvin)*

❧ BROWNIES

   2 eggs
   1 cup sugar
   ½ cup butter, melted
   2 squares unsweetened chocolate, melted
   ½ cup flour

1 teaspoon vanilla

1 cup chopped walnuts

Melt chocolate and butter in a saucepan over very low heat, or in a double boiler. Cool slightly. Beat eggs, sugar, and vanilla in large mixer bowl. Beat in chocolate mixture. Add flour, beating just to blend. Add nuts. Spread dough in greased, wax paper–lined 8 × 8-inch pan. Bake at 325 degrees for 25 to 30 minutes, or until cake tester inserted into center comes out almost clean (do not overbake). Remove from pan, cut in squares or bars. Makes 18 brownies.

—*Margaret Greenewalt Cross (Mrs. Urie)*

COFFEE BLOND BROWNIES

1 pound dark brown sugar

1½ sticks unsalted butter

2 tablespoons instant coffee powder

1 tablespoon hot water

2 eggs

2 tablespoons vanilla extract

2 cups flour

2 teaspoons baking powder

½ teaspoon salt

1 cup chopped pecans

1 cup semisweet chocolate bits

Heat the brown sugar and butter in a medium saucepan over medium-low heat until the butter melts. Dissolve the coffee in hot water and stir into the butter mixture. Let cool. Preheat oven to 350 degrees. Butter an 11 × 8-inch baking pan. When the butter mixture is cool, beat in the eggs and vanilla with a hand-held mixer. Sift the flour, baking powder, and salt together and stir into the butter mixture with a wooden spoon. Stir in the pecans and chocolate. Spread the mixture evenly in the prepared pan with a rubber spatula. Bake until lightly browned, 25 to 30 minutes. Do not overbake! Cool completely and cut into 2-inch squares. Enjoy! Makes 20 brownies.

—*Sally Clark (Mrs. John T., III)*

✸ BUTTERSCOTCH SQUARES

    1 pound brown sugar
    ¾ cup butter or margarine
    2 eggs
    1 cup flour
    1 cup pecans
    1 teaspoon vanilla

Preheat oven to 350 degrees. Cream sugar and butter thoroughly. Add eggs one at a time and mix well. Add flour, pecans, and vanilla. Spread in greased 9 × 13-inch pan. Bake for 10 minutes at 350 degrees, then lower heat to 300 degrees for 35 minutes. Remove from oven. Cool before cutting into bars. Makes 24 bars.

—*Marjorie Belt Turner (Mrs. Edward)*

✸ EMILIA'S OLD-FASHIONED BUTTERSCOTCH COOKIES

These are plain, good cookies—wonderful for children in hot weather.

4½ cups flour
  1 pound brown sugar
  1 teaspoon baking soda
  1 cup butter
  4 eggs, beaten
      pecans (optional)

Mix flour, sugar, and soda. Work in butter by cutting in, then with fingers. Then add beaten eggs. Drop on cookie sheet, ½ small spoonful of batter per cookie for small cookies. Place pecan half in center and bake at 350 degrees for about 15 minutes. Makes 148.

—*Lynette Morgan Nielsen (Mrs. Orsen)*

✸ CHERRYETTES

    ¾ cup shortening
    ¼ cup margarine
    ½ teaspoon salt
    ½ cup powdered sugar

    2 tablespoons vanilla

    2 cups sifted flour

    1 cup finely chopped pecans

  20 candied cherries for decoration

Mix all ingredients, except cherries; then measure out level tablespoon of dough and roll to form ball. Press hole in center with fingertip and insert half a cherry. Bake at 325 degrees for 25 minutes. Makes 40.

—*Barbara H. Mason (Mrs. William)*

In 1937, the "Ladies" asked the Vestry to look into the matter of draft on the candles in the altar area and to see to the condition of the windows. (It was reported the windows had been repaired, at the next Vestry meeting.)

CHIP A NUT BARS

    1 cup margarine

  1¾ cups firmly packed light brown sugar

    2 eggs

    2 teaspoons baking powder

   ½ teaspoon salt

    2 cups flour

    1 teaspoon instant coffee (optional)

    1 teaspoon vanilla

    1 6-ounce package chocolate chips

    1 cup chopped nuts (optional)

Put all ingredients except chocolate chips and nuts in large mixer bowl. Mix on lowest speed of mixer until well blended. Stir in half the chocolate chips and nuts. Spread mixture evenly in 10 × 15-inch greased pan. Sprinkle top with remaining chocolate chips and nuts. Bake at 350 degrees for 20 to 25 minutes. Cool and cut into bars. Makes 48 bar cookies.

—*Barbara H. Mason (Mrs. William)*

❧ *MINT CHOCOLATE CHIP KISSES*

> 2 egg whites
> ¼ teaspoon vanilla
> ¼ teaspoon cream of tartar
> ⅔ cup sugar
> ⅔ cup mint chocolate chips (heaping)

Beat egg whites until frothy. Add vanilla and cream of tartar. Keep beating as you add sugar. When mixture is stiff, stir in mint chocolate chips. Drop by teaspoonsful onto well-greased cookie sheet. Bake for 20 minutes at 300 degrees. Makes about 36.

—*Lois Gompf Radcliffe (Mrs. Edmund)*

❧ *COCOA BARS*

> ¼ cup butter or margarine
> 1 cup sugar
> 1 teaspoon vanilla
> 2 eggs
> ¼ cup milk
> 1 cup sifted all-purpose flour
> 2 tablespoons cocoa
> ¼ teaspoon salt
> ½ cup chopped walnuts

Cream butter and sugar. Add vanilla, creaming well. Add eggs, one at a time, beating well. Stir in milk, then dry ingredients which have been sifted together. Add nuts. Pour in a greased 9 × 9 × 2-inch pan. Bake 20 minutes at 375 degrees. Remove from oven and frost at once. Cool and cut in bars or squares. Makes 15 bars.

Frosting

> 1½ tablespoons cocoa
> 1 tablespoon milk
> ¼ teaspoon vanilla
> 1½ teaspoons soft butter
> ⅔ cup confectioners' sugar

Mix all ingredients together well.

—*Anna Grace Keith (Mrs. Ronald)*

COCONUT CHEWS

½ cup shortening
½ cup brown sugar
1 cup sifted flour
2 eggs
1 cup brown sugar
1 teaspoon vanilla
1 cup black walnut meats
3 tablespoons flour
½ teaspoon salt
1½ cups shredded coconut
powdered sugar

Cream shortening and sugar until fluffy and then work in flour. Pat this mixture into an 8 × 13-inch pan. Bake for 10 minutes at 350 degrees. Beat eggs and blend in brown sugar and other ingredients. Remove pan from oven and pour coconut mixture over the top. Return to oven and bake 20 minutes longer. Cut into slender fingers and roll in powdered sugar. Makes 20 bars.

—*Mildred Smith Thompson (Mrs. Philemon Hopper)*

CHOCOLATE SQUARES

⅔ cup shortening
2½ cups brown sugar
3 eggs
2¾ cups flour
½ teaspoon salt
2½ teaspoons baking powder
1 teaspoon vanilla
1 cup nuts, chopped
1 6-ounce package chocolate bits

Melt shortening, add brown sugar. Add unbeaten eggs, one at a time. Sift flour, salt, and baking powder together and add to first mixture. Add vanilla, nuts, and chocolate bits. Spread in greased 10 × 15 × 3-inch pan. Bake 35 minutes at 350 degrees. Cut in squares while warm. Makes 21 bars.

—*Mrs. Barclay Stanton*

🍃 DATE BARS

    2 eggs
    1 scant cup sugar
    5 tablespoons flour
    1 teaspoon baking powder
    1 pound English walnut meats (cut or rolled fine)
  ½ teaspoon salt
    1 pound dates, cut fine
       confectioners' sugar

Mix ingredients together well and spread in a 9 × 9-inch pan. Bake for 25 minutes at 325 degrees. Cut and roll in confectioners' sugar. Makes 18.

—Louise Lewis Grubb (Mrs. Ernest W.)

🍃 HELEN'S DATE AND NUT SQUARES

  ½ cup shortening
    1 cup sugar
    2 eggs
  ½ cup flour
    1 teaspoon salt
    1 teaspoon cinnamon
  ½ teaspoon nutmeg
  ¼ teaspoon cloves
    2 tablespoons orange juice
    1 teaspoon vanilla
  ½ cup chopped nuts
  ½ cup finely chopped, pitted dates

Thoroughly mix together shortening, sugar, and eggs. Sift flour, salt, cinnamon, nutmeg, and cloves together into first mixture. Add orange juice and vanilla. Mix well. Stir in nuts and dates. Spread mixture evenly in pan approximately 7 × 11 inches. Bake at 350 degrees for 20 or 25 minutes. While still hot, cut into squares. Makes 24 to 36 pieces, depending on size.

—Helen Sleasman (Mrs. A. R., Jr.)

❧ DOG BISCUITS

2½ cups whole wheat flour
½ cup dry milk solids
1 teaspoon salt
1 teaspoon sugar or molasses
6 tablespoons margarine
1 egg
3 tablespoons of one of the following: liver powder, chicken powder, beef bouillon, or dried soup greens or soup mix
½ cup cold water

Mix all ingredients with cold water. Knead 3 minutes. Dough should form a ball. Roll ½ inch thick. Cut with bone-shaped cookie cutter or cut in squares. Bake 25 minutes at 350 degrees. Watch carefully so they don't burn. Makes approximately 24 dog biscuits.

—Mary Dougherty (Mrs. Michael J.), "Kildee Kennel"

❧ DROP SUGAR COOKIES

2 cups sugar
½ cup shortening
3 eggs
1 teaspoon soda
1 cup buttermilk
3 cups unsifted all-purpose flour
1 teaspoon baking powder
1 teaspoon salt
1 teaspoon lemon extract

Cream sugar, shortening, and eggs. Dissolve soda in buttermilk. Add to mixture alternately with flour, baking powder, and salt. Add flavoring. Drop on greased pans, sprinkle with sugar. Bake 10 minutes at 350 degrees. Makes 140 cookies.

—Dorothy Keith Perkins (Mrs. Louis H.)

✌ FLORENTINES

     3½ ounces sliced and chopped almonds
     ¼ cup candied orange peel
     ¼ cup candied lemon peel (or ½ cup of lemon or orange peel)
     ¼ cup sugar
     ⅓ cup butter
     ¼ cup light corn syrup
     1 teaspoon cream
     ½ cup flour
     4 ounces semisweet chocolate
        cold milk
     1 teaspoon butter

Combine first eight ingredients, reserving chocolate for frosting later. Cook mixture in pan for two minutes. Line cookie sheet with parchment paper and drop by teaspoon on sheet, flattening with fork dipped in milk. Bake at 350 degrees for 10 minutes, watching carefully. Remove from oven; take off parchment as soon as cookies can be handled. Cool; then frost with melted chocolate to which butter has been added. This recipe can be doubled and the cookies frozen with waxed paper between layers. Makes 24.

—Amelia Dell Booze (Mrs. Robert)

✌ FUDGE COOKIES

Good accompaniment for sherbet, parfait, or fruit.

     1 16-ounce package chocolate bits
     1 14-ounce can condensed milk
     1 cup nuts (preferably black walnuts)
     2 tablespoons margarine
     1 cup sifted all-purpose flour

Blend all ingredients in double boiler. Drop by the teaspoonful to cookie sheet. Bake exactly 5 minutes at 350 degrees. Cool. Keep in airtight container. Makes 4 dozen.

—Janet Gadd Doehler (Mrs. William F.)

❧ GINGER COOKIES

   2 cups unsifted flour
   2 teaspoons ginger
   1 teaspoon cinnamon
   ½ teaspoon salt
   2 teaspoons soda
   ¾ cup shortening
   1 cup sugar
   1 egg
   ¼ cup Brer Rabbit molasses

Sift dry ingredients together. Cream shortening and sugar well. Add egg, molasses. Beat until smooth and add dry ingredients. Chill well. Roll into balls the size of walnuts. Roll in sugar and place on greased cookie sheet, allowing room to spread. Bake at 350 degrees for 12 minutes or until they crack on top. Makes 48.

—Marion Merrick Brower (Mrs. Frank)

❧ HERMITS

   1 cup sugar
   ½ cup molasses
   ½ cup butter, melted
   ½ teaspoon soda
   1 teaspoon cinnamon
   ½ teaspoon allspice
   ¼ teaspoon nutmeg
   ½ cup sour cream
   1 egg
   2 cups flour
   1 cup nuts
   1 cup raisins

Mix all ingredients together and drop, allowing room to spread, on greased cookie sheets. Bake at 350 degrees for 10 to 20 minutes. Makes 60.

—Eliza Brown (Mrs. Hampton)

🌿 GOLDEN TASSIES

These freeze beautifully, so may be used in small amounts if you wish.

1 cup margarine
1 8-ounce package cream cheese
2 cups sifted all-purpose flour

Cream margarine and cream cheese; add half the flour at a time; mix well. Form dough into ball and chill. Divide dough into fourths when ready to bake, keeping unworked dough chilled. Flour a pastry cloth and covered rolling pin and roll less than ⅛ inch thick. Cut circles with a cutter and fit into muffin tins (small tins with top diameter of 2 inches).

Pecan Filling

4 eggs
3 cups light brown sugar
4 tablespoons margarine, melted
  salt
1 teaspoon vanilla
1 cup pecans, walnuts, or coconut may be used

Beat eggs; add sugar, margarine, salt, and vanilla. Pour this mixture into lipped dispenser (I use syrup dispenser). Sprinkle broken nuts into dough-lined cups. Pour egg mixture over nuts to almost full. Sprinkle a few nuts on top. Bake at 375 degrees for 20 minutes. Makes 40 tassies.

—*Edna Sultenfuss (Mrs. Vernon)*

🌿 EMILIA'S ICEBOX COOKIES

½ cup butter
1 cup brown sugar (preferably dark)
1 egg
½ teaspoon vanilla
1½ cups flour
½ teaspoon baking soda
¼ teaspoon salt
½ cup nutmeats

Cream butter, add sugar, then add egg and vanilla. Sift flour, soda, and salt, and add to butter mixture. Add nuts dredged in a little flour. Mold dough into long rolls. You may need to add more flour. Add just enough so that dough can be handled. Put in icebox 24 hours. Cut in thin slices and bake at 400 degrees. They burn easily, so watch carefully.

The taste of the cookie can be quite changed by adding ½ cup of finely chopped nuts instead of the whole nuts. We like it with finely ground pecans.

This freezes well. I double the recipe and store the dough in plastic containers. In damp weather I bake only what is needed for the day, as they get soggy easily. Makes 48.

—Lynette Morgan Nielsen (Mrs. Orsen)

MIN'S CHOCOLATE FINGERS

½ cup shortening
½ cup sugar
1 egg, beaten
¼ teaspoon salt
1 cup flour
5 tablespoons shortening
1½ ounces unsweetened baking chocolate, melted
¾ cup sugar
1 egg, beaten
½ cup plus 1 tablespoon flour
⅛ teaspoon salt
½ teaspoon baking powder
1 teaspoon vanilla
1 cup broken walnut meats

Combine shortening, sugar, egg, salt, and flour, and mix well. Spread in an 8-inch-square pan. Combine remaining ingredients and spread over first mixture. Bake 30 minutes at 375 degrees. Cut into rectangles while still warm. Makes 16 bars.

—Marian Andrus (Mrs. Leon)

❧ LEMON SQUARES OR BARS

        2 cups flour
        ½ cup powdered sugar
        ¾ cup butter or margarine
        2 cups sugar
        ½ cup flour
        ½ teaspoon baking powder
        4 eggs, beaten
        ⅓ cup lemon juice

Cut flour, powdered sugar, and butter together until crumbly. Pat into 9 × 13-inch pan; bake at 350 degrees for 20 minutes or until crust is lightly browned. Mix together remainder of ingredients and pour over crust. Bake for 25 minutes. Sprinkle with powdered sugar. Makes 32 bars.

—*Lois Gompf Radcliffe (Mrs. Edmund)*

❧ LEMON SUGAR COOKIES

        ¾ cup butter
        1 cup sugar
        2 eggs
        2 teaspoons lemon rind
       2½ cups flour
        1 teaspoon baking powder
        1 teaspoon salt

Cream butter and sugar. Add eggs and lemon rind, and mix. Then add sifted dry ingredients. Chill. Roll out and cut with cookie cutters, or roll and chill, then cut thin. Bake on ungreased cookie sheets at 400 degrees for 6 to 8 minutes. Makes about 4 dozen.

—*Margaret Gadd Ashley (Mrs. John M.)*

❧ IB'S MERINGUES

        4 egg whites
       1½ cups sugar
        2 teaspoons baking powder
        2 brown paper–lined cookie sheets

Beat egg whites stiff but not dry, gradually adding ¾ cup sifted sugar. Then fold in ¾ cup of sugar and baking powder (sifted together 3 times). On wet, brown paper, place mounds of meringues using a teaspoon. If the cookie sheet is large enough you can get 30 meringues on each sheet: 5 across and 6 down. Bake at 250 degrees for 30 minutes, then switch cookie sheets (bottom one on top shelf). Continue baking at 250 degrees for about 45 minutes. Try to pick meringue off paper. If they are still sticky, bake a little longer.

When you are able to pick meringues off paper, do so, placing them on their sides on same paper. Turn off oven, leaving meringues in oven to cool and dry. Keep in airtight container. Use as cookies or crush over chocolate ice cream sundaes. (These have been used, crushed over sundaes, at a parish supper.)

—Mary Ib Ober Todd
—Sue Watson (Mrs. John G.)

❧ SPICE 'N' COFFEE SQUARES

    2 cups light brown sugar, packed
    2 cups all-purpose flour, sifted
    ½ teaspoon salt
    1 teaspoon ground cinnamon
    ¼ teaspoon ground mace
    2 tablespoons instant coffee
    ½ cup butter or margarine
    1 egg
    1 cup sour cream
    1 teaspoon baking soda
    ½ cup California walnuts, chopped

Preheat oven to 350 degrees. Grease, then flour 9 × 9 × 2-inch baking dish. In large bowl combine brown sugar, flour, salt, cinnamon, mace, coffee, and butter or margarine. With pastry blender (or 2 knives used scissors-fashion), blend these until crumbs are size of large peas. Pat one-half of crumbs into bottom of prepared baking dish. In small bowl beat egg, stir in sour cream and soda, then combine with remaining crumbs. Spread this mixture over crumbs in baking dish and sprinkle with nuts. Bake for 45 to 50 minutes or until cake tester inserted in center comes out clean. Cut into squares and serve alone or with fruit. Makes 12 servings.

—Marybelle Weatherford Henry (Mrs. Elmer T.)

🌿 LOCUST HILL CHRISTMAS JUMBLES

1½ cups butter
2 cups sugar
6 cups flour
2 eggs
1 grated nutmeg
3 or 4 tablespoons rose water

Cream butter and sugar. Add flour and eggs alternately. Grate nutmeg. Add to dough with rose water. Mix and allow to sit overnight in cool place, but not in refrigerator. Roll paper thin or roll in small balls, then roll out with hands like a pencil. Form into a U, crossing the ends at the bottom. Bake at 350 degrees for about 10 minutes. Makes about 6 dozen.

—*Reba Wright Turpin (Mrs. J. R. E.)*

🌿 CHOCOLATE CRUNCH COOKIES

1 cup shortening
¾ cup sugar
¾ cup brown sugar
2 eggs, beaten
2½ cups sifted flour
1 teaspoon salt
1 teaspoon soda
1 teaspoon hot water
1 teaspoon vanilla
1 cup chopped nuts
14 to 16 ounces semisweet chocolate chips

Cream shortening. Add sugars gradually and cream well. Add beaten eggs and beat well. Sift flour and salt together and add to first mixture alternately with soda, which has been dissolved in hot water. Add vanilla. Fold in nuts and chocolate chips. Drop from teaspoon on cookie sheet. Preheat oven to 375 degrees. Bake for 10 to 15 minutes. Makes 8 dozen cookies.

—*Nellie Brown Whiteley (Mrs. J. Harman)*

🍂 NIGHT OWLS

    2 egg whites
       pinch salt
    ⅔ cup sugar
    ½ teaspoon almond extract
    1 teaspoon vanilla extract
    1 cup chocolate chips
    1 cup finely chopped nuts (optional)

Beat egg whites until frothy. Add salt and continue beating until stiff. Gradually add sugar. Beat until *very* stiff. Add extracts. Fold in chocolate chips and nuts. Line cookie sheet with foil and drop mixture by the teaspoon onto sheet. Place into preheated 350-degree oven, close door tightly, and turn off heat. Next morning (time in oven should be at least 1 hour), peel meringues gently from foil. Store in tin can; these keep well. Makes 25.

—Arline Goodwin Mayer (Mrs. Charles E.)

🍂 OATMEAL LACE COOKIES

    ½ cup cake flour
    ¼ teaspoon baking powder
    ½ cup sugar
    ½ cup quick-cooking oats
    2 tablespoons milk
    2 tablespoons dark molasses
    ⅓ cup melted butter
    1 tablespoon vanilla

Sift flour, baking powder, and sugar together into a bowl. Add remaining ingredients and mix together until well blended. Drop onto ungreased baking sheet, 4 inches apart, using ¼ teaspoon as a measure. Bake at 375 degrees for 6 to 8 minutes until lightly browned. Let stand a few seconds before removing from cookie sheet. Makes about 6 dozen cookies.

—Anne Warner West (Mrs. Charles M.)

❦ STREUSEL BARS

  1¾ cups unsifted flour
  1½ cups confectioners' sugar
  ½ cup unsweetened cocoa
  1 cup cold margarine or butter
  8 ounces cream cheese
  1 8-ounce can Eagle Brand Sweetened Condensed Milk
  1 egg
  2 teaspoons vanilla extract
  ½ cup chopped nuts (optional)

Preheat oven to 350 degrees. In large bowl, combine flour, sugar, and cocoa; cut in margarine until crumbly (mixture will be dry). Reserving 2 cups of crumb mixture, press remainder firmly on bottom of 13 × 9-inch baking pan. Bake 5 minutes. In large mixer bowl, beat cream cheese until fluffy; add sweetened condensed milk, egg, and vanilla. Beat well. Pour over prepared crust. Add nuts to reserved crumb mixture and sprinkle over cheese mixture. Bake for 25 minutes or until bubbly. Cool. Chill, cut into bars. Store in refrigerator. Makes 24 to 36 bars.

                                            —Arline Goodwin Mayer (Mrs. Charles E.)

❦ KAY'S BROWNIES

  ¼ cup butter, melted
  1 cup brown sugar
  2 squares unsweetened chocolate, melted
  1 egg, unbeaten
  ¾ teaspoon vanilla
  ½ cup broken nutmeats
  ½ cup flour

Melt butter and, while hot, pour over brown sugar to melt. Stir well. Add melted chocolate. Beat in egg, add vanilla, nutmeats, and flour in that order. Line a 7-inch-square pan with foil. Grease foil and spread batter in pan. Bake at 325 degrees for 20 minutes. Turn brownies out of pan a few minutes after taking from oven and cut while warm. Makes 9.

                                            —Marian Andrus (Mrs. Leon)

❧ BUTTER-PECAN COOKIES

       1 cup butter
     ⅔ cup brown sugar
       1 egg yolk
       2 cups flour, sifted
          pecan halves

Thoroughly cream the butter and sugar together. Beat in egg yolk, add flour, and mix well. Drop by teaspoonful on ungreased cookie sheet 2 inches apart. Top each with pecan half. Bake at 375 degrees for 12 to 15 minutes until lightly browned. Remove from cookie sheet while warm. Makes 4 to 5 dozen.

—Mary Davy Pippin (Mrs. James. O., Jr.)

❧ DOROTHY'S PRALINE COOKIES

Old family recipe of my mother, Dorothy J. Baldwin.

       ⅔ cup butter or shortening
       1 cup sugar
     ½ cup molasses
       2 eggs
     ½ teaspoon vanilla extract
     1¾ cups sifted flour
     ½ teaspoon baking soda
     ¼ teaspoon mace
   1½ to 2 cups chopped pecans

Melt shortening. Cool. Add sugar and molasses, eggs, vanilla, sifted dry ingredients, and nuts. Mix well and drop by scant teaspoonful on buttered and floured cookie sheets, about 2 inches apart. Bake at 375 degrees for 8 to 10 minutes. Remove from sheet immediately. The cookies will stick if you do not work quickly. However, they are worth the extra effort! Makes about 8 dozen.

—Carolyn Armstrong (Mrs. Louis)

❦ RICH WAFER THIN COOKIES

½ cup butter (no substitutes)
⅓ cup sugar
1 egg, well beaten
¾ cup flour
½ teaspoon vanilla

Preheat oven to 375 degrees. Cream butter and sugar. Add egg and mix well. Add sifted flour and vanilla. Mix well. Drop from tip of teaspoon onto greased baking sheet 2 inches apart. Spread out with knife first dipped in cold water. Bake for 7 to 10 minutes until edges are nicely golden. Watch carefully. Makes 4 dozen cookies.

—*Louisa Smith Heilman (Mrs. Benjamin G.)*

❦ ROCKS

1 tablespoon butter
1 cup sugar
2 eggs, not beaten
2½ teaspoons cinnamon
1½ teaspoons cloves
1½ cups flour
2 teaspoons baking powder
½ teaspoon salt
¼ cup milk
1½ cups nuts
1½ cups raisins

Cream butter and sugar. Add eggs. Sift dry ingredients. Add to creamed mixture with milk. Stir in nuts and raisins. Drop with teaspoon on greased cookie sheet. Bake at 325 degrees for 10 or 12 minutes. Makes 48 cookies.

—*Marian Merrick Brower (Mrs. Frank)*

❦ MISS ALICE TURPIN'S SPICE COOKIES

2 eggs
1 pound sugar
1 teaspoon soda in milk
1 cup butter

6 cups flour

1 cup milk

1 tablespoon lard

2 teaspoons cinnamon

Mix well. Roll small balls in granulated sugar and mash flat with tines of a fork. Bake at 350 degrees. Makes about 6 dozen.

—*Miss Caroline Wilson*

❧ *COCONUT MACAROONS*

3 egg whites, beaten dry and stiff

¼ teaspoon salt

1½ cups confectioners' sugar

2 3½-ounce cans dry, shredded coconut

¾ teaspoon vanilla

Put salt in egg whites and beat well, until quite stiff: beat in part of sugar and fold in rest. Fold in coconut and vanilla. Drop from teaspoon onto lightly greased cookie sheet and bake at 350 degrees for 15 to 20 minutes. Watch them; they should not color too much and should be dry and light. If they stick to pan when you try to remove them after taking from oven, return to oven for a few more minutes of cooking. Makes 36.

—*Mackey Perry Beck*

❧ *VEEDER NUTTER (Swedish Cookies)*

1 cup butter

1 cup sugar

4 egg yolks

1 teaspoon almond extract

½ pound almonds, ground fine

3 cups flour

Cream butter, beat in sugar, egg yolks, and almond extract. Stir in almonds and flour; then work with hands until soft enough to make into small balls. Place balls on a greased cookie sheet and flatten with fingertips. Bake at 350 degrees for about 10 minutes or until just slightly brown. Makes 100 to 110 cookies.

—*Sara Warren Kidd (Mrs. A. L.)*

❧ MOTHER'S VIENNESE COOKIES

1 cup butter
¼ pound powdered sugar
3 egg yolks
vanilla
¼ pound chopped nuts
1 pound (4 cups) flour, sifted
egg white

Cream butter and sugar. Add egg yolks, vanilla, and chopped nuts. Then, using your hands, add enough flour so dough can be rolled out thin. Cut with cookie cutters. Brush with egg white. Sprinkle a few chopped nuts on top. Bake at 300 to 325 degrees for 8 to 10 minutes or until golden. Makes 72 cookies.

—Isabel Atkinson Lieber (Mrs. Albert C.)

❧ NUTMEG ICEBOX COOKIES

¼ pound butter
1 cup sugar
1 egg
1¾ cups flour
1 teaspoon nutmeg
½ teaspoon baking powder
¼ teaspoon baking soda

Cream butter, add sugar and egg, cream. Sift together flour, spice, baking powder, and soda. Mix with cream mixture. Form into long rolls and wrap in waxed paper. Chill overnight. Cut thin and bake at 425 degrees for 10 to 12 minutes. Makes 40 cookies.

—Ruth Newell (Mrs. Robert)

❧ QUICK RUM TOFFEE CORNFLAKE COOKIES

12 pieces rum toffee
3 teaspoons whipping cream (2 of thin cream if no thick cream available)
1 teaspoon butter
1 generous cup cornflakes, or 1 small box

Melt toffee, add cream and butter, stir in cornflakes, and form into cookie-like balls. Makes 14 to 16 cookies.

—*Lynette Morgan Nielsen (Mrs. Orsen)*

❧ RUM OR WHISKEY BALLS

    1 cup ground pecans or walnuts
    1 cup ground vanilla wafers
    1 cup confectioners' sugar
    2 tablespoons light corn syrup
    1 jigger rum or whiskey, rum preferred

Combine all ingredients. Make into small balls and roll in confectioners' sugar. Makes 2 dozen.

—*Isabel Atkinson Lieber (Mrs. Albert C.)*

❧ QUICK SHORTBREAD, DAVID'S DELIGHT

  ½ cup sugar
    1 cup butter
    2 cups sifted flour

Mix and spread in a 9-inch-square baking pan. Bake 10 minutes at 350 degrees; then reduce heat to 300 degrees and cook 10 minutes. Cut in squares and cool. Makes 18 squares.

—*Harriet Willcox Gearhart (Mrs. David)*

❧ ICEBOX COOKIES

    1 cup butter or margarine
    1 pound brown sugar
    2 eggs
 3½ cups flour
    1 teaspoon soda
    1 teaspoon vanilla
    1 cup chopped black walnuts

Cream butter and sugar. Add eggs and mix well. Blend in rest of ingredients until thoroughly mixed. Put in ice cube tray or roll into two logs. Wrap in waxed paper and chill overnight. Slice very thin. Bake on cookie sheet at 375 to 400 degrees for 6 to 12 minutes. Makes 6 dozen.

—*Genevieve Hall Valliant (Mrs. Edwin S., Sr.)*

❦ ST. PAUL'S COOKIE EXCHANGE

The following recipes were shared at a cookie exchange. An Episcopal Church Women's meeting was scheduled near the Christmas holidays. Everyone was instructed to bring a batch of their favorite cookie and a copy of the recipe. When they went home, everyone's cookie tins were filled with a selection of the festive morsels. You might want to try this with your friends.

❦ CHOCOLATE CHERRY CREAMS

  1 6-ounce package semisweet chocolate chips
  ⅓ cup evaporated milk
1½ cups sifted powdered sugar
  ⅓ cup chopped nuts (preferably pecans)
  ⅓ cup chopped maraschino cherries
1½ cups shredded coconut

Melt chocolate chips and evaporated milk together in double boiler. Stir in powdered sugar, nuts, and cherries. Chill. Roll into balls. Roll in coconut. Makes 36.

—Marybelle Weatherford Henry (Mrs. Elmer T.)

❦ QUICK MUNCHIES

Also good with regular chocolate.

1 pound white chocolate
2 cups thin pretzels, broken into small pieces
1 cup peanuts without skins

Melt chocolate in a double boiler. When soft, add pretzels and nuts. Stir until coated. Drop by teaspoonsful on waxed paper and cool. Yields 80 to 100 pieces.

—Marty Pippin LaGiglia (Mrs. Michael, Jr.)

❦ DATE BARS

1 cup powdered sugar
3 eggs
2 cups chopped dates

1 cup chopped nuts
1 scant cup bread flour
1 teaspoon baking powder (optional)
⅛ teaspoon salt (optional)
¼ teaspoon each cloves and cinnamon (optional)
1 teaspoon vanilla
  extra confectioners' sugar for rolling

Sift sugar. Beat eggs until light. Add sugar gradually. Blend these ingredients until they are very light. Add dates and nuts. Sift flour before measuring. Resift with baking powder, salt, and spices. Add the dry ingredients to the egg mixture along with the vanilla. Beat batter until ingredients are well blended. Pour into a greased 9 × 13-inch pan. Bake at 325 degrees for 25 minutes. When cool, cut into bars and roll in powdered sugar. Makes 36.

—Dorothy Keith Perkins (Mrs. Louis H.)

PEANUT BLOSSOMS

Great for children. These do not stay around long.

½ cup butter
½ cup peanut butter (chunky or smooth)
½ cup sugar
½ cup brown sugar, firmly packed
1 egg
2 tablespoons milk
1 teaspoon vanilla
1¾ cups flour
1 teaspoon baking soda
½ teaspoon salt
  sugar
  chocolate kisses for topping

Cream butter, peanut butter, and sugars. Add egg and beat well. Add milk and vanilla; stir in flour, baking soda, and salt. Mix well. Chill if necessary for handling. Form into 1-inch balls and roll in sugar. Place one chocolate kiss on top of each ball and press in firmly. Bake at 375 degrees for 10 to 12 minutes until golden brown. Cool on rack. Makes 4 dozen.

—Stephanie Michalec Thompson (Mrs. Robert)

❧ SAND TARTS

½ cup butter
1 cup sugar
1 egg, beaten
1¾ cups sifted flour
2 teaspoons baking powder

Cream butter and sugar and stir in beaten egg. Sift flour and baking powder together. Blend with creamed mixture to make a soft dough and set in refrigerator to chill. When cold, place a portion of dough on a well-floured board and roll out ⅛ inch thick. If dough is too soft, knead in a little more flour and roll again. Cut with cookie cutters and place on a greased sheet. Brush with egg white and sprinkle with Christmas crystal sugar. Bake at 350 degrees for 10 to 15 minutes. Store in a cookie tin. Makes about 3 dozen.

—*Lou Snyder Eby (Mrs. J. Walter)*

❧ DATE-FILLED BUTTERSCOTCH COOKIES

½ cup shortening
2 cups brown sugar
2 eggs, well beaten
1 teaspoon vanilla
3½ cups flour
½ teaspoon salt
1 teaspoon soda
1 teaspoon cream of tartar

Thoroughly cream shortening and sugar, add eggs and vanilla. Add sifted dry ingredients. Beat well. Form into 3 small rolls, 1½ inches in diameter, and chill overnight (I freeze mine). Slice as thin as possible to make a sandwich type cookie. Place filling on each slice, press edges together with a fork. Bake at 350 degrees for 12 to 15 minutes. Makes 5 dozen small cookies.

Date-Nut Filling

1 to 2 pounds dates, pitted and chopped
¼ cup brown sugar
¼ cup water
⅓ cup broken nutmeats

Combine dates, sugar, and water in a saucepan and cook until thick. Add nutmeats and cool.

—*Louise Layton (Mrs. C. Rodney)*

❧ PEANUT BUTTER CANDY

      2 cups sugar
    ¾ cup milk
      2 tablespoons peanut butter
      2 tablespoons butter
         pinch of salt

Boil sugar and milk until a soft ball forms when dropped in water. Add peanut butter. Remove from stove and beat in butter. Add salt. When cool, pour into a square buttered candy pan (about 7 × 7 inches). Cut later. Makes about 1 pound.

—*Mabel Walls Valliant (Mrs. T. Rigby)*

❧ LEMON NUT COOKIES

> *This is a rich cookie suitable for a special occasion such as a tea, wedding reception, or Christmas party.*

    ½ cup soft shortening
    ½ cup granulated sugar
      1 egg yolk, unbeaten
  1½ teaspoons grated lemon rind
      1 tablespoon grated orange rind
      1 tablespoon lemon juice
    ½ teaspoon vanilla
      1 cup cake flour, sifted
      1 egg white, unbeaten
    ¾ cup chopped walnuts
         candied cherries

Mix first 7 ingredients with mixer until light and fluffy. At low speed beat in flour just until mixed. Chill until easy to handle. Preheat oven to 350 degrees. Form dough into ½-inch balls. Roll in egg white, then nuts. Press a piece of cherry on each ball to flatten somewhat. Bake for about 20 minutes or until lightly browned. Makes 3 dozen.

—*Janet Gadd Doehler (Mrs. William F.)*

✺ MISSISSIPPI PRALINES

        5 cups granulated sugar
        1 tablespoon butter
        1 cup milk
        1 cup light corn syrup
           pinch of salt
        1 cup granulated sugar (not part of 5 cups)
        2 cups pecans

Boil together first 5 ingredients. Place the other cup of sugar in a skillet and brown, stirring constantly. When brown, add to first mixture and cook to soft ball. Beat until creamy and light in color. Add pecans. Drop from spoon onto buttered plates. Makes about 3 pounds of candy.

—*Isabel Atkinson Lieber (Mrs. Albert C.)*

✺ NEVER FAIL CHOCOLATE FUDGE

This makes a perfect icing if cooked only to soft ball stage.

        2 ounces unsweetened baking chocolate
        3 tablespoons butter
        1 cup milk
        2 cups sugar
        1 teaspoon vanilla
           pinch salt

Melt chocolate and butter together; add milk slowly, stirring until thick and smooth. Add sugar gradually, still stirring until dissolved. Cook, stirring occasionally, until a firm ball is formed when dropped in cold water. Remove from heat and place in cold water. Add vanilla and salt. Beat until it begins to lose the glaze. Pour into buttered 9-inch-square pan or onto a buttered platter. Cool and cut in squares. Nuts, marshmallows, or raisins may be added. Makes about 1¼ pound of fudge.

—*Ruth Branner Gadd (Mrs. A. Sydney, Jr.)*

CHOCOLATE CARAMELS

    3 tablespoons butter
    ¾ cup milk
    2 ounces unsweetened chocolate
    2¾ cups sugar

Brown butter first. Add milk, chocolate, and sugar. Cook until soft ball forms in water. Let cook 5 minutes, then add vanilla. Beat, and add nuts. Makes about 1 pound of candy.

—Margaret Fesmyer Wolcott (Mrs. Milton)

MINT CANDY

An old recipe!

    3 cups sugar
    ½ cup light corn syrup
    ⅔ cup cold water
    2 egg whites
    ½ teaspoon salt
    1 teaspoon mint extract

Boil together the sugar, syrup, and water until it forms a ball when dropped in cold water. Beat egg whites in large bowl until stiff, and add salt. Pour hot mixture slowly into egg whites and beat until cool, finally adding the mint extract. Pour into buttered 9-inch-square pan. Cut in squares. Makes about 1½ pounds of candy.

—Mabel Walls Valliant (Mrs. T. Rigby)

It was suggested to the Vestry in 1933 "that certain pews be assigned the pupils from Gunston School, as it was thought it would (encourage) much confession."

❧ CANDIED GRAPEFRUIT PEEL

This is a nice Christmas recipe.

peels of 2 large or 3 medium grapefruit
water
3 cups sugar
red, green, and yellow food coloring

Cover peel with cold water. Bring to boil and cook until tender, pouring off water and adding fresh cold water several times. Drain. With spoon, remove white inner portion of peel. With knife or tiny star cookie cutter, cut a few stars from peel if desired. With scissors or sharp knife, cut rest of peel in thin strips. Make a syrup by boiling 2 cups sugar with 1 cup water. Add a little red or green food coloring. A drop or two of yellow food coloring with red improves the finished color. Add peel to syrup and cook over low heat until peel has a clear, candied appearance. Remove peel, two or three pieces at a time, allowing excess of syrup to drain back into the saucepan. Roll strips separately in remaining 1 cup of sugar until well coated. Place on rack to cool. Store in lightly covered container in cool, dry place. Keeps at least a month and makes about 1 pound grapefruit peel.

—*Margaret Gadd Ashley (Mrs. John M.)*

❧ PANUCHI

2 cups brown sugar
1 cup water
2 tablespoons butter
¾ cup milk
1 tablespoon vanilla
pinch salt
1 cup chopped nuts

Mix brown sugar, water, 1 tablespoon butter, and milk together in saucepan. Boil to soft ball stage. When soft ball is reached, add vanilla. Add another tablespoon of butter and a pinch of salt. Beat until thick. Add chopped nuts and pour into buttered 9-inch-square pan. Cut in squares. Makes about ¾ pound of candy.

—*Isabel Atkinson Lieber (Mrs. Albert C.)*

❧ *SPRITZ*

  2½ cups all-purpose flour
  ½ teaspoon baking powder
  1 cup butter, softened
  ¾ cup sugar
     dash of salt
  1 egg, unbeaten
  1 teaspoon vanilla

Sift flour and baking powder together. Cream butter, sugar, salt, egg, and vanilla; mix well. Add sifted ingredients in small amounts to butter mixture. Use cookie press to place cookie on a cold ungreased cookie sheet. Bake at 375 degrees for 12 to 15 minutes. You can add a sprinkle of nuts to the tops before baking; however, they are delicious plain. Makes 4 dozen cookies.

—Barbara Seaman Efland (Mrs. Herman)

❧ *MICROWAVE PEANUT BRITTLE*

  1 cup raw peanuts
  1 cup sugar
  ½ cup light corn syrup
  1 teaspoon vanilla
  1 teaspoon margarine
  1 teaspoon baking soda

Mix first three ingredients in microwave-safe bowl and cook on high 4 minutes. Stir. Cook on high 3½ minutes. Stir, then add vanilla and margarine. Cook on high 1½ minutes. Add soda. Pour onto warmed, greased cookie sheet. Cool, then break up. Makes ½ pound.

—Susan McFadden Miller (Mrs. Mark)

PICKLES AND JAMS

This day be bread and peace my lot
All else beneath the sun
Thou know'st if best bestowed or not
And let thy will be done.
—Alexander Pope (1688–1744)

🍃 *BREAD AND BUTTER PICKLES*

      1 gallon firm cucumbers, unpeeled, sliced very thin
      8 small white onions, skinned
      1 quart crushed ice
     ½ cup salt
      5 cups sugar
      5 cups vinegar
     1½ teaspoons turmeric
     ½ teaspoon ground cloves
      1 teaspoon celery seed
      2 teaspoons mustard seed

Place cucumber slices, onions, and ice in layers in a pan with salt. Cover with weighted lid and place in refrigerator for 3 hours. Drain well. Make a syrup of remaining ingredients. Add cucumbers and onions to this mixture. Heat slowly, with little stirring. Scald, do not boil. Place in sterilized jars and seal at once. Makes 10 pints.

—*Louise Thurston Stanton (Mrs. Barclay R.)*

🍃 *SWEET PICKLE FIGS*

      1 teaspoon ground cloves
      2 teaspoons ground allspice
      4 teaspoons cinnamon
      7 pounds ripe black figs
         soda water (1 tablespoon soda to a kettle of water)
      1 pint vinegar
      4 pounds sugar

Put cloves, allspice, and cinnamon in a bag. Scald figs in soda water. Drain. Boil vinegar, sugar, figs, and spice bag all together slowly about 3 hours. Skim out figs, remove spice bag, and boil down syrup with pinch of salt. Pour with figs into hot sterilized jars and seal at once. Makes 8 to 10 pints.

—*From the collection of Mrs. Luther Gadd*

❧ CORN RELISH

- 1 dozen ears corn
- 8 medium size onions
- 1 good size head cabbage
  salt
- 4 red peppers
- 2 stalks celery
- 3 pints vinegar
- 2 pounds brown sugar
- 4 tablespoons prepared mustard
- 2 tablespoons flour
- 1 tablespoon turmeric

Cut kernels off the cobs and cook until tender, about 8 to 10 minutes. Chop cabbage. Pour over it cold water and add handful of salt. Let stand 10 minutes, then drain well. Chop onions and peppers together in food chopper. Cut celery by hand. Put all together in kettle with vinegar and brown sugar. Make a paste of mustard, flour, and turmeric. Take some of vinegar and mix with this. Cook all 30 minutes and put in sterile glass jars. Makes 8 to 10 ½-pint jars, depending on size of ears of corn.

—*Ruth Newell (Mrs. Robert)*

❧ CANTALOUPE PICKLE

- 7 pounds cantaloupe
- 4 pounds sugar
- 1 pint vinegar
- 1 ounce mace
- 1 ounce stick cinnamon

Pare fruit. Cut in slices and let stand in weak vinegar water (1 pint vinegar to 1 pint water) overnight. Drain in morning. Put fruit, sugar, vinegar, mace, and cinnamon into kettle and boil very slowly until transparent. Put boiling hot in jars and seal tight. Makes 9 or 10 pints.

—*Katherine Nicols Grove (Mrs. J. Robert)*

🌿 *PICKLED FIGS*

    3 quarts firm, ripe figs
    2 quarts boiling water
    1 cup water
    6 cups granulated sugar
 1½ cups cider vinegar
    1 tablespoon grated orange rind
    1 tablespoon whole cloves
    2 tablespoons broken cinnamon sticks

Cover figs with boiling water. Let stand 5 minutes. Drain. Mix 1 cup water, sugar, and vinegar in enamel saucepan and add orange rind and spices (in a bag). Bring to boiling point and cook 10 minutes. Let stand 'til the next day and cook 10 minutes again. Do the same the third day. Remove spice bag and pack in hot sterilized jars. Process in hot water 10 minutes. Makes 9 or 10 pints.

—A. M. B.

🌿 *PEPPER RELISH*

    12 red peppers, seeded
    12 green peppers, seeded
    12 onions
    12 green tomatoes
     2 cups apple cider vinegar
  1½ cups sugar
     2 teaspoons salt
     2 tablespoons mustard seed
     2 tablespoons pickling spice (tied in a bag)

Cut vegetables coarsely and chop in food processor. (You may need to do this in batches. Watch for a fine grind, not a puree). Drain well. Mix vinegar, sugar, and salt in stainless steel saucepan and bring to boil. Add relish, mustard seed, and spice bag. Simmer uncovered for 30 minutes. Remove and discard spice bag. Pour the relish into hot, sterilized jars and seal. Makes 11 pints. Recipe may be halved.

—Mary Davy Pippin (Mrs. James O., Jr.)
—Janet Gadd Doehler (Mrs. William F.)

🍂 *MUSTARD PICKLE*

  1 quart onions, chunked before measuring, scalded
  1 quart lima beans, cooked with a little salt added
  1 quart cauliflower, separated into small pieces, scalded
  1 quart sour cucumber pickles, cut before measuring
  1 tablespoon celery seed
  1 pint corn, scalded
  1 quart sweet peppers, cut before measuring
  1 hot pepper, cut up; or a dash of red pepper
  1 quart sugar
  1 quart vinegar
  1 cup flour, scant
 ¾ cup ground mustard
  2 tablespoons white mustard seed
  1 tablespoon turmeric

Put flour, mustard, celery seed, and turmeric together and smooth with some of the vinegar. Thicken the pickle with this paste when it comes to a boil. Boil for 5 minutes. Vacuum seal while boiling. Makes 10 pints.

—*Mrs. Edwin P. Meredith*

🍂 *PICKLED COCKTAIL ONIONS*

A Pennsylvania Dutch recipe (Saurea Tswiwla).

  2 quarts small onions (onion sets)
 ¼ cup sugar
 ¼ cup vinegar
  1 teaspoon salt
 ½ cup water
 ½ teaspoon black pepper

Boil onions in water until not quite done, and onions haven't started to come apart. Drain. Place in a large dish and add the remaining ingredients. Mix. Let sit for short time, 15 to 30 minutes. Serve either hot or cold. Makes 4 pints.

—*G. Myron Latshaw*

❧ *SPICED GRAPES*

> 7 pounds grapes
> 3 pounds sugar
> 1¼ tablespoons ground cloves
> ¾ tablespoon ground cinnamon (or to taste)
> ¾ tablespoon ground allspice (or to taste)
> 1¾ pints vinegar

Wash, pick grapes from stems. Squeeze pulp from grape skins. Boil pulp a few minutes. Strain through colander to eliminate seed. Grind skins through meat grinder (large knife). Catch juice under grinder and use. Mix pulp and skins. Add sugar, spices, and vinegar. Boil all for 45 minutes. Stir frequently while cooking to prevent skins from settling and scorching. Skim foam before jarring in hot, sterilized jars. Makes 5 pints.

—*Louise McFeely Perry (Mrs. John W.)*

❧ *SPICED PEACHES*

> 7 pounds prepared peaches
> 3½ pounds sugar
> 2 cups vinegar
> 2 tablespoons whole cloves
> 2 tablespoons whole allspice
> 1 stick cinnamon
> 6 to 8 peach pits cooked with fruit

Cut firm peaches in halves, peel, remove seeds, and weigh. Place in large kettle and cover with sugar. Let stand overnight. Tie spices in a bag. Add vinegar, bag of spices, and peach seeds and bring to a boil. Cook gently until peaches seem to turn transparent. If thicker syrup is desired, remove fruit, spice bag, and seeds, and cook syrup longer. Pack in sterilized jars and cap tightly. Makes 3 to 4 pints depending on how much syrup is cooked down.

—*From recipe of Paul C. Merrick*
—*Miriam P. Chambers*

❧ *SPICED CHERRIES*

  1 1-pound can dark sweet cherries, drained and pitted,
        reserving juice
  3 tablespoons sugar
  ¼ cup white vinegar
  ¼ teaspoon salt
  ½ teaspoon mixed pickling spices (optional)
  4 whole cloves

In a saucepan stir together ¾ cup cherry juice and sugar, vinegar, salt, and all spices. Bring to a boil. Let simmer 5 minutes. Strain and pour over pitted cherries in a pint jar. Cool, cover, and refrigerate overnight before using. Serve with baked ham or chicken. Makes 4 servings.

—Margaret Gadd Ashley (Mrs. John M.)

❧ *SWEET-SOUR PICKLE CHIPS*

  6 cups water
  ¼ cup salt
  6 large cucumbers, pared and thinly sliced
1½ cups sugar
  ¼ cup flour
1½ teaspoons celery seed
1½ teaspoons turmeric
  ¼ teaspoon cayenne
  2 cups vinegar
  6 medium-sized onions, thinly sliced
  1 medium-sized sweet red pepper, chopped

Combine water and salt in large bowl. Stir to dissolve salt. Add cucumbers; cover bowl and let stand overnight. Next day, drain cucumbers.

Combine sugar, flour, celery seed, turmeric, and cayenne in a large kettle; gradually stir in vinegar. Add drained cucumbers, onions, and red pepper. Bring vegetables to boiling. Cook over low heat, stirring often, for 10 minutes or until the vegetables are just tender. Remove from heat. Pack at once into sterilized jars. Seal. Makes about 4½ pints.

—Genevieve Hall Valliant (Mrs. Edwin S., Sr.)

❧ *TOMATO JUICE*

>   12 cups tomatoes
>   2 cups water
>   4 celery leaves
>   ¼ cup chopped onion
>   2 bay leaves
>   1 teaspoon granulated sugar
>   6 whole cloves
>   2 teaspoons salt
>   ½ teaspoon paprika

Wash, but do not peel the tomatoes. Cut into quarters. Add rest of ingredients. Cover and let simmer for 30 minutes. Strain. Reheat the juice and let boil for 3 minutes. Pour into sterilized jars and seal immediately. Makes 3 quarts.

—*Genevieve Hall Valliant (Mrs. Edwin S., Sr.)*

❧ *WATERMELON PICKLE*

> *This is an old recipe belonging to my mother-in-law, and is the best I have ever eaten.*

>   6½ pounds thick watermelon rind
>   5 pounds sugar
>   4 cups water
>   4½ cups vinegar
>   2½ tablespoons stick cinnamon
>   2 small slices lemon

Cut pink and green (skin) from rind and cut rind in small squares. Cover with water and cook until tender. Make syrup with sugar, water, and vinegar. Add cinnamon sticks, tied in a bag; lemon slices, and watermelon rind. Cover and boil slowly until rind clears, about 1 hour. Seal in jars. Makes 3 quarts (6 pints).

—*Frances Wright Hilleary (Mrs. Robert)*

🌿 *PRESERVED WATERMELON RIND*

Best melon with thick rinds to preserve is large and round, with a dark green skin—a variety named "Excel."

8 pounds watermelon
  salt water
3 tablespoons powdered alum
7 pounds sugar
1 ounce dry gingerroot, washed
1 lemon

Cut watermelon in 1½-inch squares. Cut off all green skin and soft pink meat. Cover in salt water to taste with alum for 24 hours. Drain and soak in clear cold water to cover for 24 hours. Drain and add 1½ gallons clear, boiling water and gingerroot. Boil until fruit can be pierced with a straw, but not too soft. Pour off ginger water into a bowl. Measure a quart of reserved water and pour back into fruit (keeping rest in case your syrup boils away in preserving). Add sugar. Boil fruit, ginger, and sugar slowly about an hour. Slice lemon into 4 or 5 thick slices. Add to fruit and cook until transparent (about 2¾ hours in all, depending on thickness and ripeness of rind. It should be amber color. It colors a little as it cools.) Jar cold. Fill to overflow with syrup, releasing air bubbles with knife blade and wiping threads of jar clean. You can substitute boiling ginger water if syrup runs out. Use hot sterilized jars, rubbers, and tops. It yields about 6 pints.

—*Louise McFeely Perry (Mrs. John W.)*

🌿 *DAMSON PRESERVES*

4 pounds (3 quarts) plums
½ cup water
8 cups sugar

Pierce plums and add to sugar and water. Heat slowly, stirring gently every few minutes, until sugar dissolves. Increase heat, cook briskly for 10 minutes. Reduce heat to simmer. Strain out seeds as they float to top. Cook until syrup gives the jelly test (2 drops sheet from edge of metal spoon). Preserves require 40 to 50 minutes' cooking. Pour into hot sterilized jars. Seal. Makes 5 pints.

Committee note: A dollop of this tart jam is delicious with white potato pie.

🌿 HEAVENLY CONSERVE

    4 pounds Kieffer pears, cored and diced in 1-inch squares
    4 pounds sugar
    1 pound raisins
    1 pound English walnuts

Mix pears and sugar and let stand overnight. Boil until pink. Add raisins and walnuts. Cook until thick. Makes 5 pints.

—Julia Goldsborough Long (Mrs. H. L.)

🌿 APRICOT MARMALADE

    1 pound dried apricots
    3 cups water
    1 20-ounce can crushed pineapple
    1 orange
    1 lemon
       sugar

Grind the dried apricots. Add the water and cook until tender. Add the pineapple. Grind the orange and the lemon. Add these to the apricots. Weigh, and add equal amount of sugar. Cook 20 minutes, stirring constantly, as it is easily scorched. Put into clean, scalded glasses and cover with paraffin. Makes 4½ pints.

—Louise C. Layton (Mrs. C. Rodney)

🌿 OLD-TIME LEMON BUTTER

This was always taken on family picnics when I was a child.

       grated rind and juice of 6 lemons
    6 egg yolks, slightly beaten
    2 cups sugar
   ¼ pound butter

Mix lemon rind and juice with egg yolks in top of double boiler. Add sugar and butter. Cook in double boiler, stirring constantly, until it thickens. Use as jelly. Makes 3 cups.

—Ruth Willis Draper (Mrs. Frank W., Jr.)

❧ PRESERVED STRAWBERRIES

1 heaping quart berries
2 pounds sugar
1 tablespoon vinegar

Let sugar dissolve on very slow heat. Add strawberries and vinegar; boil slowly 20 minutes. Skim off all foam while hot. To prevent sugar and fruit from sticking or burning, twist pan occasionally. Do not stir. Cook 1 quart only at a time; as each quart gets done, pour all in large bowl and let sit. Next morning, gently mix berries evenly through thick syrup by wooden spoon or by hand. Put cold in jars. Usually 1 quart of berries will yield 1 quart of preserves.

—*Louise McFeely Perry (Mrs. John W.)*

❧ RHUBARB CONSERVE

2 pounds rhubarb
4 pounds sugar
1 lemon
1 large orange
⅓ cup walnuts

Cut rhubarb into 1-inch pieces. Slice lemon and orange thin. Combine all ingredients in a saucepan and cook until thick. Makes 5 pints.

—*Julia Goldsborough Long (Mrs. H. L.)*

❧ PEACH CONSERVE

3 pints peaches, peeled and diced
6 cups sugar
1 10-ounce jar maraschino cherries, cut up with juice
  juice of 2 lemons
  grated rind, pulp, and juice of 2 oranges

Cook 45 minutes. Put in hot, sterile jars. Seal. Makes 7½ pints.

Committee note: This is very juicy, and bright as a sunset. A nice sauce over hotcakes, waffles, or ice cream.

367

$\mathcal{L}$OAVES AND FISHES

Come, Lord Jesus, be our guest,
And bless what thou hast given us.

Buying Guide for Approximately 50 Servings

For 100 servings, multiply quantities by 2; for 25 servings, divide by 2.

BREAD AND BUTTER, AND SANDWICHES

Sliced bread: 4 to 6 about 1-pound loaves

Butter (50 pats): 1 pound

Bread for sandwiches: 2 3-pound loaves

Crackers: 1 pound

Rolls: 7 dozen

Cheese slices: 3¼ pounds

Sliced baked ham: 5 pounds

DESSERTS

Apples for pie: 20 pounds

Apples for sauce or salad: 15 pounds

Cherries, fresh, for pie: 7 quarts or 15 pounds

Cream, heavy, to whip for dessert topping: 1 quart

Ice cream with #12 dipper: 2½ gallons

Pies: 9 9-inch pans

Sherbet with #16 dipper: 6 quarts

DRINKS

Coffee, instant: 1½ 4-ounce jars

Coffee, regular: 1¼ pounds

Cream for coffee: 2½ pints

Fruit juice, frozen concentrate: 9 6-ounce cans

Lemonade, frozen concentrate: 13 6-ounce cans

Lemons, to slice for tea: 6 large

Milk: 3 gallons

Punch: 2 gallons

Sugar cubes for coffee or tea: 1⅛ pounds

Tea: ¼ pound

Tomato or fruit juice: 4 46-ounce cans

FISH

Fish fillets, frozen: 13 to 14 1-pound packages
Oysters for stew: 6 quarts
Salmon for salad: 8 1-pound cans
Tuna for salad: 16 6- to 7-ounce cans

MEATS AND POULTRY

Bacon, 2 slices per serving: 6 pounds
Frankfurters: 100
Beef, ground for hamburgers: 15 pounds
Beef, ground for meat loaf: 12 pounds
Beef, rolled roast, before boning: 25 pounds
Beef, standing rib roast: 35 pounds
Ham, canned, boneless: 1 14-pound can
Ham, ground for loaf: 12 pounds
Leg of lamb to roast: 25 pounds
Pork chops, ¾-inch thick: 17 pounds
Pork loin, to roast: 25 pounds
Sausage, bulk or link: 12½ pounds
Veal loin chops: 14 to 15 pounds
Chicken, to roast (drawn): 40 pounds
Chicken, to stew and cut up: 25 pounds
Turkey, to roast and cut up to use in dishes: 16 to 17 pounds
Turkey, to roast and slice: 40 pounds

RELISHES

Carrots for sticks: 6 large
Celery: 5 to 6 bunches with 12 stalks each
Cranberries, fresh, for sauce: 3 pounds
Cranberry sauce: 6 1-pound cans
Jam and jelly: 8 8-ounce jars
Ketchup: 3 14-ounce bottles
Olives: 2 quarts
Pickles: 2 quarts
Radishes: 8 to 16 bunches

SALADS AND SALAD DRESSINGS

Cabbage for coleslaw: 15 pounds
Chicken: 6½ quarts
French dressing: 1½ quarts
Fruit: 9 quarts
Lettuce for salad: 10 to 12 heads
Lettuce leaves for garnish: 6 large heads
Mayonnaise or salad dressing: 1 quart
Potato: 6½ quarts
Tomatoes, small: 15 to 18 pounds

VEGETABLES

Carrots without tops: 16 pounds
Instant potatoes: 1 1-pound 10-ounce package
Potatoes, to mash: 25 pounds
Potatoes, to scallop: 12 to 16 pounds
Squash, to mash: 10 to 12 pounds
Sweet potatoes, to candy: 25 pounds
Vegetables, canned: 14 1-pound cans or 11 1-pound 4-ounce cans
Vegetables, frozen: 15 to 18 10- to 12-ounce packages

Loaves and Fishes Events

For Lenten Suppers, auctions on the south lawn, Farmer's Markets, and other autumn functions, these combinations pleased masses of people.

MENU ONE

Vegetable Beef Soup*
Tossed Green Salad*
Vinaigrette Dressing*
Red French Dressing*
Tea Biscuits*
French Bread
Assorted Desserts
Beverages

* See large-quantity recipe below.

❧ *VEGETABLE BEEF SOUP*

For the Lenten Supper, 9 gallons of soup were made: 3 gallons were served and the rest was sold in pint and quart containers. For the Farmer's Market, 18 gallons of soup were made: 3 canners and 2 large stockpots full.

30 pounds trimmed beef
 5 pounds tomatoes
 5 pounds potatoes
 4 pounds onion
 2 heads cabbage, chopped
 2 pounds peas, frozen
 2 pounds corn, frozen
 2 pounds green beans, frozen
 2 pounds lima beans, frozen
 4 pounds carrots
 2 bunches celery
 1 pound turnips
    water to half fill stockpots
    stock from beef
 2 tablespoons Worcestershire sauce
 1 teaspoon Tabasco
 2 bay leaves
    salt and pepper to taste
    small amount of oil

Cut beef in cubes. Distribute beef among 5 large stockpots or canning kettles; enamel or stainless steel. Brown beef in small amount of oil to prevent sticking. Add water to cover beef. Simmer for 45 to 60 minutes or until beef is tender. Add vegetables and seasonings. Cover and simmer until vegetables are tender. Remove bay leaves. Cool. Refrigerate. To serve, adjust seasonings and simmer until hot. A variety of herbs and spices will enrich the character of the soup. (See Vegetable Soup, St. John's Church, on page 82 of Soup Chapter for suggestions.)

Notes about soup making: For basic stock, simmer 4 pounds of bones in 2½ quarts of water for 45 to 60 minutes or until meat is cooked. Cut meat from bones after cooling. Defat stock and refrigerate. Makes 2 quarts. Add 2 cubes of bouillon to each quart of stock to enhance beef flavor. Two gallons of soup provide approximately 30 1-cup servings or 25 1¼-cup servings.

🍂 *TOSSED GREEN SALAD FOR 50*

    2 heads of lettuce
    1 pound spinach
    ¾ pound radishes (2 cups sliced)
    1 pound cucumbers (2 cups thinly sliced)
    2 large green peppers (2 cups chopped)
    1 medium onion (1 cup chopped)

Break lettuce into bite-sized chunks. Tear spinach. Make layers of greens, radishes, cucumbers, pepper, and onion in 1 or 2 large bowls. Refrigerate.

🍂 *VINAIGRETTE DRESSING*

    1 cup lemon juice
    ½ cup sugar
    1 tablespoon salt
    1 tablespoon paprika
       dash of cayenne
    3 cups salad oil

Combine all ingredients in large jar with tight-fitting top that can be stored in refrigerator. Shake well before serving. Makes 1 quart.

🍂 *RED FRENCH DRESSING*

    ¾   cup sugar
    1⅓ cups vinegar
    4   teaspoons Worcestershire sauce
    4   teaspoons dry mustard
    2   teaspoons salt
    2   10½-ounce cans tomato soup, undiluted
    ¼   teaspoon Tabasco
    1   clove garlic, minced
    2   cups vegetable oil

Blend all ingredients except oil in blender for 1 minute. Add oil in steady stream as you blend again. Store in refrigerator. Makes 1 quart.

❧ TEA BISCUITS

*For the Farmer's Market, 4 loaves of French bread, cut to make 20
to 24 servings each, and brushed with melted butter or margarine,
supplemented the 6 dozen tea biscuits, also brushed with butter or
margarine.*

- 10 cups all-purpose flour
- 2 tablespoons plus 1 teaspoon baking powder
- 1½ teaspoons salt
- 1½ cups shortening
- 2½ teaspoons sugar
- milk, approximately 1¾ cups, more if needed

After mixing dry ingredients with hands or pastry blender to break up
shortening, add milk. Mixture should have dry, rough texture. Beware
of "drowning the miller" by adding too much milk. Divide into three
parts for rolling out. Keep dough covered while rolling out in thirds.
Flour the rolling pin and work surface. Roll and cut biscuits. Place fairly
close on baking sheet. Prick tops.

Place biscuits on lower shelf in oven and bake at 425 degrees for
10 minutes until bottoms are browned and biscuits rise. Now place on
upper shelf in oven for about 12 minutes. Butter when easy to handle.
Makes 75 small 1½-inch cocktail biscuits or 4 dozen 2-inch biscuits.

Usually assorted desserts are prepared and brought in for large
events. Sheet cakes, bar cookies, and pies are easily apportioned and
served.

MENU TWO

Fit for a spring get-together

Potage St. Germain*
Chicken curry sandwiches* on whole wheat bread
Cucumber sandwiches on white bread
Strawberry Squares*
Beverages*

* See recipe below.

Rochambeau's French troops, in the spring of 1781, began the long march south from Newport, Rhode Island, to Yorktown, Virginia. On the march, the troops prepared a soup utilizing what was available at the time, in the same way their countrymen had for centuries.

❧ POTAGE ST. GERMAIN

1 chicken for poaching
1 cup chopped onion
¼ cup chopped celery
2 big sprigs parsley
1 head spring lettuce, chopped
3 tablespoons butter or oil
5 cups chicken stock
2 pounds frozen peas
1 teaspoon basil
   salt and pepper to taste
   cream (optional)

Poach chicken in salted water. Cool; remove meat from bones and reserve for chicken sandwiches. Cool and defat stock. Sauté vegetables in butter. Heat 5 cups of stock. Add sautéed vegetables and frozen peas. Simmer to cook peas. Strain vegetables and process or run through food mill. Add to stock. Add seasonings. Soup may be frozen at this point after it is cooled. Cream may be added when reheated for a richer soup. Doubles easily. This recipe is for 10 or 12 servings.

❧ CHICKEN CURRY SANDWICH FILLING

5 cups cooked, finely chopped chicken
1 cup toasted, finely chopped almonds (or celery)
2 tablespoons finely minced onion
1½ teaspoons salt
2 tablespoons finely minced parsley
2 teaspoons lemon juice and zest to taste
1 teaspoon curry powder
¼ teaspoon white pepper
1½ cups lite mayonnaise

Blend all ingredients together thoroughly. Spread on sandwiches. Trim off crusts. Makes 10 to 12 servings.

STRAWBERRY SQUARES

    2 cups sifted flour
    ½ cup brown sugar
    1 cup chopped walnuts
    1 cup margarine, melted
    4 egg whites
    1⅓ cups sugar
    2 10-ounce packages frozen strawberries, partially thawed
    4 tablespoons lemon juice
    2 cups heavy cream, whipped

Mix flour, brown sugar, nuts, and margarine. Spread evenly in shallow pan. Bake at 350 degrees for 20 minutes, stirring occasionally. Remove from oven and sprinkle ⅔ of these crumbs in 11½ × 15½-inch jelly roll pan or similar pan with sides. Combine egg whites, sugar, berries, and lemon juice in large bowl. Beat at high speed to fluffy peaks, about 10 minutes. Fold in whipped cream. Spoon over crumbs. Top with remaining crumbs. Freeze overnight. Serve directly from freezer. Recipe may be halved. Serves 24.

ICED TEA CONCENTRATE

    1½ quarts water
    ¼ pound loose tea or 16 tea bags or 2 1-quart size bags

Cover tea with boiling water and steep for 5 minutes. Add 5 quarts cold water. Herbs may be added with tea: mint, lemon verbena, rosemary, or lavender. Makes enough for 30 to 35 ice-filled glasses.

COFFEE IN QUANTITY

Water	Ground coffee
12 cups	1⅓ cups
18 cups	2 cups
24 cups	2⅔ cups
30 cups	3⅓ cups

LOAVES AND FISHES

Smithsonian Luncheons

When Smithsonian Institution–sponsored tours came to Queen Anne's County, the Episcopal Church Women prepared luncheon for them in Donaldson Hall on a beautiful autumn day.

MENU

Forty-two luncheons were served on each of 2 Saturdays.

Chablis
Cider
Cheese Wafers
Crab Imperial*
Country Ham
Pickled Carrots*
Green Beans with Mushrooms
Maryland Beaten Biscuits
Tea Biscuits
Apple Pie* with cheddar cheese wedge
Coffee and tea

WORKERS

Seven people were needed to prepare luncheon, set up, and arrange flowers the day before. Seven people were needed the day of the luncheon plus one helper to make tea biscuits and help clean.

PREPARATIONS

Friday: Prepare crab casseroles, apple pies, cheese wafers, butter curls, and pickled carrots. Refrigerate carrots, ham, crab, pies, and cream. Set up 12 card tables, buffet table, table for sale items (baskets, dried flower arrangements, cookbooks, remainders from Farmers' Market). Place salt, pepper, and sugar on tables. Arrange flowers for tables and buffet (12 small, 1 centerpiece).

Saturday: Make tea biscuits; slice cheese; crisp cheese wafers briefly in oven; make coffee (100-cup coffeepot). Cook beans, sauté mushrooms, and combine. Cut pies and put on plates. Bake crab (allow 30 to 35 minutes in preheated oven). Heat water for tea; put cream on tables; take flowers from refrigerator and set on tables.

*See recipe below.

Purchase Chablis (2 3-liter jugs for each luncheon); arrange for wineglasses to be brought into church. Purchase cider (¾ gallon) at local orchard. Buy 4 pounds country ham needed for each luncheon. Arrange to have Maryland beaten biscuits ordered well in advance and picked up at 9 AM Saturday morning, still warm from the oven. Purchase 10 pounds green beans from local freezer plant (5 pounds for each day). Twenty pounds carrots, 6 pounds coffee, 5 pounds butter, 15 pounds flour (5 pounds for crust, 10 pounds for biscuits) were purchased at a warehouse market. The rest of the food was bought at the local market. In addition, one dozen gold triple-ply paper tablecloths were bought at a paper company and cut in half for the card tables.

❦ *PICKLED CARROTS*

Ten pounds of carrots were prepared for each luncheon, for 5 times this recipe.

2	pounds carrots
1	10-ounce can tomato soup, undiluted
⅓ to ½	cup sugar
½	cup vinegar
¼	cup oil
1	teaspoon salt
½	teaspoon pepper
	dash Worcestershire sauce
½	teaspoon dry mustard
1	tablespoon dried parsley
1	large onion, chopped
1 or 2	small green peppers, chopped

Cut carrots on bias or into sticks or coins. Cook firm, about 5 to 7 minutes. Drain. Combine remaining ingredients, except onion and pepper, in a separate pan and boil for 2 to 3 minutes. Add chopped onion and green pepper. Pour dressing over hot, drained carrots. Marinate 3 to 4 days. Serve hot or cold.

❧ CRAB IMPERIAL

> 1 pound margarine
> 2 cups flour
> 1 gallon milk
> 2½ tablespoons salt
> 1 teaspoon pepper
> 4 teaspoons celery salt
>   cayenne (red pepper)
> 8 egg yolks
> 1 cup sherry
> 8 cups soft bread crumbs
> 8 pounds crabmeat (6 pounds regular, 2 pounds lump)
> 2½ tablespoons parsley
> 2½ tablespoons minced onion
>   salt and pepper
> 2 cups buttered crumbs
>   paprika

Melt margarine, add flour to blend. Add milk slowly. Add seasonings. Cook over low heat, stirring constantly until thickened. Gradually add egg yolks. Cook 2 minutes more. Remove from heat. Add sherry, soft bread crumbs, crabmeat, parsley, onion, salt, and pepper. Gently mix and pour into 4 well-greased casseroles. Top with buttered bread crumbs. Sprinkle with paprika. Casseroles can be prepared to this point and refrigerated until baking. Bake at 400 degrees for 15 to 20 minutes or until hot.

❧ PIECRUST

> *Three quantities of this recipe were used for each luncheon to make 7 9-inch pies. This is more than required, but provides extras for helpers or tour additions.*

> 3 cups flour
> 1 cup shortening

1 teaspoon salt

2 teaspoons vinegar

1 tablespoon sugar

1 large egg, slightly beaten

4 to 6 tablespoons ice water

Process all ingredients except ice water in food processor until blended. Add 4 tablespoons ice water at first, then last two if needed. Chill well. Makes 3 crusts.

APPLE PIE

This recipe makes enough filling for 7 9-inch pies.

12 pounds apples, peeled and sliced

5 cups sugar

½ cup flour

1 teaspoon salt

2 tablespoons cinnamon

7 tablespoons lemon juice

7 tablespoons butter

cheddar cheese (optional)

Mix sugar, flour, salt, and cinnamon. Reserve 1¼ cups. Mix the remaining sugar mix into the apples. Roll crusts into pie pans. Fill with apple mixture. Sprinkle each pie with a tablespoon of lemon juice and dot with a tablespoon of butter. Cover pies with a top crust and sprinkle with 3 tablespoons of the sugar mixture. Bake 15 minutes at 450 degrees, then 35 minutes at 325 degrees. Each pie makes 6 or 8 slices. Garnish with cheddar cheese if desired.

Large Quantity Recipes

🍃 SUSIE'S CABBAGE SALAD

    4 cups cut-up cabbage
    1 small onion, chopped
    1 green pepper, chopped
    1 red pepper, chopped
    1 cup sugar
    ½ teaspoon salt
    ½ cup vinegar
    ½ cup water
    ½ cup salad oil

Chop onions and peppers separately in a food processor. Mix remainder of ingredients in a large bowl. Add vegetables and mix together. Keep in a gallon jar. Let stand at least six hours. Will keep for two weeks. Serves 4 to 6.

—*Mary Ashley Long (Mrs. Paul)*

🍃 CHICKEN SALAD

    8 whole chicken breasts
       juice of 1 lemon
    1 cup dry vermouth
    2 cups mayonnaise
  1½ cups sour cream
    1 tablespoon Dijon mustard
    1 teaspoon Pickapeppa Sauce
    1 cup sliced celery
    1 cup finely sliced onion
    1 cup black, pitted, medium size olives, each cut in half
    1 cup slivered almonds
    1 tablespoon tarragon or herbes de Provence
    ½ teaspoon salt
    ½ teaspoon white pepper
       lettuce leaves
       Hungarian paprika

Simmer chicken breasts in salted water until done. Cool and cut into large cubes. Combine chicken, lemon juice, and vermouth, toss well, and marinate several hours, mixing every now and then. Mix together mayonnaise, sour cream, mustard, and Pickapeppa Sauce. Drain all but about 1½ tablespoons liquid from the chicken. Add celery, onion, olives, and almonds to chicken. Add tarragon or herbes de Provence, salt and pepper. Add mayonnaise–sour cream mixture. Fold together all ingredients carefully and chill. Serve on a bed of lettuce leaves. Sprinkle Hungarian paprika on the chicken salad before serving. Serves 12 to 16.

—*Garry E. Clarke*

FRUITED CHICKEN SALAD

    2 cups mayonnaise
    ⅓ cup sour cream
    1 teaspoon Worcestershire sauce
    2 tablespoons lemon juice
   12 cups cooked cut-up chicken
    4 cups diced celery
    2 large cans Mandarin oranges, drained
    2 cups Thompson grapes

Combine mayonnaise, sour cream, Worcestershire sauce, and lemon juice. Add to chicken and blend well. Stir in celery and fruit and chill. Serves 24.

—*Jane Corey (Mrs. R. Reece)*

POTATO SALAD

    7 pounds potatoes
    4 cups sliced celery
    ¾ cup finely chopped onion
    1 tablespoon salt
    1 quart salad dressing

Boil potatoes. When cooked, peel and cut into cubes. Add celery, onion, and salt, and toss together. Gently stir in salad dressing and refrigerate. Serves 20.

🐟 THREE BEAN SALAD

    2 1-pound cans green beans
    2 1-pound cans wax beans
    2 1-pound cans dark red kidney beans
    1 cup chopped green pepper
    1 cup chopped onion
    1 cup salad oil
 1½ cups sugar
    1 cup vinegar
 1½ teaspoons salt
    1 teaspoon pepper

Drain beans, then combine with pepper and onion. Mix oil, sugar, vinegar, salt, and pepper, and stir into vegetables. Chill before serving. Serves 24.

🐟 CRANBERRY SALAD MOLD

    1 large package cherry-flavored gelatin
    4 cups pineapple juice
    2 packages unflavored gelatin
    2 cans cranberry sauce
    1 orange, finely ground (in a blender, grinder, or food processor)
    2 unpeeled apples, coarsely ground
       Pam
       lettuce
       mayonnaise

Dissolve cherry gelatin in 3 cups hot pineapple juice. Dissolve un-flavored gelatin in 1 cup cold pineapple juice. Add to hot mixture when dissolved. Mash cranberry sauce with fork. Add orange and apples. Add gelatin mixture and pour into flat pans which have been sprayed with Pam. Refrigerate. Serve on lettuce leaf with a dollop of mayonnaise. Makes about 25 servings.

🐟 WHITE WINE VINAIGRETTE FOR A CROWD

    ½ cup dry white wine (or 3 tablespoons fresh lemon juice)
    1 cup red wine vinegar

3 tablespoons Dijon mustard

2 cups canola oil

1 cup extra-virgin olive oil

1 cup chopped fresh parsley

½ cup snipped fresh basil leaves

2 teaspoons salt

2 teaspoons freshly ground pepper

2 cloves of garlic, pressed

Mix wine, vinegar, and mustard with a whisk. Add oils slowly, in a stream, until well blended. Fold in herbs and seasonings. Store in lightly covered jar. Makes about 5 cups.

❦ *BEEF BOURGUIGNONNE*

12 slices bacon, cut in small pieces

8 pounds lean sirloin or top round of beef, cut in strips ½ × 4 inches

4 garlic cloves, crushed

4 pounds mushrooms, sliced

2 teaspoons salt

4 bay leaves, crushed

4 tablespoons parsley, chopped

2 teaspoons thyme

¼ teaspoon pepper

1 cup butter or margarine

1 cup flour

5 10½-ounce cans condensed consommé or 3 cans and balance in Burgundy

Sauté bacon in a large Dutch oven or casserole. Remove cooked bacon and, in remaining fat, brown beef a small amount at a time. Add garlic and mushrooms. Add salt, bay leaves (remove later), parsley, thyme, pepper, and cooked bacon pieces. Make a roux by melting butter or margarine in a skillet and working in flour with a whisk. Cook in skillet until flour turns light brown. Add consommé slowly. Combine roux with beef mixture. Cover and simmer or bake at 300 to 325 degrees for about 1½ hours or until beef is tender. Serve with broad noodles. Makes 16 servings. May be doubled.

—Mary Ashley Long (Mrs. Paul)

🍃 *HOT TURKEY SALAD FOR FIFTY*

> 4 quarts cooked chopped turkey
> 4 quarts chopped celery
> 2 cups chopped pecans
> 4 teaspoons salt
> 4 teaspoons minced onion
> 6¾ ounces lemon juice
> 5 cups mayonnaise
> 10 cups mashed potato chips

Mix first 7 ingredients and top with potato chips. Bake at 450 degrees for 20 minutes, covered, and then for 10 minutes,uncovered. Serves 50.

For 300 to 325 people, make the above recipe 6 times. You will need 6 to 8 turkeys, chopped, bagged and frozen ahead; and 18 bunches celery. Bag the chopped turkey, 4 quarts per bag, and freeze in 6 bags. Bag the chopped pecans and freeze in 6 equal bags.

🍃 *CALICO HAM CASSEROLE*

> 2 16-ounce packages mixed frozen vegetables
> 1 cup margarine
> 3 cups ½ inch squares of fresh bread
> 1 cup flour
> 1 teaspoon salt
> ½ teaspoon pepper
> 2 teaspoons dry mustard
> 2 teaspoons Worcestershire sauce
> 6 cups milk
> 1 medium onion, finely chopped
> ½ to ¾ pound sharp cheddar cheese, grated (2 to 3 cups)
> 2 pounds cooked ham, cut into ¼ × 1½ inch strips

One day ahead, cook vegetables, drain, and set aside. In large pan (such as Dutch oven) melt ¼ cup margarine, then add bread and toss well. Remove and set squares aside. In large bowl, mix flour, salt, pepper, mustard, and Worcestershire. Slowly stir in about 2 cups milk. Heat remaining milk in same Dutch oven, then stir in flour mixture and ¾ cup margarine. Cook, stirring often, until smooth and thickened; add onion and cheese and continue to cook, stirring often until cheese is melted. Remove from heat, stir in vegetables and ham. Pour into 2 12 × 8 × 2-inch baking pans. Refrigerate overnight. About 1 hour before serving, preheat oven to 350 degrees, sprinkle buttered squares over top of mixture and bake uncovered 40 minutes or until hot. Serves 25.

"The Ladies have been most energetic in trying to help pay off the Indebtedness from Suppers given each month at the Parish House, and other entertainments." (1925)

GALLON JUG MUFFINS

This wholesome muffin is a nice accompaniment to fruit salad.

2 cups quick oats
2 cups All Bran cereal
1 cup 40% Bran
1 cup Grape Nuts
1 cup margarine, melted and cooled
4 cups buttermilk
2 cups sugar
4 eggs, beaten
2 cups whole wheat flour
3 cups all-purpose flour
1 teaspoon salt
5 teaspoons baking soda

Combine oats, All Bran, 40% Bran, Grape Nuts, and margarine. Mix buttermilk, sugar, and eggs; stir into oat mixture. Add flours, salt, and soda. (Batter will keep in closed container in the refrigerator for two months.) Pour into muffin pans. Bake at 375 to 400 degrees for 15 minutes. Makes 5 to 6 dozen medium-sized muffins.

❧ CHEESE/TURKEY STRATA

          12 slices white bread
           2 pounds diced turkey
           1 pound cheddar, grated
          ½ cup melted margarine
          ½ teaspoon dry mustard
           6 eggs, beaten
           1 quart milk
              salt and pepper to taste

Arrange turkey, bread, and cheese in no more than 2 layers each in high-sided, flat-bottomed casserole. Pour melted margarine over layers. Beat eggs. Add mustard, salt and pepper, and milk. Pour over casserole, but do not fill casserole too deep, as it puffs up and runs over if pan is too full. Cover and let stand overnight in refrigerator. Bake at 350 degrees for 1 hour. If recipe is doubled, bake for 2 hours in larger pans. Makes 12 servings.

❧ CHICKEN COUNTRY CAPTAIN

          10 cups (5 pounds) canned tomatoes, drained and chopped
           1 teaspoon salt
           1 teaspoon pepper
  1 to 1½ tablespoons curry powder
           1 teaspoon thyme
           1 cup raisins
           1 cup chopped onion
           2 cloves of garlic, crushed
           2 chopped green peppers
           2 tablespoons oil
  5 to 6 cups cooked cubed chicken (approximately 6 to 8 pounds
              chicken)

To tomatoes, add salt, pepper, curry powder (use 1 tablespoon, then add more if needed), thyme, and raisins. Sauté onions, garlic, and pepper in oil and add to tomato mixture. Simmer for 10 minutes, stir in chicken; simmer until heated. Do not continue cooking. Serve over or with rice. Makes 12 servings.

❧ PINEAPPLE ICEBOX CAKE

    1 stick butter
    1 cup powdered sugar
   ½ teaspoon salt
    2 eggs
    1 can crushed pineapple, drained
       graham crackers
       sherry
   ½ cup shredded coconut
   ½ cup chopped pecans
       chocolate syrup

Cream butter, powdered sugar, salt, and eggs until light and fluffy. Add pineapple and mix. Line bottoms of 2 9-inch-square buttered pans with whole graham crackers. Sprinkle with a small amount of sherry. Spread half of creamed mixture on top of crackers. Add half of shredded coconut and chopped pecans. Repeat with second layer of crackers and creamed mix, pineapple, coconut, and nuts. Top with finely crushed graham crackers. Trace top with fine line of chocolate syrup. Refrigerate or freeze. Serves 16 to 18.

❧ PUNCH

       juice of 18 lemons, rind of 6
       juice of 6 oranges, rind of 2
    5 cups granulated sugar
    1 ½-gallon can pineapple juice
    1 quart strong tea (1 tablespoon tea to quart of water), boiling hot
    1 quart hot water
    1 pint maraschino cherries and juice
    2 quarts of carbonated water
    2 quarts rum, champagne, or sauterne

Pour boiling tea on first 4 ingredients. Add the quart of hot water. Cool. Add maraschino cherries and juice. When ready to serve, place cracked ice in punch bowl. Pour punch over ice. Add carbonated water and liquor last. Bits of pineapple and more cherries may be added. Serves 50.

—Isabel Atkinson Lieber (Mrs. Albert C.)

Weights and Measures

For adapting a foreign recipe it may be necessary to experiment a little, since the ingredients may be slightly different from American ones.

A few grains, pinch, dash, etc. (dry) = less than ⅛ teaspoon
a dash (liquid) = a few drops
3 teaspoons = 1 tablespoon
4 tablespoons = ¼ cup
2 cups = 1 pint
2 pints = 1 quart
4 quarts (liquid) = 1 gallon
8 quarts (dry) = 1 peck
4 pecks (dry) = 1 bushel
1 ounce = about 28 grams
1 pound = about 454 grams
1 kilogram = about 2¹⁄₁₀ pounds
1 liter = about 1 quart
1 jigger = 1½ fluid ounces or 3 tablespoons
1 large jigger = 2 fluid ounces or ¼ cup

Temperatures

180°: Simmering point of water
212°: Boiling point of water
220°: Jellying point for jams and jellies
234 to 240°: Soft ball stage for syrups
255°: Hard crack stage for syrups
320°: Caramel stage for syrups

At altitudes above 3,000 feet, lower air pressure causes differences in the boiling point of water and syrups. Consult government bulletins for details.

OVEN

250°: Very slow
300°: Slow
325°: Moderately slow
350°: Moderate
375°: Moderately hot
400°: Hot
450° to 500°: Very hot

TIMETABLE FOR ROASTING

Have all meats at room temperature. Roasting times vary according to the shape of the cut and its fat content. Begin testing well before the suggested time is up. For accuracy use a meat thermometer. You may vary the temperature by as much as 25 degrees to suit other food being cooked at the same time; adjust the time accordingly. For a crisp brown surface, raise the temperature to 400 degrees about 15 minutes before the roasting time is up and baste several times with the fat in the pan.

MEAT	*OVEN HEAT*	*MINUTES PER POUND*	*INTERNAL TEMPERATURE*
BEEF Sirloin Rump Eye of Round Rib *(Add 10 minutes per pound for boned roasts. Never more than 3 hours total time.)*	325°	Rare 18 to 20 Medium 22 to 25 Well done 30 to 35	Rare 140° Medium 160° Well done 180°
Tenderloin *(Usually preferred very rare)*	Preheat to 450°, put in roast and reduce to 350°	Rare 35 to 45	Rare 140°
VEAL Leg Cushion Loin Boned	325°	40	180°
LAMB Leg Loin Shoulder *(Add 5 minutes per pound for boned roasts.)*	325°	Medium well done 25 to 35 Medium rare about 2 hours	175 to 180°

MEAT	*OVEN HEAT*	*MINUTES PER POUND*	*INTERNAL TEMPERATURE*
PORK (Always well done)	350°	Under 4 pounds, 45; over 4 pounds, 35	Under 4 pounds, 185°; over 4 pounds, 185°. For suckling pig, cook 4 hours longer, internal temperature of 185°
HAM (Cured)	Under 8 pounds, 325°; over 8 pounds, 325°	Under 8 pounds, 25; over 8 pounds, 16-18	150°. Precooked ham: to heat and glaze, bake about 30 minutes at 400°
CHICKEN (Stuffed)	325°	30 to 35; without stuffing, 25 to 30	180° for both
DUCK AND GOOSE (Domestic)	325°	25 to 30	175°
TURKEY	325°	Under 8 pounds, 3 to 4 hours; 8 to 12 pounds, 4 to 5 hours; 12 to 16 pounds, 5 to 6 hours; over 16 pounds, up to 7 hours	180°

Equivalents

BREAD CRUMBS

4 ounces = ¾ cup less 1 tablespoon
100 grams = ½ cup

BUTTER, LARD, OTHER FATS, AND CHEESE

1 pound = 2 cups
1 ounce = 2 tablespoons
100 grams = 7 tablespoons (½ cup less 1 tablespoon)

CURRANTS AND RAISINS

1 pound = 2⅜ cups
100 grams = ⅝ cup less 1 tablespoon

FLOUR

1 pound = 3½ to 4 cups
1 ounce = 3 tablespoons
100 grams = ¾ cup less 2 tablespoons

NUTMEATS (CHOPPED)

4 ounces = ⅔ cup
100 grams = ⅝ cup

RICE

1 pound uncooked = 2½ cups
1 pound uncooked = 8 cups cooked

BROWN SUGAR

1 pound = about 2¼ cups
100 grams = ¾ cup less 2 tablespoons

CONFECTIONERS' SUGAR

1 pound = about 3¾ cups
100 grams = ¾ cup

GRANULATED SUGAR

1 pound = 2 cups
100 grams = ½ cup less 1 tablespoon

EGG WHITES

1 = 1½ tablespoons
4 to 6 = ½ cup

EGG YOLKS

1 = 1 tablespoon
6 to 7 = ½ cup

FOOD FACTS—HOW ITEMS MEASURE UP

Wondering how many bananas to mash for a quick bread? Need to know how much rice to cook to make 2 cups? Take the guesswork out of measuring while you cook by using these ingredient equivalents.

CEREALS

Macaroni: 1 cup uncooked (3½ ounces) = 2½ cups cooked
Noodles, medium: 3 cups uncooked (4 ounces) = 3 cups cooked
Spaghetti: 8 ounces uncooked = 4 cups cooked
Rice, long-grain: 1 cup = 3 cups cooked
Rice, quick-cooking: 1 cup = 2 cups cooked
Popcorn: ¼ cup = 5 cups popped

CRUMBS

Bread: 1 slice = ¾ cup soft or ¼ cup fine dry crumbs
Cracker: 28 saltines, 24 round crackers, or 14 graham cracker squares = 1 cup finely crushed crumbs
Cookie: 15 gingersnaps or 22 vanilla wafers = 1 cup finely crushed crumbs

FRUITS

Apples: 1 medium = 1 cup sliced
Bananas: 1 medium = ⅓ cup mashed
Cranberries: 1 pound (4 cups) = 3 cups sauce
Lemons: 1 medium yields 3 tablespoons juice, 2 teaspoons grated peel
Limes: 1 medium yields 2 tablespoons juice, 1½ teaspoons grated peel
Oranges: 1 medium yields ¼ to ⅓ cup juice, 4 teaspoons grated peel
Peaches, pears: 1 medium = ½ cup sliced
Strawberries: 4 cups whole = 3½ cups sliced

VEGETABLES

Beans (dry): 1 pound (2½ cups) = 6 cups cooked
Cabbage: 1 pound (1 small) = 5 cups shredded
Carrots: 1 pound (6 to 8 medium) = 3 cups shredded or 2½ cups chopped
Celery: 1 medium bunch = 4½ cups chopped
Green beans (cut up): 1 pound (3 cups) = 2½ cups cooked
Sweet peppers: 1 large = 1 cup chopped
Mushrooms: 1 pound (6 cups) = 2 cups sliced and cooked

Onions: 1 medium = ½ cup chopped

Potatoes: 1 medium = ⅔ cup cubed or ½ cup mashed

Spinach: 1 pound = 1½ cups cooked

Tomatoes: 1 medium = ½ cup cooked

NUTS

Almonds: 1 pound in shell = 1¼ cups shelled

Pecans: 1 pound in shell = 2 cups shelled

MISCELLANEOUS

Chocolate chips: 1 12-ounce package (2 cups) = about 1 cup melted

Eggs: 4 whole, 8 yolks, or 8 whites = about 1 cup

Substitutions

Arrowroot: 1 tablespoon = 2 tablespoons flour (as thickening)

Baking powder (tartrate or phosphate): 1 teaspoon = ⅔ teaspoon double-action type or ¼ teaspoon baking soda plus ½ teaspoon cream of tartar

Chocolate: 1 ounce (1 square) = 3 tablespoons cocoa plus 1 teaspoon to 1 tablespoon shortening (less for Dutch cocoa)

Cornstarch: 1 tablespoon = 2 tablespoons flour (as thickening)

Pastry flour: 1 cup = 1 cup all-purpose or bread flour less 2 tablespoons (for baking)

Potato flour: 1 tablespoon = 2 tablespoons flour (as thickening)

Milk, fresh, whole: 1 cup = ½ cup evaporated milk plus ½ cup water or ½ cup condensed milk plus ½ cup water (reduce the sugar in recipe) or ¼ cup powdered whole milk plus 1 cup water or ¼ cup skim milk powder plus 2 tablespoons butter and 1 cup water

Milk, fresh, skim: 1 cup = ¼ cup skim milk powder plus 1 cup water

Milk, sour: 1 cup = 1 cup lukewarm fresh milk (less 1 tablespoon) plus 1 tablespoon vinegar. Let stand 5 minutes.

$\mathcal{I}$NDEX